MARLBOROUGH
HIS LIFE AND TIMES

VOLUME III

1702–1704

BY WINSTON S. CHURCHILL

———

THE WORLD CRISIS, 1911-1914

THE WORLD CRISIS, 1915

THE WORLD CRISIS, 1916-1918

THE WORLD CRISIS, 1911-1918
  (Abridged, in one volume)

THE AFTERMATH

A ROVING COMMISSION

THE UNKNOWN WAR

AMID THESE STORMS

THE RIVER WAR

MARLBOROUGH

MARLBOROUGH
Sir Godfrey Kneller
By permission of the Duke of Marlborough

MARLBOROUGH

HIS LIFE AND TIMES

By

THE RIGHT HONOURABLE

WINSTON S. CHURCHILL, C.H. M.P.

VOLUME III

1702–1704

NEW YORK

CHARLES SCRIBNER'S SONS

MCMXXXV

PREFACE

WHEREAS the records of Marlborough's earlier life are singularly scanty, we now enter a period where information is baffling because of its abundance. Lediard's admirable biography presents a continuous account of all the campaigns told with spirit, in detail and well documented. Archdeacon Coxe, writing in 1818–19, had access to all the Blenheim archives that were then known, and produced a comprehensive and monumental work in which large numbers of the personal letters of Marlborough and of his wife, as well as of Queen Anne and many other correspondents unknown to Lediard, were freely quoted. In 1842 a new discovery was made in remarkable circumstances. The sixth Duke of Marlborough in the course of repairing Blenheim built a muniment-room, and collected all the family papers in it. Some of these papers had been stored in Hensington House, at the gates of Blenheim Park, in a record-room used by former stewards. In this room were three large chests, unlocked, placed one upon another, which no one had troubled to open in living memory. The Duke's solicitor, a Mr. Whateley, was more curious. Although he was told that they contained nothing but useless accounts, he continued to pry. The first two chests were filled with old militia accounts and other papers of no importance, but in the third chest, which was undermost, "I found eighteen folio books bound in vellum." These books contained the dispatches and official or secret letters written by John Churchill to the princes of the Grand Alliance; to the Ambassadors and agents of the various states; to the Ministers of the English Crown; to the leaders, agents, and generals of the Dutch Republic, and to the hostile commanders, during the whole of his ten campaigns.

His descendant was not unworthy of this amazing treasure-

5

trove. He entrusted the editing and publishing of the papers to General Sir George Murray, one of Wellington's Peninsular officers, who was at that time Master-General of the Ordnance. Three years later Murray published the greater part of this material, which might so easily have been consigned as rubbish to the flames, in five large, closely printed octavo volumes, comprising considerably over a million words. This enormous collection of original documents is called *The Letters and Dispatches of John Churchill, First Duke of Marlborough, from 1702 to 1712.* It also contains the frequent bulletins of the Duke's armies in the field, and affords a detailed record of the military operations as they actually occurred. A further examination of the Blenheim papers during the last five years has revealed a large number of letters of great historic interest which either escaped Coxe's notice or were excluded from his history for want of space. Among these are the long series of holograph letters written by him to his two most profound intimates, Godolphin and Sarah. They reveal the personality of Marlborough, his inward hopes and fears, his secret thoughts, in a degree never before achieved; and they tell, in his own words, the story of his greatest enterprises far better than his ponderous official correspondence, conducted in the main by the immense abilities and labours of Cardonnel. In this work I have reprinted from Coxe only those documents which are essential to the story, and have used the dispatches only as a guide. These two copious sources, together with Lediard, should be resorted to by students to confirm, explain, and supplement what is written here. I have sought rather to throw a new light upon Marlborough's character and toils by using whenever possible his own words which have remained up till now unknown, written under stress of events from camps and quarters to those who were dearest to him and were also his most trusted colleagues.

No one can read the whole mass of the letters which Marlborough either wrote, dictated, or signed personally without being astounded at the mental and physical energy which it attests. The entire range of European affairs, all

6

PREFACE

the intricate personal relations of the heads of States and
Governments, all the vital connexions with Holland, with the
Empire, with Prussia, with the Archduke Charles, and with a
score of minor potentates, all the anxious shifting combinations of English politics, all the ceremonious usage which
surrounded the Queen, her husband, and her Court, are
disposed of day after day by a general manœuvring equal or
smaller forces in closest contact with a redoubtable enemy,
who often might engage in a decisive battle "at no more than
one hour's notice." After twelve or fourteen hours in the
saddle on the long reconnaissances often under cannon-fire;
after endless inspections of troops in camp and garrison;
after ceaseless calculations about food and supplies, and all
the anxieties of direct command in war, Marlborough would
reach his tent and conduct the foreign policy of England,
decide the main issues of its Cabinet, and of party politics at
home. He thought for all, he acted for all. But when
the longest day was done, and its hours of hazard had
faded into the night, it was not seldom that he wrote his
letter to his beloved Sarah or to his great colleague and
lifelong friend, Godolphin. It is these most interesting
simple records, never meant for any eye but those to which
they were addressed, that tell his tale in its most compulsive
form, and vindicate alike the greatness, warmth, and virtue
of his nature.

But while the wars of Marlborough are set forth by his
bulletins in full and continuous detail, we are singularly
lacking in stories of his campaigns from those who served
in them. The age of military diarists and memoir-writers
had not begun. Very few officers on either side who fought
in those brave armies have left records which have come
down to us. There is, of course, in the first place the Journal
of Marlborough's Chaplain, Dr Francis Hare, which covers
the campaign of 1704. This journal further contains eight
long letters describing the campaign of 1705 which have not
been published. There is the handful of letters of Colonel
Cranstoun, of the Cameronians, in the Bath Papers, and
the few but vivid letters of Lord Orkney. There are a

7

few letters of Captain Richard Pope, of the 7th Dragoon Guards. Samuel Noyes, chaplain to Orkney's Regiment, has left a hitherto unpublished diary for 1705 and 1706, now in the possession of his descendants. A number of Cardonnel's letters have recently been acquired by the British Museum, while a series of Cadogan's letters, chiefly covering the later years, has also been put at my disposal by the Hon. Edward Cadogan. There is the journal of Colonel Blackadder, which, as has been well said, tells us more about the state of his soul than the course of the war. But it would be difficult to paint a lively picture of these memorable campaigns were it not for three diarists who all served throughout with the Royal Regiment of Ireland. None of them published anything in his lifetime. Their writings lay forgotten in family chests. It was only in another generation and under the impulse of another war that they were printed. The accounts of Colonel, afterwards Major-General, Kane and Captain Robert Parker are in the main one. In page after page they follow each other textually. It would seem that they kept a joint regimental record which each embellished, expanded, or corrected for his own version. The third diarist, Sergeant John Millner, has left us a well-written soldierly account, especially valuable for its detail of marches, camps, and numbers.

Captain Robert Parker was a Protestant gentleman from Kilkenny whose heart in early youth was turned to a military life. He fought in all the campaigns of King William both in Ireland and in Flanders. He was now to serve almost continuously through the second great European war under Marlborough. His book is the more valuable because it was written with no thought of publication, and is singular for the aptness and pith of its style. It was penned only as a record for his friends. It lay neglected for many years after his death, and was published by his son in 1746, as a stimulus, according to the preface, for our army then fighting the French in the War of the Austrian Succession. The captain—for he rose no higher—tells us that he had no reason to like Marlborough, whom he often saw, but to

8

whom apparently he never spoke, and who had, as he thought unjustly (though he did not blame him), passed him over for promotion. Yet if we had to choose one single record of Marlborough's campaigns and of his personality we might well be content with the journals of this marching captain, whose grasp not only of the war, but of the great causes which stirred the world, so far exceeded his station. The testimony of ordinary regimental officers is often a truer guide to the qualities of generals than the inscriptions on their monuments. We shall often recur to him as we tramp the fields of Flanders behind "the surly drums."

We also owe a debt to Ailesbury, whom we have already met in the personal circle around King Charles and King James, and whose troubles during the trial of Sir John Fenwick have been mentioned. This lord had been exiled for Jacobitism during the late King's reign, and William had left a written direction that he should never be allowed to return to England. We find him therefore in the Low Countries, a figure of affluence and social distinction. He had been graciously received by Louis XIV, and shortly before the actual outbreak of the war had been hospitably entertained by the French in their camps in Belgium and at their headquarters in Liége. Indeed, flattering proposals had been made to him to throw in his lot with the Court of Saint-Germains and the party of the Two Crowns. But the old Earl had an English heart, and as the armies gathered and fighting drew near he detached himself from his French hosts with many frank explanations, which were accepted in good part, and betook himself within the Dutch lines. Henceforward Ailesbury was an agreeable figure in the society behind the front. Marlborough's relations with him were characteristic. Ailesbury longed to return home, and perpetually entreated Marlborough to enable him to do so. As he was a banished man who steadfastly refused to take the Abjuration Oath, his return would have embarrassed the Government by laying them open to accusations of favouring the Jacobites. "So in plain English I was sacrificed out of State policy and for no other reason, and which lasted so very many years." Marlborough liked the poor Earl and sympathized with him, and actually, as a letter at Blenheim reveals, played fairy godfather at his daughter's marriage, but he had no wish to have the Government involved on his account. He treated him always with a personal courtesy and tenderness which captivated, if it did not console, the exile. Travelling to and from the army, he often dined with him and his amiable Belgian second wife, and paid him any small attention or service that was possible; but he never let him go home. On one occasion, when Ailesbury in exasperation omitted to call upon the Comander-in-Chief, it was Marlborough's part the next day to visit him at his house and take great pains to soothe him. But on the public issue he was adamant. Thus for a series of years we have a number of contacts between these two former courtiers of Charles II, which Ailesbury in his *Memoirs* has set in a light that brings them near to us.

There are scores of histories of Marlborough in the English language, but no modern English work on this subject can compete with Taylor's *Wars of Marlborough.* This writer devoted the closing decade of his life to the most detailed study of the campaigns, which he invested with a colour and movement that lose nothing from his obvious admiration for his hero.

It is, however, the Continental historians who give the most complete picture of this world war, and who reveal upon a European background the dominating part which England played under Marlborough's leadership. The standard French history by Pelet unrolls the panorama as it appeared from Versailles. The original documents of the highest consequence which are presented in this long series of massive volumes will repay the reader, apart altogether from the valuable comments by which they are pointed. The *Histoire de Jean Churchill,* by Madgett, assisted by the Abbé Dutems, is of interest because it was written by the direction and under the supervision of Napoleon, whose appreciation of Marlborough as a soldier was profound.

The Austrian Catholic historian Klopp in *Der Fall des Hauses Stuart* has bequeathed us a monumental work. For

twenty years he trailed through the archives of Europe
tormented by the inherent contradictions of his theme. As
an Austrian patriot he championed the Empire, its statesmen,
and its generals. As a convert to Rome his heart lay with
the house of Stuart in exile at Saint-Germains. In fourteen
volumes still preserved in Continental libraries he recorded his
dislike of Marlborough as a foreigner and a Protestant. He
can hardly bring himself to recount his victories. Blenheim
was an accident caused by some French cavalry squadrons
being pushed into the Danube and leaving their infantry cut
off behind them. Ramillies, to which he devotes one paragraph in several thousand pages, was occasioned by a change
of the wind. On the other hand, whole chapters are devoted
to mocking at the correspondence about Marlborough's
principality, or proving him unfair in his treatment of the
Imperial commander, Prince Louis of Baden. A whine
and drone of baffled spite arises from these wearisome,
laborious chronicles; but more curious still is Klopp's
lack of proportion in judging events and of responsibility
to his country's cause. Never for one moment does he
perceive that but for the life-effort and tireless scheming of
Marlborough the whole structure which resisted Louis XIV
would have fallen to pieces. If the cannon-ball at Blenheim
or the sabre-cut at Elixem, or any one of the hundred
chances amid which Marlborough rode from day to day upon
his duty, had removed him from the scene, the driving-force
of the coalition was dead. His will and his craft alone
drew the English, the Dutch, and the German states to the
rescue of the Empire upon the Danube. His authority and
comprehension sought to marshal an army upon the Moselle
which might have dictated peace. Whenever he is for the
time frustrated, the poor Klopp, fit scribe for an Empire which
has sunk in the abyss, can only clap incontinent hands. Yet
Marlborough had but to relax his efforts, so strenuous and
intense year after year, for the Dutch, with all their wealth
and armed power, to fall back eagerly, thankfully, behind their
own fortress-barrier, and for England to wash her hands of
Continental entanglements and blithely pursue trade and

plantations across the seas. And that would have entailed the ruin of both the causes to which Klopp seems to bear a thin but persistent allegiance. The Holy Roman Empire would have crumbled to pieces before its time, and Gallican Catholicism would have dominated the Papacy.

The race of Klopps is not extinct in modern days, but few of them make so acceptable an apology for their existence as this writer, with his industry in unearthing and transcribing documents and with his magpie shrewdness in picking out all sorts of glittering novelties from among the dusty ruins of the past.

The German von Noorden is an authority of equal diligence, but with far greater discernment and literary power. His comprehension of English statesmen and politics is upon the highest level, and he is equally master of the European scene. An immense mass of original documents collected by the Dutch historian Lamberty affords a quarry in which very few English picks have clinked. But probably the most valuable work is the Austrian official history, the *Feldzüge des Prinzen Eugen von Savoyen*.[1] I was fortunate enough by advertising in Germany to procure a copy of this very rare book, which contains so many of the original secret dispatches of Prince Eugene, Wratislaw, and other high personages written from the headquarters of the armies, and of the Imperial replies, as well as military comments based upon intimate knowledge of the ground and of the conditions of the operations.

I mention these few authorities from among the host of witnesses whose names and works will be found in the appended bibliography.

In my former volumes I have dealt with the first fifty-two years of Marlborough's life and traced his rise under three successive sovereigns to the general recognition that he was the leading Englishman in the realm. The crimson thread of his biography has already in the last year of King William broadened into English history. In the reign of Queen Anne it spreads beyond our own annals, and enters, often decisively,

---

1 Commissioned by the Imperial General Staff, 1871; vol. i appeared in 1876.

during ten tremendous years into the strange, gigantic story of Europe.

Upon this stage we see Marlborough as an Olympian figure making head against innumerable difficulties and opponents in every quarter, and preserving by his genius and his exploits the religious and civil liberties of England and of Europe against French domination in Church and State. Certainly he is revealed by his letters, by every reported utterance, and by his deeds, as a majestic, sagacious, benignant personality, making allowances for everybody, enduring every vexation with incredible patience, taking all the burdens upon his own shoulders, tirelessly contriving and compelling victory, running all risks and always ready, as he phrased it, to die "for Queen and country."

During the four years (1702–1705) covered by the present volumes, Marlborough led England as Captain-General and, with Godolphin, as virtual Prime Minister. He conducted by personal negotiation with sovereigns and potentates the essentials of England's foreign policy. He was the mainspring of the Grand Alliance and its many signatory States. His tent or headquarters were the clearing-house for all the ceaseless disputes and tangles of the whole confederacy against Louis XIV. He was the central link on which everything was fastened. He supplied whatever there was of unity of command, of cohesion and design. We know from our own experience the difficulties of achieving these elements of success. His life was a ceaseless triple struggle, first to preserve the political foundation in England which would enable her to dominate the Continental war; secondly, to procure effective military action from the crowd of discordant, jealous, and often incompetent or lukewarm allies; and thirdly—and this was the easiest part—to beat the French in the field. Nothing like this concentration of business and effective action upon a single man had ever been seen before in Europe, or was soon to be seen again. King William III had filled the diplomatic and political spheres with kingly authority; but he had not the military genius which could compel the turbulent course of war. Frederick the Great possessed military gifts of the first order; but for all his sovereignty he did not preside over affairs comparable in their width and complexity to the domain of Marlborough. It is not till we reach Napoleon, the Emperor-statesman-captain, that we see this threefold combination of functions—military, political, and diplomatic—which was Marlborough's sphere, applied again upon a Continental scale.

Never have such influence and such power been brought to bear upon Europe by any man not possessing a kingly title. Marlborough was but a subject—a "private man," as Bolingbroke calls him. He moved and acted in an aristocratic period, when the world was still set in a formal frame. To pretend that the triumphs of England in the age of Anne were the sole work of Marlborough would be an exaggeration. But it would only be an exaggeration. Had he been given the power to design and command which Frederick and Napoleon exercised so fully, there is little doubt, apart from the chances of his being killed in battle, that he would have brought the world war of the eighteenth century to a decisive, absolute victory before the end of the period which these volumes describe.

His powers were nevertheless very varied and extensive. Monographs could be written about the relations of Marlborough and Queen Anne; on his connexion with the friend of his life, Godolphin; on his military brotherhood with Eugene, a comradeship unmatched in the annals of war between commanders of equal fame and capacity; on his relations with the Grand Pensionary Heinsius and with Wratislaw, the plenipotentiary of the Emperor. These were the five great personalities with whom and through whom he acted. Beyond them and beneath them lay a throng of kings, princes, commanders, ambassadors, and politicians, many of whom upon occasions came to the centre of affairs. But these five stand out throughout the whole period in the supreme circle of those with whom he had continually to work.

Behind him was his own family and his own military family. First stood his beloved wife, and in a sense Cabinet colleague, Sarah, whose intimate relations with the Queen at times vastly helped and at others vastly hindered harmonious action. He himself was not only Captain-General of the British Army and its commander in the field, he was also the Master-General of the Ordnance, which gave him complete control over all those services of munitions and supplies upon which the army lives. Through Godolphin as Lord Treasurer he was sure of the finances. His brother George Churchill, advising his friend the Prince of Denmark, controlled for the first six years the Board of Admiralty. His other brother, Charles Churchill, a good, competent soldier, commanded the English infantry. Always there was his right-hand man, Cadogan, a devoted, unswerving adherent who seems to have combined the functions of Chief of the Staff and Quarter-master-General in the field with those of principal intelligence and reconnoitring officer. Cadogan was very often Marlborough's eye. He went out in advance to see the situation for himself and to report to his chief, who knew he could act upon what Cadogan said was true. Hard by Marlborough's tent or coach was always Cardonnel, who made it possible for him to conduct from his constantly moving headquarters the diplomacy and politics of the Grand Alliance. And then there was Dr Hare, already mentioned, who followed the Duke in all the campaigns and actions, administered the sacrament before the battle, and was at hand to perform the last offices in case some sabre-cut or cannon-ball laid his leader low. Dr Hare was besides what was then called a 'journalist.' He kept the staff diary of the army, assisted Cardonnel with the bulletins, which were remarkably good reading, and much more informing than the ones we used to have in the Great War; and he also probably helped in composing the communiqués on controversial issues which were sometimes launched, or allowed to leak out by calculated indiscretion from nowhere in particular.

Such, in brief, is the personal apparatus by which Marlborough was surrounded and through which he addressed himself to Europe and moved the armies against the enemy. It is remarkable and revealing, so far as Marlborough's character is concerned, that practically none of this entourage

15

was altered during the ten campaigns. George Churchill, indeed, had to be turned out of the Admiralty in 1708, but all the others went through the whole course with Marlborough, shared his marches and dangers, shared his triumphs, and also his misfortunes and ill-usage at the end. It is quite true that the Duke was not popular with his leading contemporaries. He followed his own hard maxim, "It is best to have to do with as few people as possible." But those who knew him best and through whom he worked held to him always through thick and thin, and he for his part never found any occasion to change his opinion of them.

These volumes close at a moment when Marlborough's place among the greatest captains of history was still disputed. Although in 1704 on Blenheim field he had rescued the Empire from ruin and the Grand Alliance from collapse, the fruits of victory were largely cast away by the jealousies of the allies and the fatal caution of the Dutch in 1705; and it was possible for rivals and detractors to maintain that he was an imprudent, unorthodox general with one stroke of luck. His authority was still flouted by other allied commanders; his judgment was still trammelled by endless councils of war. Although the instinct of both the English and the Dutch peoples acclaimed him as their champion, he was beset on all sides by a host of critical functionaries and personages. Blenheim had aroused the spirit of the English to a degree of warlike enthusiasm scarcely ever equalled in our records. But other proofs were needed before Marlborough obtained that plenary power at the head of his armies which has always been deemed indispensable to success. By the time his authority in the field was no longer challenged, the basis of his political power at home had been undermined. But to recount this curious double process must be the task of later volumes.

I have been greatly helped in unravelling the four campaigns described in these volumes by Colonel R. P. Pakenham-Walsh who has during the last five years made a detailed

study of them in their technical aspects. Together we have
visited the battlefields and traversed the marches, and I have
enjoyed the advantage of his excellent professional opinion.
The greatest pains have been taken with the diagrams and
maps which illustrate most of the situations. If the reader
will but glance at them as they occur page after page he
will find no difficulty in understanding what happened.
Commander J. H. Owen, R.N., has assisted me in naval
matters.

I must renew my thanks to all of those who have so
kindly allowed me to reproduce pictures and portraits in
their possession, and also to those who have placed original
documents at my disposal. I make my acknowledgments
in every case.

I had looked forward to presenting these volumes, like their
forerunners, to my cousin, the late Duke of Marlborough.
His interest in the story was keen, and without his ardent
co-operation and the freedom of the Blenheim archives
which he accorded me for so many years my task would
never have been thus far accomplished. It is with lasting
sorrow that I recall in these pages the breaking by death
of a lifetime's friendship.

WINSTON SPENCER CHURCHILL

CHARTWELL
WESTERHAM
August 13, 1934

CONTENTS

VOLUME III

ILLUSTRATIONS

PLATES

FACSIMILES OF LETTERS

MAPS AND PLANS

MAPS AND PLANS

ABBREVIATIONS

B.M. = British Museum Library.
H.M.C. = *Report of the Royal Historical Manuscripts Commission.*
S.P. = State Papers at the Public Record Office, London.

For further details as to footnote references see the Bibliography (pp. 257–261, Vol. IV).

In quoting from old documents and letters the original text has been preserved wherever it is significant. Letters of Marlborough and Sarah which enter directly into the narrative have been modernized in spelling, grammar, and punctuation so far as is convenient to the reader. But the archaic style and setting has been preserved, and occasionally words are left in characteristic spelling.

Documents never before made public are distinguished by an asterisk (*). In the case of unpublished letters to and from Marlborough preserved in the Blenheim collection no further reference is given.

All italics are the Author's, unless the contrary is stated.

In the diagrams, except where otherwise stated, fortresses held by the allies are shown as black stars and those occupied by the French as white stars.

METHOD OF DATING

Until 1752 dates in England and on the Continent differed owing to our delay in adopting the Reformed Calendar of Gregory XIII. The dates which prevailed in England were known as Old Style, those abroad as New Style. In the seventeenth century the difference was ten days, in the eighteenth century eleven days. For example, January 1, 1601 (O.S.), was January 11, 1601 (N.S.), and January 1, 1701 (O.S.), was January 12, 1701 (N.S.).

The method used has been to give all dates of events that occurred in England in the Old Style, and of events that occurred abroad in New Style. Letters and papers are dated in the New Style unless they were actually written in England. In sea battles and a few other convenient cases the dates are given in both styles.

It was also customary at this time—at any rate, in English official documents— to date the year as beginning on Lady Day, March 25. What we should call January 1, 1700, was then called January 1, 1699, and so on for all days up to March 25, when 1700 began. This has been a fertile source of confusion. In this book all dates between January 1 and March 25 have been made to conform to the modern practice.

MARLBOROUGH
HIS LIFE AND TIMES

VOLUME III

CHAPTER I

THE SUNSHINE DAY

(1702, March)

THE accession of a sovereign is rightfully an occasion for rejoicing; but seldom has a great and virtuous prince been so little mourned as King William III. The long foreign compression of his reign was over. A personality always dominating and active, but never likeable, was gone. A queer, unnatural interlude in English history had reached its end. Bishops and courtiers who watched the couch upon which William of Orange gasped and choked on his journey into silence vied with each other in sending or carrying accurate bulletins of his death-agony to his successor. In the morning of March 8 Anne had become ruler of the three kingdoms. There was a sigh of relief throughout the capital, and then, with scarcely the pause which decorum enjoined, a very general jubilation for Her Majesty Queen Anne.

Little cause had she or her friends, the high personages with whom we are concerned, to cherish the memory of William. Anne had been at one time almost persecuted by him, often vexed in petty ways, and always excluded from the slightest share in public affairs. She "should not," he had reminded her, "be Queen before her time."[1] He had treated her husband with cordial, unspoken contempt. Marlborough, though in the end handed Elijah's mantle, had been imprisoned in his reign and denied a fair part in the war while he was in his military prime. Godolphin, who stood next to Marlborough in experience and authority, had been newly driven from office as the result of the wanton dissolution of 1701. All these three, certainly Anne and Marlborough, were conscious of the lifting of a great weight. The whole of the Tories, smarting from their recent but partial defeat, reviled the late King's memory, and

1 Vol. II, p. 194.

the Whigs were deeply conscious of the national reaction against him and all his works.

But far beyond the bounds of the ruling political circles there was satisfaction throughout the country at the disappearance of an alien ruler who, though he had faithfully discharged his duties to England, had scarcely troubled to conceal his dislike for her and his preference for his native land. Dignified ceremonial but no public funeral was accorded to the corpse of the world-famous prince by the island he had saved. His Dutch favourites—Bentinck, Keppel, and the rest—were brushed out of English affairs. We shall meet them in Holland. All the policies of his reign were searchingly called in question. Soon seven commissioners from the Tory Opposition, "the hottest men in the House, who had raised as well as kept up the clamour with the greatest earnestness," will be appointed to examine his accounts and finances. The addresses which from all parts of the country saluted Queen Anne made little or even slighting reference to his services. Although a more correct, if frigid, demeanour was observed by the Court, and the customary verbal tributes were paid, the vindication of King William's memory was left to history, which has not failed him.

The Privy Council repaired to the new Queen, and for the first time her subjects heard in official declarations that melodious, well-trained voice which always charmed and often thrilled. She spoke of the Protestant Succession, of the Church of England, of resistance to France, of her resolve to do her constitutional duty and to fulfil the obligations entered into by her predecessor for the common good of Europe. She was acclaimed. By the time she met the Houses of Parliament on March 11 the feeling of the nation was revealed to the London world. We are told that the Queen repeated "more copiously" to Parliament what she had said to the Privy Council. But there were some significant additions. "I know my own heart to be entirely English," she declared, and added in marked and challenging repetition of her father that "you shall always find me a strict and religious observer of my word."[1] The royal attire was also deemed remarkable. She wore a robe of red velvet lined with ermine and edged with gold galloon, and over it a royal mantle of the same materials, and around her neck a heavy gold chain with the badge of St George hanging on her bosom. Upon Anne's head was the red velvet cap surmounted by the crown of England. On her left arm she bore the ribbon of the Garter. It was said that she had used a portrait of Queen Elizabeth as a model.[2] The impression produced by her declarations, her voice, and her appearance was profound. Many, taking the cue, spoke of a second Queen Elizabeth, and felt the presage of great days to come.

To Marlborough belongs the responsibility for the impulse given to the whole policy of the State and for the note struck by Queen Anne. In these first momentous hours and days he was not only the chief but the sole guide of the Queen, and the decisions to which he obtained her assent shaped the future. Anne relied on Marlborough. Moreover, in the main she agreed with him. She liked his innate Toryism. She admired his strong religious strain. His high, tolerant outlook upon the fierce factions of the times, his desire for national unity, all seemed to her to harmonize with her own duties as sovereign. There was the wise, great, and good man who had always stood by her; the captain who had steered her ship through so many storms and shoals, who always knew what to do, and never made a mistake. He would protect her from "the mercyless men of both parties." He understood all about Europe and this terrible war into which she must now plunge. And was he not also the husband of her dearest personal friend? So Queen Anne and her ablest subject, the man whom she knew best and liked and trusted most, sat down together to bring prosperity and glory to the realm.

Marlborough's ascendancy was well received at home and in

[1] *Parliamentary History of England* (Hansard), edited by William Cobbett and J. Wright, vi (1810), 5.

[2] Dispatches of Wratislaw (the Imperial Ambassador Extraordinary) and Hoffmann (the Imperial Minister Resident in London), March 11.

friendly states abroad. In spite of some sneers he was recognized as the outstanding Englishman, on whom the Queen would rightly bestow her favour, even if long service and friendship had not made this natural. Both parties accepted him for his gifts, and for a time because he stood above their warfare. The foreign envoys and agents were from the beginning deeply impressed with his qualities. "The greatest consolation in this confusion," wrote Wratislaw on the day of the demise, "is that Marlborough is fully informed of the whole position and by reason of his credit with the Queen can do everything."[1] Others dwelt upon his honesty and financial strictness. "There is a general conviction," wrote L'Hermitage, "of Marlborough being a very clever man whose character is honest, simple and conciliatory, and whose whole interest is in making things go well";[2] and Bonet a little later, "Milord Marlborough, the 'grand ministre,' is a great lover of order, so that people promise themselves that the finances will be strictly regulated."[3]

It was well understood in the Army that if Marlborough had the power he would pursue unswervingly the Protestant and warlike foreign policy of King William III. It is curious how these impressions communicated themselves to persons of high character in military discipline but far removed from politics or the Court. Captain John Blackadder, of the Cameronian Regiment, was, like his father, a man of iron, if iron can be so strong. According to our records, where religion, honour, or patriotism were concerned neither ever blenched under the malice of domestic government or the fire of the foreign enemy. Both sustained without any perceptible sign of weakness, the one in his pulpit or in proscribed conventicles, the other in the forefront of British battles, every pressure, violent or prolonged, that man may be born to endure. The father was dead. He had expired in 1686 upon the Bass Rock after four years of rigorous imprisonment. But the son remained to plead with his sword

1 Wratislaw's dispatch, March 8, 1702.
2 L'Hermitage (Dutch Agent in London), March 17, 1702.
3 Bonet (Prussian Minister Resident), April 10, 1702.

in a gallant regiment the causes to whose service he conceived himself born. When Captain Blackadder heard of William's death he was grieved to the roots of his being. His faith sustained him, and he wrote in his diary on March 12:

> But the same God who raised up for us a Moses to bring us out of Egypt and the house of bondage sits at the helm still, and can, after him, raise up a Joshua to perfect the deliverance, and lead his people into the promised land.[1]

The new reign opened amid a blaze of loyalty. It was the "sunshine day" for which the Princess Anne had waited with placid attention. In her mind were a number of particular things she had long wished but lacked the power to do. She hastened to appoint her husband Generalissimo and Lord High Admiral. She made the Earl of Marlborough Captain-General of her armies at home and abroad. More than ten years had passed since she had begged in vain a Garter for him from William. She was now, on the fifth day of her reign, able to confer it herself. For nearly ten years also Henry Sidney, now Lord Romney, had enjoyed by William's favouritism the lucrative position of Quartermaster, or Master-General of the Ordnance, which Marlborough had needed and too much desired. Upon the death of his patron Sidney was stripped of his unmerited, though not ill-borne, advantages, and Marlborough put in his stead. An emblem from the Sidney family arms, the Broad Arrow, has, however, left its mark upon our country.

At every point we see intermingled the policy of Marlborough and the wishes of the Queen. It was the Queen's wish to load him and his wife with honours and wealth; and we need not suppose that either of the recipients made much objection. The Queen had old friends to honour and old scores to pay. The reader will remember that young Lord Mulgrave who had courted her with poems in the jovial days of Charles II and been sent in a leaky frigate to Tangier for his presumption. Mulgrave—Normanby he had become—was soon to be appointed Lord Privy Seal and thereafter Duke of Buckingham. Thus romance received a belated dividend

---

[1] A. Crichton, *Life and Diary of Lieutenant-Colonel J. Blackadder* (1824), p. 174.

with compound interest. Wharton, William's Comptroller of the Household, was made to surrender his staff of office to his successor in the Queen's presence by her express arrangement because she disapproved of his licentious and ungodly modes of life and speech. The aged Earl of Macclesfield nearly a quarter of a century before had supported his brother in accusing Anne's father, afterwards James II, of responsibility for the suicide of Essex in the Tower. He was incontinently turned out of office. In the making of bishops and the preferment of all clergymen the Queen was deeply interested. She advanced to such vacancies as occurred—for longevity is fashionable in ecclesiastical hierarchies—zealous High Churchmen. She dealt with the Archbishop of York, Dr Sharp, who was High, rather than with the Archbishop of Canterbury, Dr Tenison, who was Broad. She even endeavoured to persuade Bishop Ken, the Non-Juror, whose conscientious convictions challenged her sovereign right, to resume his spiritual office. In all this both in likes and prejudice the Queen's will and pleasure were made manifest.

Anne gratified many special desires. Marlborough had one general purpose. No sooner had the Queen met the Privy Council on March 8 than he informed the Imperial Ambassador, Wratislaw, that the Queen, like the late King, would support unswervingly the interests of the Emperor. He also authorized the Ambassador to make this public by every channel. That night he sent a personal message of the same character to the Grand Pensionary of Holland.[1] Wratislaw seems to have urged Marlborough to go to The Hague forthwith himself. For the moment this was impossible. He could not leave the Queen. But after the Queen had met Parliament and announced the broad lines of her policy Marlborough turned immediately to Holland. On the 13th he visited Wratislaw again, bringing Godolphin with him.[2] Marlborough told the Ambassador that earlier in the day he had been appointed Captain-General of the English forces, and that in the evening the Order of the

[1] See von Noorden, *Europäische Geschichte im achtzehnten Jahrhundert* (1870), i, 193.
[2] Wratislaw's dispatch, March 13.

Garter would be conferred on him. He announced that no
official notification of the accession would be made to the
King of France; and that the Queen had instructed him to
proceed as soon as possible to The Hague. If the wind were
favourable he would start the next day. Lord Godolphin
would act for him in all matters during his absence, and
Wratislaw should have recourse to him. As Godolphin was
not yet a Minister the arrangement was for the moment
informal. It was none the less effective. Sarah was the
link between Godolphin and the Queen. Mrs Freeman reported to Mrs Morley what Mr Montgomery—for so Anne
called Lord Godolphin—mentioned in his talks with her.
Never was the English Constitution found more flexible.

These events were watched by one who was by now
no more than a profound observer. Sunderland, old and
declining, read in his library at Althorp the Queen's Speech.
He had also received a friendly message from Marlborough
reassuring him about his pension under the new régime.
Considering his kinsman's anger against him for having
counselled William's unlucky dissolution of 1701, the token
of amity must have been a sensible relief to this straggler
from the reign of James II. He wrote him a mellow letter.

> Whatever coldness has been between us of late, I am sure on
> my side, and I believe on yours, was from thinking differently
> of the public; which, as it is at an end, so I dare confidently
> say it will never be again. To convince you of this, I need only
> tell you, that I wished all yesterday, that every article might be
> in the Queen's Speech, which, when the letters came, I found.
> This may appear vain, but it is true, and my wife can wit-
> ness it.[1]

These sentences, proving that Sunderland had had no
hand in the Speech, dispose of the report, so misleading to
foreign historians, which Hoffmann made to Vienna, that
Marlborough, Godolphin, *and Sunderland* would "form a
triumvirate in the Ministry."[2] Sunderland had no longer
any part in affairs, but Marlborough with a kindness

1 Coxe, *Memoirs of John, Duke of Marlborough* (second edition, 1820), i, 144.
2 Hoffmann's dispatch, March 13; Klopp, *Der Fall des Hauses Stuart*, x, 16.

which family ties may perhaps discount sought to put him politically at his ease in the closing months of his life.[1]

Of all the wishes which Anne nourished on her accession none was more ardent than to make her dearly loved husband King Consort of England. It fell to Marlborough to persuade her that this could not be done. The whole impression which the Queen, no less than her counsellor, wished to give of an English reign would be destroyed by such a project, which Parliament would never have sanctioned. There remained the question whether King William's offices in Holland of Stadtholder and Captain-General might not be transferred by the Dutch to Prince George of Denmark. No doubt the Queen dwelt on this hope. Marlborough was still Ambassador and plenipotentiary to the Dutch Republic. It was natural that he should announce Queen Anne's accession to her ally. The Queen wished that he should see what could be done on the spot in her husband's interests. She even sent an autograph letter to the States-General proposing Prince George as the new Stadtholder. The States-General found after long thought no better answer than silence. For Marlborough himself the obvious and vital need was to gain control of the European situation and grip the Grand Alliance together; and this could only be done from The Hague.

The personal influence of Anne upon history has been much disputed. The modern impression of the important part she played is due to foreign rather than national historians. The portrait of a weak, feeble-minded, narrow being, managed by her female intimates or by Marlborough has never been recognized abroad. Nor does it represent the character of

1 "The moral quality of these three personages," writes Klopp, "is sufficiently apparent from previous events. Even Godolphin, though not surrounded by such deep shadows as Sunderland or Marlborough, does not appear in an altogether favourable light. But if we put in the other scale their intellectual ability, the triumvirate represented the finest flower of contemporary English statesmanship, and that in the opinion of an unquestioned expert, King William III. As, then, these three men combined to carry on his work and Queen Anne, whether fully aware or not of what she was doing, lent them the concurrence of the royal authority, the question might well be raised from the first in Versailles as to whether the death of William III, when he had once completed his work of the Grand Alliance, could still be regarded as a gain" (Klopp, *ibid.*). The argument is excellent, but the fact erroneous.

36

one of the strongest personalities that have reigned in these islands. The politics of England, in fact, revolved around Queen Anne. Her intellect was limited, but her faith, her conscience, her principles, and her prejudices were for ten years a factor in the life of England and in the fortunes of Europe which held its own with the growing power of Parliament and the victories of Marlborough. She was a simple, brave, constant woman, and she formed a fairly stable pivot upon which the passions and the fortunes of the parties turned. Anne cared about some of the largest and some of the smallest things, and for the sake of these she was ready to make exertions and run risks which might shake the realm. Anne cared about the Church of England, the Tory Party, Marlborough, her faithful servant, guide, and champion, and Sarah, her dear bosom friend from childhood onward. Besides these she cared intensely about the glory of England, which mattered a great deal, and about her husband Prince George, who mattered very little except to her.

Nothing ever stirred her mind more deeply than her right and duty to wear the crown. At heart she was a Protestant-Jacobite. While in her person and in her policy she barred the return of the rightful heir, she embodied the claims of blood and affirmed the Divine Right of Kings. She reverenced the principles the overthrow of which had brought her the crown. But she did not mean to give up the crown. She desired to have it, to keep it, and to transmit it to an heir of her own body. There was therefore an innate discordance in the bosom of this virtuous and pious woman. She had grieved for her exiled father. She had sought his forgiveness. At the same time she had taken every step in her power to turn him out and keep him out. From the very beginning she had disputed the legitimacy of the Prince of Wales. We remember how she had written in June 1688, "I shall never now be satisfied whether the child be true or false. Maybe 'tis our brother. . . . Where one believes it, a thousand do not. For my part . . . I shall ever be of the number of unbelievers." Like the England

37

she typified so closely, she clung to the warming-pan. She held it between her and the pricks of conscience. But the warming-pan was wearing thin. By 1702 it was regarded throughout Europe as a fraud, and in good society in England as a salutary fiction. Anne could not escape the atmosphere which she breathed. But never for a moment even in her fullest self-revelations did she lay down her defence. Sarah wrote later on:

> When I saw she had such a partiality to those I knew to be Jacobites, I asked her one day whether she had a mind to give up her crown; for if it had been her conscience not to wear it, I do solemnly protest I would not have disturbed her, or struggled as I did. But she told me she was not sure the Prince of Wales was her brother; and that it was not practicable for him to come here without ruin to the religion and country.[1]

As the first of these objections seemed to weaken, Anne leaned the more heavily upon the practical and unanswerable force of the second. On the death of her father her step-mother, Mary of Modena, had written, on September 27, 1701, a challenging letter:

> I think myself indispensably obliged to defer no longer the acquainting you with a message which the best of men as well as the best of fathers left with me for you; some few days before his death he bid me find means to let you know that he forgave you all that's past from the bottom of his heart, and prayed to God to do so too, that he gave you his last blessing and prayed to God to convert your heart and confirm you in the resolution of repairing to his son the wrongs done to himself.[2]

Under this assault the Queen found sanctuary in the Church of England. Was she to betray that holy instrument to Roman idolatry? Was she to deliver her realm to civil war? Above all, was she, as Sarah put it bluntly, to give up her crown? No—a thousand times no! She would make the conscientious sacrifices which her public duty required, and she would take every step to make them effective. In their anger at Louis XIV's recognition of the Prince of Wales

1 October 29, 1709; Coxe, i, 142.   2 Clarke, *Life of James II*, ii, 602.

38

as rightful King, the English nation demanded that an article should be added to the treaties of the Grand Alliance pledging all its original members to the absolute exclusion of the Pretender. Anne was resolute for this additional article. She gave the fullest expression to her people's will, which was also her own. But at the same time she hated the Whigs for being the driving-force of such ideas, and she clung all the more tightly to the Church of England, whose sacred mission alone could preserve her from self-reproach, and to the Tories, who guarded that Church from agnosticism or Dissent. Thus it followed that the Queen had a sentiment for the Jacobite cause, against which she warred, and a liking for the Tories, who felt as she did; and she nursed a resentment against the Whigs, because if there had not been such people there never would have been such problems. As long as she lived she meant to reign. She had already buried many children. But she still prayed, and invoked the prayers of the Church of England, for an heir. If that failed—and miracles were rare—then it must be an open question who should succeed her at her death. Certainly above all things she was determined that, however ill the fates might lie, the detestable Hanoverian who for reasons of State had spurned her youth and maidenhood should not obtrude himself within her bounds. Conscience and kinship, in revolt from such possibilities, turned to Saint-Germains. After all, "maybe 'tis our brother."

Among the sympathies which united the Queen to Marlborough and Godolphin was their mysterious respectful attitude towards the exiled house. Like her, they seemed to wish for forgiveness without making reparation. Like her, while waging ruthless war, they laboured to preserve not only polite relations but some human contact with the opponent they were destroying. Never was such sincere deceit, such studied effort to enjoy both sides of the argument, such airy indulgence of sentiment, while purpose and action flowed inexorably down the opposite channel.

But Sarah was different, and the changes in her position from the beginning of the reign deserve close study. Anne on her coming to the throne still loved Sarah fondly. Nothing gave the Queen more pleasure than to bestow honours and wealth upon her friend and those who were dear to her. Sarah was once made Groom of the Stole, Mistress of the Robes, and Comptroller of the Privy Purse, and both her married daughters became Ladies of the Bedchamber. William's death deprived the Earl of Portland (Bentinck) of the Rangership of Windsor Park, and a few weeks later, in May, the Queen, remembering that Sarah had often admired the Lodge, wrote:

> Mentioning this worthy person puts me in mind to ask dear Mrs Freeman a question which I would have done some time ago; and that is, if you would have the Lodge for your life, because the warrant must be made accordingly; and anything that is of so much satisfaction as this poor place seems to be to you, I would give dear Mrs Freeman for all her days, which, I pray God, may be as many and as truly happy as this world can make you.[1]

These appointments and bounties were more than the moving of furniture about by an incoming tenant who had long had her own views upon its previous arrangement; they expressed the sincere affection and friendship which glowed in Anne's generous heart for one who had shared the joys and sorrows of her life and its bleak years.

Nevertheless we must not overrate the influence of Sarah upon national affairs. On the contrary, her relations with Anne were definitely, though at first insensibly, impaired. At the accession the ties which joined them were of nearly thirty years' growth, and their differences of political opinion and temperament were frankly and sympathetically recognized on both sides. But these differences were fundamental. Sarah's logical mind and downright character offered no shelter for the internal dualism which oppressed the Queen. She was not troubled by spiritual conflict. She despised the warming-pan myth as much as she abhorred the Church of Rome. England would not have Popery or Absolutism, and the sooner kings and queens were taught this, the better for them and their subjects. Sarah was an inveterate Whig, with

1 Anne to Sarah, May 19, 1702; Coxe, i, 143.

a detached, disdainful, modern outlook upon life, except where her interests were touched, and a tolerance and rationalism on religion which would now class her as an agnostic. Her salt common sense, her pithy conversation, and her pungent judgment of men, women, and politics, had long fascinated, fleetingly convinced, and at times terrified the Queen. The two women had hitherto lived in the most sincere and natural comradeship possible between persons of the same sex. Till now they had dwelt in a small society in the Cockpit or at St James's, generally under an official cloud and without responsibility or power. The sharp contrasts in politics and religion between Mrs Morley and Mrs Freeman had not been of much importance so long as they lived together in private life. But now Anne was Queen. She was forced from day to day to make grave choices of men and things: and here immediately opened a constant discordance and friction between the two by which in the long run their wonderful friendship was slowly but surely worn away. Indeed, it is amazing that it survived for several years.

From the outset and for nearly six years Marlborough through one agent or another managed nearly everything. Anne yielded herself gladly and often unconsciously to his guidance; and thus the main direction of British, and presently of European, affairs came to reside in Marlborough's hands. The Queen had always her own wishes, and these had almost invariably to receive satisfaction. Often they centred upon minor matters, and did not touch the supreme needs of the State. The more clear-cut and vital decisions of war and policy were largely beyond her comprehension. Great actions in the field, the webs or clashes of politics, the long, deep furrows of strategy, were necessarily outside her sphere. But Queen Anne knew without the slightest doubt what she wanted, and where she wanted to go, and she knew still better where she would never be made to go.

We must at the outset establish her relations with Marlborough. They were always the relations of mistress and servant. Never, in private or in public, in the dark times of

41

William and the Tower, or in the European glories of Blenheim and Ramillies, never on the flowing tide of over-lavish favour, or in the hour of injustice and dismissal, did John Churchill lose for one moment the instinct of sub-mission to the august personage he served. A servant con-fronted with impossible tasks or subjected to undue strain might claim to retire; a mistress might beseech him to remain—or might not; but the relation was dominant, tacit, and immutable. We must recognize this, for it is the keynote of the reign. The Queen was the crowned embodi-ment of the nation, and she often interpreted in a shrewd and homely way to a degree almost occult what England needed and, still more, what England felt. We portray her as a great Queen championed by a great Constable.

Thus was inaugurated the age of Anne. A gulf in national life separates it from the times of Charles II. That gulf had been traversed almost unperceived during the alien interlude of William III. Many unspoken conclusions had gathered in these fourteen years which now emerged as the accepted facts of society. We have entered a period less antique, less harsh, less grim, but with more subtle complications. The struggle of parties continued in the midst of war with an inconceivable bitterness and vigour which were, however, far removed from the brutalities of the Popish Plot and its revenges. The personal stakes for which sovereigns and their Ministers were forced to play were more limited. It was now only nominally that their heads were brought into question. Their property and even their liberty stood on a more assured foundation. All men breathed a gentler air. But the problems with which they were vexed were more baffling because more refined. A large instructed audience, comprising many different classes in the State and a great number of independent notables, watched with lively atten-tion the marches of the armies and the movements of the fleets, the course of trade, the debates in Parliament, and the great personalities at the head of the nation. All classes rose together in the rapid expansion of England. The nobility were recovering an almost feudal splendour after a century and a half of eclipse. The Parliamentary Constitution and the Cabinet system developed with extraordinary speed. The coffee-houses buzzed and throbbed with an activity of thought, speech, and pamphleteering unprecedented in the past, unparalleled in contemporary Europe, and not approached again for a long period in England itself. The City merchants and financiers became a factor in world affairs. Science, learning, architecture, literature, and painting continued to herald all along the line the general advance of the islanders. Public opinion and national consciousness moved forward hand in hand. The masses of the people shared in the national gains.

For two hundred years, during which the sway of Britain became world-wide, we were ruled by an oligarchy. Although the population was but an eighth of its present numbers, there were probably under Anne twenty persons of consequence and of independent standing who had to be considered for every one who counts to-day. On every side were magnates, authorities, and institutions conscious of their rights and duties, and resolute to defend them on every occasion. Even in the most exciting crises the nobility, the gentry, the clergy, and the merchants, or, corporately, the Lords and Commons, the Church and the City, already advanced their opinions with obstinacy and effect. The structure of the body politic was massive and rigid. A vigilant and jealous patriciate, as proud as any which had ruled in Rome or Venice, brooded with jealous eye upon all exceptional personal power. None of those sweeping effects with which the French Revolution and Napoleon have made us acquainted, none of those sudden mass-impulses by which dictators rise and are acclaimed to-day, were possible then. The common people were allowed no share in the high public opinion of the period; to court them would have been adjudged a crime. The names of Cromwell and of Monk were fresh and deep in the memories of the governing classes. Marlborough almost crept home after his victories to avoid any form of popular demonstration other than the formal thanksgivings prescribed by Parliament and the Crown. The

43

field in which he acted, and upon which he had to encounter the despotic power of Louis XIV in sole control of twenty millions of the French, was one thickly occupied by pegs driven firmly into the ground as well as by many potent factions in movement. These forces he must combine, deflect, or cancel against each other before any of his real work could begin. Through all the pegs he must make his way to meet the foreign enemy, and choose some place between them for every sabre-stroke.

We may claim this period as on the whole the greatest in our history. In ten years England rose to the leadership of Europe. She gained the mastery of the seas, including the control—never since lost—of the Mediterranean. The ocean roads to trade and empire in the New World were opened. Her soldiers, according to their enemies, were the best in Europe. Her wealth and prosperity seemed for a while to rise upon the tide of war. By the union with Scotland the island became one. The might of France was abated, and a balance was established in Europe to correct her exorbitant power. The Dutch ally, crippled in the long war, ceased to be a rival at sea, and, weakening under the financial strain, soon ceased to be a rival in trade.

The foundations were laid of that power which fifty years later enabled Lord Chatham by the victories of Wolfe and Clive to drive all challengers alike from America and India.

CHAPTER II

THE REPUBLIC OF THE DYKES

(1702, April)

THE accession of Anne had raised Marlborough to the first position under the Crown in England, but across the Narrow Seas, in the Dutch Republic, he gained a domain of power and influence which was hardly less important and proved at the end of ten years more durable. The foundations of this had been laid during 1701, when as King William's plenipotentiary he had negotiated the treaties which constituted the Grand Alliance. Then it was that Marlborough, already for twenty years behind the scenes of European politics, acquired that direct, authoritative, personal knowledge of how its rulers and peoples stood towards one another. Then he had established contacts with the leading Dutchmen which were based upon broad political harmonies and fostered by mutual understanding and respect. These bonds were to be strained by the inherent divergences of interest and sentiment and the domestic stresses of England and Holland during so many years of unremitting struggle side by side. But they were never broken. Always, in spite of everything that vexed or tempted, Marlborough was true to the principle of the Anglo-Dutch alliance, and always the statesmen of the Republic trusted him as their anchor and salvation. At the very end, when he was hounded out of his own country and stripped of every vestige of power or favour, the fathers of the Republic and the populace of its cities treated him with the honours of a sovereign prince. The union thus formed in his person, as formerly in that of William of Orange, of the two Great Powers of the sea, of trade, and of the money market, was found capable of breaking the ambition of Louis XIV and humbling the might of France. It thus preserved that freedom for the Protestant religion and those rights of Parliamentary government which lighted and

45

guarded the Age of Reason and prepared the civilization of the nineteenth centry.

This was the great period of the Dutch Republic. The Seven Provinces, which had been forged in the fires of Spanish persecution and tempered by heroic warfare against France on land and England by sea, were now become a wonderful instrument and force in Europe. They embodied a victory over suffering, tyranny, and dead-weight bulk which was of precious consequence to the future of mankind. But the very freedom which had preserved them, and the strength and tradition of the resulting organism, bore all the marks and characteristics of the protracted ordeals which had brought them forth. The Dutch Republic perhaps was the most perfect manifestation of obstinacy—constitutional, moral, temperamental—which has ever been known. Obstinacy, stolid, valiant, harsh, even brutal, dwelt in every fibre of the nation; and the humblest burghers and the smallest villages confronted the problems of Europe and the puzzles of men with their own narrow, potent, and unyielding convictions. Their service to the western world was at once sublime and matter of fact. They wished to be free, by which they meant—Protestant and democratic; prosperous, by which they meant—masters of seaborne commerce; and above all safe, by which they meant—behind a dyke, well guarded. The dyke embodied the national idea. On the one side it kept back the hungry seas; on the other the French armies. Behind their dykes they would dwell, and from this shelter they would trade. These and no more were their aims, and for their sake they gave forth over a prolonged period an immense volume of sacrifice and toil.

It is important to survey at this point the articulation of the Dutch States. The whole internal history of the United Provinces is the struggle between the centralized monarchy of the Oranges and the decentralized oligarchy of the bourgeois republicans. The structure of the Constitution was at once complex and rigid. The Dutch municipalities elected representatives, called Regents, from their burghal panels. These Regents, when assembled, formed the Provincial States.

46

The Provincial States chose the delegates who formed the States-General. Each of the seven provinces had only one vote in the States-General, although there was no limit to the number of delegates who might be present. If there were not enough seats in the chamber they had to stand. Each municipality had a salaried officer, the Pensionary. Each province also had a Pensionary, who was in fact governor. The Pensionary of Holland, by far the largest province, paying 60 per cent. of the federal taxes, was known as the Grand Pensionary, and was generally the most powerful man in the Republic. Such was the frame of the Dutch State.

The Stadtholderate, with which was combined the function of Captain-General, was an elective executive office in each province. There was no constitutional reason why there should not be at one time seven Captains-General; but the almost invariable custom was for all the provinces to elect the same man, the heir of the first Dutch hero, William the Silent, to this post; and he became in fact hereditary monarch and war-lord, limited in his actions by the need of procuring the agreement of the oligarchy. The executive body of the States-General was the Council of State, which contained such officers as the Veldt-Marshal, the Treasurer-General, and the Greffier, or Clerk. But practically every detail of policy, every important appointment, every large movement of troops and ships, was referred to the States-General, while all main issues required consultation with each of the Provincial States. This cumbrous machinery hampered all war measures, and was only rendered tolerable through the earnest patriotism enforced upon its components by the gravity and imminence of the national danger. Indeed, when we contemplate the Dutch polity it seems marvellous that it could ever have endured the shocks of war. A confusion of authorities, a Babel of debate, a vehement formalism, a paralysis of action, endless half-measures, compose the picture. And yet this same divided, self-hampered state, with less than three million citizens, maintained year after year armies of a hundred and twenty thousand men against France, the second navy afloat, and an active, far-reaching commerce; and financed all these during ten years of war following on a century of struggle for life.

By the death of William of Orange the entire structure of the Dutch oligarchy and republic was riven or shaken. Their long power, their internal feuds, their elaborate foreign policy, their connexion with England, and their safety in a world war to which they were already committed, all were called to the most searching account. Although this event had been for some time expected, its shock was no less severe. Of the five supreme offices of State the two most important in a foreign crisis fell vacant. Heinsius the Syndic, Fagel the Clerk, and Hop the Treasurer were at their posts. But the Stadtholder and the Captain-General were buried in the tomb of King William III.

Who would lead the armies against the gathering foes? Who would preserve the common action of the Sea Powers? All seemed in dissolution and jeopardy. "When they had the first news of the King's death," wrote Burnet of the States-General,

> they assembled together immediately; they looked on one another as men amazed; they embraced one another and promised they would stick together and adhere to the interests of their country: they sat up most of the night and sent out all the orders that were necessary upon so extraordinary an emergency.[1]

Hard upon the news of William's death came the message from Marlborough to Heinsius promising in the name of the Queen the resolute prosecution of the war and adherence to the treaties. This caught the mood of the assembly at its most tense phase. Sorrow, perplexity, and alarm all took the channel of stern action. Through the long debate there resounded the unanimous determination to march forward unitedly upon the path the dead Stadtholder had opened and prescribed.

Nevertheless, within the Seven Provinces King William's death had unsealed many bitter discontents. In Holland, as in England, he had advanced his personal favourites far

---

[1] Burnet, *History of His Own Time*, vii, 4.

beyond the public esteem in which they stood. In his prolonged absences in England he had "allowed his trusted
friends or creatures to rule over the country." The nation
had submitted perforce. "The Republicans had not ventured
to lift up their voice against the abuses of the prince's
favourites, not even against Odijk, who played the tyrant
in Zeeland, and enriched himself and his followers shame-
lessly."[1] The oligarchical party had waited with as much
impatience as the English Tories for the death of the
unpopular but indispensable prince. Now that the event had
happened, what was virtually a clean sweep was made throughout the provinces of William's men. Latterly his wish had
been that his young cousin, John William Frisco of Nassau,
whom we shall meet later at Oudenarde and Malplaquet,
should succeed him. But at this time the prince was a lad
of fourteen, still at his books in Utrecht. The Captain-
Generalship of the Republic therefore remained unfilled,
though a general war had begun.

A few days after their debate Marlborough was in their
midst. He was received in Holland at this juncture almost
with worship. He was already trusted as a friend, and here
was a friend in need. The Dutch instinctively regarded him
as their champion and deliverer, and much of the loyalty and
trust they had given to William of Orange was directed
almost unconsciously to this gleaming English figure which
appeared in a dark hour so suddenly among them, speaking
in accents of comfort and command. He was careful to
postpone all contact with the States-General until after he
had reached conclusions with Heinsius and with Count Goes,
the Imperial Ambassador. We have found no record of his
conversation with the Pensionary, but Goes, whom he visited
immediately afterwards, has left us an excellent account.
Indeed, it is in the dispatches of Goes, Wratislaw, and other
envoys that we can most plainly hear Marlborough speak, and
feel his hand closing upon affairs. Goes wrote his dispatches
only a few hours after their talks and while the impression was
still vivid. "The only change resulting from the death," said

[1] P. J. Blok, *History of the People of the Netherlands*, v, 3.

49

Marlborough, "is this, that the Queen does not take the field. In all the remaining conduct of affairs the general business against France will lose nothing. The Queen will be loyal to the alliances which have been formed. For that reason," he added, "I hope that the article of the Alliance relating to the pretended Prince of Wales will now be accepted in Vienna." On this, as will be seen, the Ambassador was not yet instructed. Goes therefore turned the conversation questioningly to the opinion which he said prevailed in Holland that the Sea Powers would conduct the war as associates rather than allies, and that consequently there would be no need for the Dutch to give up the lucrative carrying-trade which they did for France. Marlborough at once stamped upon this idea. That it was ridiculous, he said, would be proved by prompt, uncompromising declarations of war.

Upon William's offers to the Emperor about the West Indies Marlborough said the King might have gone farther. "If the Emperor can induce the West Indies to declare for him, we in England are ready to support him without making any claim for ourselves. We would rather that all these islands should fall to the Emperor than that they should be divided between the Powers. If the Emperor is not to have them all, then he would surely be agreeable that we should take as many of them from the house of Bourbon as we can." This frank and fair-seeming offer was made with the knowledge that the declarations of the West Indian islands would not fulfil the condition required. Thus, in fact, the Ambassador learned in the most courteous guise that England meant to take all she could in the West Indies. Such latitude was highly important to Marlborough, because of the Tory predilection for oceanic ventures and conquest.

About Naples and the Italian provinces Marlborough reversed William's policy. "The King," he said, "spoke to Count Wratislaw on this matter rather as hereditary Stadtholder of Holland than as King of England. I have taken it much to heart to dissuade him from his view so that it might not seem that England wished to prevent the Emperor from acting vigorously in Italy. Anyhow that is done with; and

I may now assure you that England will strain every nerve to secure that all the Spanish possessions in Italy without exception shall fall to the Emperor's share. That is the constant thought of the Queen in accordance with the opinion and interest of the English people. If the Emperor can provide the necessary forces England will stand loyally by his side and the Republic must follow our lead." The Ambassador renders these last words of Marlborough, which were no doubt spoken in French, "Die Republik muss mitgehen." They were soon found to be significant. "I have been asked," Marlborough continued, "by a member of the States-General whether England is willing to send a fleet to the Mediterranean. I have told him he can look at our preparations for naval war, and then himself answer the question whether these are intended only to hold the Channel."[1] Thus he sought to confine the Emperor's aims to Europe and direct his chief effort upon Italy, while leaving the new world overseas to England.

In those words, "the Republic must follow our lead," we have the first indication of the change wrought by the death of William III upon the relations of England and Holland. William was a Dutchman to the core. He regarded England as a valuable auxiliary which his birth, marriage, and achievements had gathered to the Republic. The arrival of Marlborough in power meant that the combination would continue —nay, it would become more forceful than ever. The same main objects would be pursued even more vigorously. England would make a greater and not a smaller contribution. But the predominance would lie in the island rather than among the dykes. The alliance would be of England and Holland, instead of the old reversed form. But of this only the four German words which the Ambassador reported gave any sign. The declaration had yet to be made good by the weight of the English effort and by events in the field. The Dutch Republic was for some time unconscious of the altered emphasis and priority, and they learned it only through the agreeable channel of aid and victory.

1 Goes's dispatch, March 31.

No longer was Holland in and through the personality of William III the leading power, but by the force of the personality, not of Queen Anne, but of Marlborough, the leadership passed to England. The position developed to the full only in the course of time. But Marlborough was from the first fully aware of it.[1]

We must look for a moment at the leading Dutchmen. Franz Fagel, the Clerk or Greffier, was the head of the Civil Service of the Republic. He was its permanent head. He was its hereditary head. For more than a hundred years the Fagel family had secured to itself by industry and loyalty this great office with plenary authority which nothing had successfully disputed. The Clerk discharged in a magnified form all those duties which nowadays fall to the permanent chiefs of the Civil Service and of the Foreign Office. All the detailed elaboration of the Central Government decisions, as well as those of its civil and military officials, all the ceremonial conduct of the communications between the Dutch executive and foreign Courts and envoys, passed through his hands; and he controlled the staff and kept the papers by which the business was transacted. Besides this, Fagel was an orator and trained politician who had for many years shone in the debates of the States-General.

Jacob Hop was Treasurer-General. He too had a life-long experience of affairs. As the supreme finance officer of the Seven Provinces he not only called on the States-General to provide the means of maintaining the Army and Navy, but also through the money power exercised a potent influence upon foreign policy. He is described as a man of proud and even haughtily provocative nature, but a whole-hearted, uncompromising patriot, a ready speaker, and a skilled writer deeply versed in the politics of Europe. He had travelled widely, he had been Ambassador in Berlin, Copenhagen, Vienna, and London. He was the implacable enemy of the house of Bourbon. He devoted the prime of his life to gathering resources for the Dutch armies and sustaining them by every aid which farseeing diplomacy might invoke.

1 Klopp, x, 23.

But the most interesting and most powerful figure in the Dutch federation was Antony Heinsius, the Grand Pensionary. In its earliest form his office was that of a tribune of the people protecting the rights of the inhabitants against the Government of the Counts. Originally there had been in Holland only a Committee of Secret Affairs, without a Foreign Minister or an organized Foreign Department. But as the Republic became a great European Power, and, indeed, through its active public discussions, the forum of international affairs, the Pensionary of the State of Holland had become Foreign Minister. Besides this, through the preponderance of Holland he was the informal but acknowledged leader of the States-General. All their deliberations could be subjected to his judgment, and he could initiate business and claim a vote. Even under the august authority of William of Orange, with the crown of England upon his brows, Heinsius had been in fact Chancellor of the State. Upon the death of the Stadtholder and as long as that office remained unfilled he became naturally and inevitably the citizen-sovereign of the Republic.

Heinsius was a lonely man, a bachelor of simple, austere habits whose whole life was one long round of official business. The discharge of his office was the tale of his existence, the unity and safety of the Republic his sole purpose. As the Dutch envoy to Versailles his resistance to the encroachments of Louis XIV after the Peace of Nimwegen had been carried to the point of Louvois' threatening him with the Bastille. Thereafter he was, like Hop, an inveterate enemy of French aggrandizement. He had entered Dutch party politics in the patrician oligarchy which saw its duty and its interest in counterbalancing the 'royalist' tendencies of the house of Orange. But after his experiences at the French Court he joined the circle in which William had gradually gathered almost all the most distinguished Dutchmen. The Stadtholder, when he became King of England, induced Heinsius to undertake the office of Grand Pensionary, with all that accession of responsibility which resulted from the prolonged absences of the ruler. The influence of

53

Heinsius had helped King William to combine the headship of the two nations. He it was who had prevailed upon the States-General to maintain the Army at the strength of forty-five thousand men after the Peace of Ryswick, when the English Parliament had shown itself so improvident in disarmament. Already regarded, even in King William's lifetime, as the most eminent statesman in Europe outside France, Heinsius in all except military operations presided over and conducted the policy of the Republic. His aims, if narrow, were definite. In his own nature he embodied the national conviction or obsession of the dyke. All his life-work was devoted to building an invincible fortress-barrier between his fatherland and France. We shall see later the part that this played in history.

His sincerity was felt by all who came in contact with him. Although a man of high courage and indomitable perseverance, he carried soberness of judgment to the point of pessimism. Nor did he care if friends who visited him in his modest dwelling in times of crisis found him in tears amid his papers over the perils of the State. His patience in discussion, his kindliness, his probity won universal respect. It was obvious to all that he must fill a large part of the void which had opened. Upon him descended the responsibility for maintaining the treaties of the Grand Alliance, and above all the special relations with England, which William's double office had enshrined. And in this his friendship with Marlborough and their mutual confidence were decisive. Heinsius looked upon Marlborough as his link with England. It was as a statesman and diplomatist rather than as a soldier that the foundations of Marlborough's influence in Holland were laid. The military command was a second stage. Thus events shaped themselves gradually and naturally, until Heinsius and Marlborough together filled King William's place, with less authority, but far greater success. The three great Dutchmen speedily accepted Marlborough as a fourth comrade. Principally he dealt with Heinsius, but there is a lengthy correspondence with both Hop and Fagel. These statesmen sat

54

THE GRAND PENSIONARY HEINSIUS
From an engraving after the copy by H. Pothoven
of the painting by G. van de Eikhout
By permission of 's Rijks Prentenkabinet, Amsterdam

almost as close to him and were as much a part of his system as Wratislaw and Eugene in dealing with the Empire, or the Queen and Godolphin and, to some extent, Harley at home.

The discussions at The Hague were now complicated by the English demand that an article should be added binding all the allies to the exclusion from the English throne of the pretended Prince of Wales—*Prætensus Princeps Walliæ*. Both parties at Westminster were open-mouthed for it. To the Whigs it was a cardinal principle and one of the main objects of the war. Very different were the motives of extreme Tory partisans in supporting a proposal which ran counter to their sentiments. Though their leaders could not refuse, they did not wish to be drawn into the European war— except upon the loosest terms. They did not believe that the Emperor could ever bring himself to apply the word *prætensus* to James II's son. It must seem from his point of view to strike both at truth and divine right. Thus the renewal of the Alliance and the outbreak of the war would be at least obstructed. Accordingly there had been seen the extraordinary spectacle of Sir Edward Seymour as one of the Tory chiefs proposing in the House of Commons this additional article, which was, of course, blithely accepted by the Whigs. This is the first of several occasions which we must note where the Tory Party overreached themselves in too clever Parliamentary tactics designed to embarrass their opponents by putting forward Whig doctrines mischievously.

Henceforward the article, almost unanimously endorsed, became a vital counter, both in English politics and in the European situation. Marlborough understood this perfectly. He had gone to Holland with the firm intention of procuring the assent of all the signatory Powers to the new article, including the word *prætensus*. But upon this word, as the Tory leaders knew, the Emperor Leopold had the deepest misgivings. The Imperial Ministers advised him to consult his confessor, a Jesuit, Menegatti. He was reluctant even to do this from a well-grounded apprehension that Menegatti was already in touch with his Ministers. At the moment when Marlborough reached The Hague he was still believed to be resisting. His Ambassador, Goes, declared himself as yet unable to make a definite statement upon the article. Heinsius added that he had learned that the Emperor would not agree to it unless the offending words were omitted. Goes has recorded Marlborough's vehement reply: "If that is the case," he said, "I cannot conclude anything here. The English nation will be so excited that I cannot agree to anything. I do not understand why the Imperial Ministers cannot appreciate the significance of the title of Prince of Wales. A Prince of Wales is, like the Dauphin in France, the recognized heir to the throne. For the very reason that in France the name of Prince of Wales is usually applied to the son of King James, the word *prætensus* has been selected in England and adopted in various Acts of Parliament. The idea of implying thereby any judgment as to the Prince's birth was not in the mind of Parliament at all. Indeed, the question of birth was carefully avoided by Parliament. But on the other hand it is quite impossible to vary the phraseology of an article which is based upon an Act of Parliament. I ask therefore for an immediate decision, or the despatch of a courier to Vienna with a correct explanation of the position."[1]

This forcible intervention shows plainly not only the importance of the issue, but once again how Marlborough stood towards the exiled house at Saint-Germains. He was always their most formidable opponent. He might, like many Tories, indulge a Jacobite sentiment; he might preserve the most agreeable relations possible with Saint-Germains; but he never allowed either his feelings towards, or his conversations with, the real Jacobites to influence in the slightest degree his State policy. And now we see him, at the very outset of his control of affairs, throwing the whole weight of England against them.

However, while the three Plenipotentiaries were sitting in conference on April 3, dispatches arrived from Vienna for both Goes and Heinsius. In the face of the Emperor's repugnance the Imperial Ministers had themselves obtained an

---

1 Goes's dispatch, April 4; Klopp, x, 29.

opinion from Menegatti. This was not at all unlike the argument which Marlborough had just used. The Jesuit fruitfully explored the word 'pretender.' It might as well be read as meaning 'claimant' as 'impostor.' "As it is quite true that the surviving son of King James pretends to be Prince of Wales, and in the additional article nothing is said as to the validity of this pretence, I am of opinion that without any injustice to King James his son can be described as the pretended Prince of Wales. . . . For the issue as to whether he is in reality what he pretends to be, or pretends without justification, is left undecided."[1] Nevertheless, the Emperor had made one final effort, and Goes found himself instructed only to agree to *prætensus* in the last resort. But Heinsius had opened his report from the Dutch Ambassador at Vienna. "I see here," he interposed, "that the Emperor has agreed to the term *prætensus* on the advice of his Confessor." Thus undermined, Count Goes made the best bargain he could, and his nimbleness deserves admiration. "Though your correspondent," he said to Heinsius, "may guess at the contents of my dispatch, it all depends on its interpretation. This is the position: if the declaration of war against France depends wholly on my answer, I am prepared to gratify Lord Marlborough, at least in the hope that my action will be approved; that is to say, I will sign the additional article. But the two things are inseparable."

Nothing could suit Marlborough better. All, in fact, fell into his hands. He obtained agreement both upon the simultaneous declaration of war and the additional article from Holland and the Empire. Not only did this serve his great purposes in Europe, but it left the high Tories with no excuse but to support the war. The condition they had pretended to desire was obtained. They had insisted that the wine they most disliked should be drawn, and now they must drink it with what grace they could.

The practical and vital question of the command of the armies of the Sea Powers was not brought to an issue during Marlborough's visit; yet it was in every one's mind. Even

---

1 The Jesuit's answer is in Latin. Klopp, x, 402.

before Marlborough had reached The Hague some steps had been taken by the Dutch Government. They apprehended, not without good information, that Queen Anne would propose Prince George of Denmark to them. The Queen was sure that her beloved husband was the very man for this responsibility and power. She was alone in her view, and, as one might say, biased; but her view was none the less important. It was well known in Holland that the Prince Consort's intellect and ability were extremely modest. In the earliest Dutch conclaves this was not felt by all to be an insuperable objection for a commander-in-chief of armies in a deadly war. Such a personage would obviously be controlled by a council of war, and this procedure was highly valued by the Republic, since it gave so many people a chance of expressing their opinion. On the other hand, it was contended that a certain amount of brains and personal force were desirable in the chief of armies about to be brought in contact with the military power of France. The more the matter was discussed, the more they realized the loss the Republic had sustained by the death of King William III. Meanwhile, as Marlborough was approaching and it was certain he would press Prince George of Denmark upon them, they thought it best to appoint the aged invalid Prince of Nassau-Saarbrück Veldt-Marshal temporarily as a stopgap. Near him stood Ginkel, whom we must recognize in the Earl of Athlone, an able and experienced officer, the limits of whose solid capacity had been established. Ginkel did not conceal his opinion that the post of Captain-General of the Dutch—and consequently of the English—Army belonged to him. Behind Ginkel there was an array of veteran Dutch generals—Opdam, Slangenberg, Overkirk—all of whom had seen far more service than Marlborough, and looked sourly upon the claims of foreigners. Such was the situation when Marlborough arrived.

No one can ever tell from the records which have survived whether at this time he expected to obtain the supreme command for himself. But it is certain that he pressed Prince George's claims in such a manner that if they had not been absurd they must have been accepted. He did not on this occasion make a direct proposal. According to Goes, he said he was not authorized to raise the question formally. If, however, the proposal were made from the Dutch side, it would seem the best way of binding the two armies together as closely as before, and he stated that as the English Captain-General he would then readily serve under Prince George as Commander-in-Chief. But this very combination of an intense and dominating personality with the Queen of England's husband in his hand as a puppet Commander-in-Chief alarmed the Dutch magnates even more than the Prince of Denmark by himself. It might well, it seemed, be destructive of the authority of councils of war—nay, of the States-General themselves. They therefore fell back into a state of indecision from which Marlborough did not at all attempt at this time to rescue them. There is no doubt that now and later at the Queen's command he paraded Prince George's claims with an earnestness which convinced that good man that he had done everything possible on his behalf; and this in spite of gossip, rumour, and suggestion in their most plausible forms.

Certain it is that he employed every argument in favour of Prince George. We have his letter to Godolphin from The Hague of April 11:

> *I have with all the care I am capable of endeavoured to incline these people to desire the honour of having the Prince to command their army as well as the English. To the Pensioner and such as I can trust I have let them see very plainly that it is His Royal Highness only that can unite [bring in] the forty thousand paid by England. The King of Prussia will be to-morrow at Wesel, in order to make all the interest he can to have the command. The Elector of Hanover underhand does all he can to have it; the Duke of Celle is also named.
>
> The difficulty of this matter is that not only every province but every town must consent before the States can make an offer. Your thought of the Archduke [Charles] the Pensioner thinks is not practicable for this year.

Once again we see a strangely characteristic instance of

Marlborough doing everything that a man could be asked to do against his own interest in complete sincerity and with force and skill, and yet none the less advancing the course which favoured his heart's desire. The extraordinary feature is that in his advocacy of Prince George's claims lay the surest route to the attainment of his own. How was he, a subject, a private man, to set himself against the kings and princes of the Grand Alliance, or against the old, trusted, proved generals of the Dutch Republic? Compared with such rivals, some of whom, like the Prussian, even hinted they might join the enemy if their wishes were not gratified, his personal merit stood no chance. But Prince George of Denmark, with the Queen of England vital and powerful behind him, was a figure large enough to scare away the crows.

We do not think he was at all sure at this juncture that the command would fall to him. In that patient, persistent, contriving mind, long accustomed to inferior solutions, there must have arisen a practical plan by which Prince George would hold the supreme command while Marlborough, from the second place, would nevertheless govern the event. Nor did he recoil from such expedients. The best obtainable was nearly always good enough for him. Besides, at this stage it was his bounden duty to press the Prince George proposition, and that proposition, backed by Queen Anne, would certainly extinguish the Continental royalties. Again and again we see him in the most correct positions, where his duty was afterwards perceived to be his interest, but was none the less his duty. After all, no one can be blamed for executing a lawful mission faithfully, merely because if his efforts failed the consequences would be good for him and for his country. So in the upshot Queen Anne was decisive against the foreign royalties, the Dutch were obdurate against her husband, and none of the generals of the Republic were acceptable to the English Government. Under extreme conflicting pressures the Dutch fell back on negative solutions. Stanhope, our envoy at The Hague, broached the choice of a generalissimo to the Pensionary, who answered that the whole question was "too nice for him to appear to concern himself any way in. . . . They shrug up their shoulders and say 'tis a slender point, and they ought to be pardoned for the preservation of their liberty. . . . It seems to me they design no other General but the old Prince of Nassau-Saarbrück."[1]

Here, then, this all-important matter rested uncomfortably for the time being. Its solution must be sought in the inherent prejudices of the Dutch. They disliked a royal Commander-in-Chief. They feared even more a combination of Marlborough plus a royal prince whom he dominated. They were seeking the impossible; they wanted a general who would be strong against the enemy, but weak and submissive towards themselves. Their ideal was a deferential dictator, a docile champion. And here the fundamental cleavages of Dutch politics reveal themselves. The Amsterdammers and all the elements least favourable to the war most wanted a weak command. It was the keynote of their politics that there should be no resurrection of the 'Royalist' offices of War-lord or Stadtholder. They therefore looked with favour upon a foreigner who was not a prince, because he would be the more controllable. Subject to this condition, they were agreeable to his being competent. Thus from the first in those very quarters where the sharpest opposition might have been expected there was a definite inclination towards this Englishman, of no great rank, but undoubtedly a remarkable person.

Marlborough allowed all this to simmer. When we consider the dazzling prize, as it must have seemed to an ardent soldier, which dangled aimlessly in the air, we must be astonished at his composure and seeming detachment. If he had lifted his hand to grasp it, a hundred voices of authority would have been raised against him. Yet can we believe that he was indifferent? Could so powerful a mental mechanism of schemes and action be combined with perfect self-effacement? However this may be, Marlborough quitted The Hague without having exposed by even the twinkle

1 Stanhope to Vernon, April 25; S.P. 84/224, f. 22.

of an eye the slightest personal interest in the question of command, while at the same time there grew throughout the high circles of the Republic the general feeling that no one would suit all purposes so well as he.

Not until after he had reached agreement upon the main lines of policy with Heinsius and Goes did Marlborough present himself to the States-General. He had wished to preserve an informal and private status. But the public temper would not be satisfied without a demonstration. Accordingly at Heinsius' insistence he assumed the character and style of an Ambassador-Extraordinary, and went to the Assembly in full pomp. He was received with the utmost honour. He addressed Their High Mightinesses in French.

"Her Majesty . . . is firmly resolved to contribute all that lies in her power towards the advancing and increasing union, friendship, and correspondence, and to make that a constant maxim of her government. . . . She will not only exactly and faithfully observe and execute the treaties and alliances made between the Kings her predecessors and your High and Mighty Lordships, but . . . is likewise ready to renew and confirm them; as also to concur with you in all the measures which have been taken by the late King of glorious memory, in pursuance of the said alliances. Her Majesty is likewise disposed to enter into such other stricter alliances and engagements, which shall most conduce to the interests of both nations, the preservation of the liberty of Europe and reducing within just bounds the exorbitant power of France.

"In the meantime Her Majesty is ready from this moment and without any delay to concur to this end, with all her forces as well by sea as by land. . . . And Her Majesty to show her zeal the more has been pleased to authorize me to concert . . . the necessary operations. These motives obliged Her Majesty to order me to depart with all diligence in order to come hither, and give . . . all possible assurances thereof, without stopping at the ordinary formalities. And I look upon it as an extraordinary happiness that Her Majesty has done me the honour to employ me in this commission, since it gives me the opportunity of expressing . . . the zeal I have for your service."[1]

Dykevelt, William's old agent, now President of the Assembly, in welcoming these bold, plain offers with thanks and "with a flood of tears,"[2] turning to Marlborough, added "that his person would be highly acceptable to them not only for the Queen's choice of him and for the sake of King William who first invested him with that character, but for his own merit."[3]

These declarations, carried as fast as the posts could ride into every capital, consolidated the Grand Alliance. All the temptations, bribes, and threats which French diplomacy was offering to every signatory Power lost their potency. Marlborough restored the vast structure which King William's death had seemed about to dissolve. And this was what King William had foreseen and prepared. We must pause to contemplate the shock to friend and foe of the King's death and the counter-shock when it was realized that the gap was filled. No one at this time dreamed that the new indispensable Man at the centre would step forward and weld the confederacy with tireless patience, or strike its enemies down with stunning blows. It was enough for rejoicing that William's cause had not perished with his breath. In this temper all the treaties and military conventions, the quotas of fleets and armies, were eagerly confirmed.

Marlborough's mission was therefore entirely successful. In ten days he had rallied all the signatories of the Grand Alliance and expressed all their engagements in strict terms. Treaties were also prepared between the Emperor and Poland, and subsidy-treaties were signed with Prussia, Münster, Hesse-Cassel, Mecklenburg, Trèves, and Lüneberg. All that had threatened to fall to pieces was now gripped together more strongly than ever; where all had been doubt and despondency there was now resolve and confidence. The

1 Boyer, *Annals of the Reign of Queen Anne*, i, 12.
2 Legrelle, *La Diplomatie française et la Succession de Espagne* (1892), iv, 263 *et seq.*
3 Lediard, *Life of John, Duke of Marlborough* (1736), i, 143.

Dutch rejected with scorn the peace proposals of Louis XIV. The three Great Powers bound themselves together secretly to declare war upon France on May 4/15. The additional article, with the word *prætensus*, was duly signed, and the English political situation was for the time being consolidated for the most vigorous action. Nothing remained when Marlborough returned to England for King William's funeral but to choose the commander, make the plans, and begin the fighting. But these were matters not to be so swiftly settled.

CHAPTER III

QUEEN ANNE'S FIRST GOVERNMENT

(1702, May)

QUEEN ANNE and Marlborough had not waited to begin their political studies until after the death of King William had been formally announced. They both knew what they wanted to do, and their aims, though different, were not in the main incompatible. The government of England had passed by lawful succession to Princess Anne and her Cockpit group. There they were, this tiny circle, bound together by common interests and by the anxieties and partisanship of many years—the Queen, sacred and at the moment of accession almost omnipotent; Marlborough, master of politics and diplomacy, and certainly the leading English general; Sarah, the much-loved link; and Godolphin, the faithful friend of the Queen and kinsman of the Marlboroughs. Here was a close confederacy which had been slowly and tensely wrought. Anne had insisted upon the equality of their intercourse, but this privilege was strictly limited. Mrs Morley, Mr and Mrs Freeman, and Mr Montgomery—there could not be a tighter thing. They formed a group as integral and as collectively commanding as anything of which there is record in our annals. Outside, beyond their privacy, prowled the magnates of the Whigs and Tories with their strident factions and the formidable processes of Parliament. Outside lay the Church of England in the highest state of effervescence, and the finances of the country, already drained and overtaxed by a long war. Across the seas loomed the European coalition and the mighty armies of France, already on the march. With all these the Cockpit must now deal. It must have seemed an unequal struggle; but the result showed them completely triumphant, and had they held together to the end it is certain that they could have continued to enforce their will in every direction.

Below this personal organism of the Queen and the genius of Marlborough came the constitutional Ministry of the realm. This had now to be formed. It must surely be Tory. The phrases of the Queen's Speech which had chilled the Whigs had made this fact public. The Queen was a Tory and a High Tory at heart. Marlborough was a Tory by origin, sentiment, and profession. But he was quite cool about whether the Government was Tory or Whig. What he sought was a political system that would support the war. He shared none of Anne's strong feelings about the High Church or Low Church bishops. Unity at home and in Parliament to sustain, with the combined resources of the nation, the war abroad against the power of France was his sole and only end. When all deference had been shown to the Queen's wishes Marlborough secured from her the larger necessities of his policy. He was still convinced that the war against France could only be waged with success by a united nation. The Tories were the peace party. Their opposition would rend the State. But if the responsibilities of office would compel them to face the task themselves, then they could make the war truly national. The Whigs would have no choice but to support them, and no wish but to do it themselves instead. It was therefore certain that, though the Whigs had a narrow majority in the existing House of Commons, the emphasis of the new reign and the character of the Queen's first Government would be Tory. Anne desired to gather Tory Ministers round her, and Marlborough sought a solid Parliamentary foundation for the war.

Both sovereign and counsellor wished by the retention of some Whigs in the less important offices to make the Government broad-bottomed, and to tinge it with a national beyond a party complexion. The Tories were moreover made aware that if they received the favour of the Crown and were entrusted with the conduct of public affairs, it must be upon the basis that they would support and prosecute the war with the whole of their party forces. These undertakings their leaders were ready to give, though with many unspoken reservations which will presently emerge about the character and scale of England's war effort. This Tory allegiance to the war was the foundation of the politics of the first half of the reign. However fierce the faction fights might be, however bitter the rivalries of the parties or the discontents of deposed Ministers, it was definitely understood that the waging of the war and the voting of the necessary supplies were above and beyond political strife. This dominant condition was on the whole punctiliously fulfilled.

The two pillars of a Tory Ministry must, of course, be Rochester and Nottingham. Their careers have both run through this account. We remember Rochester as the Laurence Hyde who had striven to convert James to Protestant conformity in the 1680's; as the Lord Treasurer whose financial irregularities had escaped from the clutches of the great Halifax through the opportune death of Charles II, and whose indifferent attitude to Anne in her troubles with King William was also not forgotten. Rochester was Lord-Lieutenant of Ireland at the moment of the demise. William had purposed his removal with the other Tories. Rochester had come to London at his summons. He was now a personage of the highest consequence. In the public eye as an uncle of the Queen he stood very near the throne. His elder brother, Clarendon, could not bring himself to take the oath to his niece against the rightful heir; but Rochester had bowed to the Act of Settlement. Upon the dynastic question his conscience was at rest. Office would confirm its repose. He was moreover the lay champion of the Church of England. The carping voice of criticism alleged against him an indulgence in liquor, with consequential bad language, as well as other vanities of various kinds which ill-accorded with his pontifical airs and public professions. Burnet describes him as "the smoothest man in the Court." Another view was "a difficult and prickly man." Certainly his impressive virtues and far-famed piety were no bar against the seductions of ambition or intrigue. Nevertheless, if anyone could be said to embody in his person what the Tory Party stood for in Church and State, it was Rochester.

At his side was Nottingham, the experienced and accomplished Minister who under William and Mary had meddled—too much to please the admirals—with the command of the fleet, and did justice to Marlborough when he was in jeopardy by the forgeries of Robert Young. Nottingham's birth, his experience, his culture, his versatile learning, his natural piety and upright life, entitled him to the respect of the Tory squires and the country clergy. Even his opponents did not accuse him of hypocrisy. They commented upon his "airs of a Spanish grandee" and upon his pompous delivery of the commonplaces of Oxford parsons. When he dwelt with unction on the Divine Right of the Anglican priest-kingship and the unity of Church and State, when he descanted upon the mystical significance of Primogeniture, and conducted his fight against the Dissenters with a display of prodigious school-learning, friend and foe fled the chamber. But no one could deny that he had kept the Tory faith. He had withheld himself from the Popery of James II. His scruples had prevented him from signing the appeal to William. He had never tainted his record by taking part in the election of a sovereign by Parliament. He commanded almost tender devotion from the most orthodox Tories. Descending to the secular sphere, Nottingham had throughout 1701 declaimed in the spirit of his party against costly intervention in Continental affairs. If this could not be avoided he fell back on Rochester's opinion "that we shall never have any decisive success nor be able to hold out in a war against France, but by making it a sea war and such a sea war as accompanies and supports attempts on land."[1]

Meanwhile the Queen's popularity, in which she rejoiced, grew by leaps and bounds. Nothing was more buoyant than her action about her Civil List. The Commons had voted her King William's revenue for life, but that revenue had included fifty thousand a year for herself, as heiress-presumptive. Might not the Whigs suggest that this sum should be passed on to the new heiress-presumptive, the Electress Sophia, and her son George? The Court at

[1] Feiling, *History of the Tory Party*, p. 368. *Cf.* von Noorden's admirable vignette (i, 202).

THE EARL OF ROCHESTER
From a copy of the painting by William Wissing
National Portrait Gallery

Hanover sat up attentive upon the point. Now this touched the old feud of the abandoned courtship in 1681. No English money while she was Queen should go to that quarter. Anne was, moreover, generous and even disdainful of money, although in a large way she had felt the want of it. The Commons were amazed to hear her announce that in view of the heavy taxes which weighed on her subjects she would restrict her expenditure in every possible way. "It is probable that the revenue may fall very short of what it has formerly produced; however I will give directions that one hundred thousand pounds be applied to the public service in this year, out of the revenue you have so unanimously given me."[1] Hoffmann reported to his Government that the enthusiasm which greeted this statement was indescribable. "Since Queen Elizabeth there had been no instance of such graciousness. . . . The Queen had completely won the hearts of her subjects."[2] Unnoticed by these subjects then and thereafter, she had won other points which also counted with her. There could certainly be no question of her being pressed to provide any money for the Court of Hanover. That hated brood could shift for themselves. We can only speculate upon the authorship of this brilliantly successful gesture. Marlborough was at The Hague. The new Ministry was not yet formed. The Queen was still surrounded by Whigs. Moreover, the act when we see it in its full light has a truly feminine quality. The abandonment of so large a sum of money was hardly what the matter-of-fact Sarah would have proposed. She makes no claim to have done so in her writings. It must have been the Queen's own plan; and if so the fact gives us a measure of the scale and force of her personal interventions in public affairs.

By the time Marlborough returned from The Hague the Queen's intention to rest upon the Tories was known everywhere, and the principal figures in the new Administration could be plainly discerned. At The Hague and Vienna the advent of the leaders of the peace party caused a natural

1 *Parliamentary History*, vi, 11.   2 Hoffmann's dispatch, April 11.

anxiety. Moreover, a Tory member, Jack Howe, one of William III's most persistent assailants, had presented to the Queen an address from the Diocese of Gloucester which in fulsome terms invited her to assume a personal rule; and in Marlborough's absence Anne had replied, "I am greatly indebted to you and your friends, and thank you for your well-intentioned address." It was unusual for the Crown to reply to a partisan address. Whig remonstrances were made to Marlborough by the indirect channel of Wratislaw. Marlborough replied that he did not approve of the address or of the answer, but the Queen had not spoken deliberately, and had merely not wanted to offend anyone who addressed her in loyal terms. Protest was made to the Queen by the Duke of Somerset, who still retained the office he had held under William and the Queen made answer that "on the public reading of the address she had not appreciated its real gist; now, on a close examination, she must openly admit that she did not approve of its substance."

Whether Marlborough had made representations, we do not know; but it is certain that he used his influence sparingly. He reserved it for essentials. Of these the first was Rochester's demand to be Lord Treasurer. If Marlborough was to lead the Army with any prospect of success he must be sure of the money for pay and supplies. He must have some one at the Treasury, and near the Queen at home, whom he could trust. We cannot doubt that before he went to Holland the Queen had promised him that Godolphin should have this key-post. At any rate, when Wratislaw early in April voiced the fears of the allies about Rochester, and asked why this troublesome personage was not sent off to his Viceroyalty in Ireland, Marlborough replied, "Have patience; he will have to go there nolens volens."[1]

Normanby's appointment as Lord Privy Seal a few weeks later caused another perturbation in Whig and allied circles. In King William's reign he had lived with Monsieur de Tallard, the French Ambassador, on the most friendly and confidential terms, and it was said that Tallard's dispatches had been

---

[1] Wratislaw's dispatch, April 7; Klopp, x, 34.

often based on information procured by Normanby. Wratislaw expressed his fears lest war secrets should be divulged
by this new Cabinet Minister. Marlborough shrugged his
shoulders and said that he had had nothing to do with
Normanby's selection. "I am aware of his bad qualities and
anxious about the results; *but it is not in my power to intervene in everything.* Anyhow the Lord Privy Seal has nothing
to do with foreign affairs."[1] These instances are sufficient to
show the separate will-power of the Queen and the care which
Marlborough observed in dealing with her.

At the desire of his Mistress Marlborough continued to
press upon the Dutch Prince George's claims to the supreme
command of the armies. The more Tory appointments
they saw in the new English Ministry the less they were
inclined to such a plan. They recalled James II's spiteful
but truthful remark upon the Prince of Denmark's departure
from the camp at Salisbury, "the loss of a single trooper
would have been of greater consequence."[2] In vain Marlborough applied his persuasive arts to Wratislaw, and dwelt
upon the stimulus that would be given to the action of
England if only the new Dutch Ambassador could bring the
patent of Prince George's appointment with him among his
credentials. Wratislaw replied:

> In accordance with your wishes I am ready to write to Goes [at
> The Hague] on the subject, but I must not conceal from you that
> I have little hope. The inclination of the republic has not been
> markedly favourable; and the Queen's movement towards the
> Tories will not help it.[3]

This forecast was well founded. The Dutch took refuge in
the folds of their quaint but sometimes serviceable constitution. Even the threats conveyed by the English agents
that England might stand out of the land war did not move
them. All the towns of Holland except Dordrecht resolved
that no Captain-General should be appointed; and Dordrecht
bowed to the general view.

1 Wratislaw's dispatch, May 3 ; Klopp, x, 34.
2 Clarke, *Life of James II,* ii, 225.
3 Wratislaw's dispatch, May 3 ; Klopp, x, 34.

The Queen and her husband had to accept such an unmistakable decision. For months Marlborough had used all his influence upon the Dutch in favour of an appointment which must certainly run counter to his dearest wish and greatest need. He had failed. But it was not his fault. Certainly he had done more than could have been claimed from mortal man. Despite all his force and tact, so faithfully forthcoming on this point, somehow or other he could not succeed. We must recognize the episode as one of his defeats. Yet the slightest suspicion that he had not tried his utmost to gain this silly point would have been fatal. Happily the project was so absurd that he could expend himself upon it without extravagant risk.

The character of the Government was not changed violently in a day. The transformation, which was ceaseless, was complete in about three months. The private funeral of King William III marked one of its stages. The coffin was conveyed on Sunday, after night had fallen, to the Henry VII Chapel at Westminster. Two days later Whig officers of the Household were replaced with Tories. Jersey became Lord Chamberlain, and Sir Edward Seymour, ailing and grumbling, with his solid block of West Country members behind him, became Comptroller. On May 2 Nottingham, in spite of his recalcitrance to the avowed main objects of the Government—namely, the maintenance of the Grand Alliance and the prosecution of the war—became publicly Secretary of State in charge of Southern Affairs at a council board which already included Rochester. Moreover, Rochester and Nottingham brought with them as their colleague in the Secretaryship of State (Northern Affairs) Sir Charles Hedges, a pleasant, adaptable man, who owed his preferment to their patronage. Soon the notorious Jack Howe of the Gloucester address, the defamer of King William, received a petty but challenging post. Marlborough had the greatest difficulty in inducing Devonshire to remain Lord Steward. Almost the only other Whigs in office were the Duke of Somerset, Master of the Horse, and Boyle, a friend of Harley, Chancellor of the Exchequer, an office then, and sometimes since, of subordination. All this was Anne. Marlborough waited for the main issues as a general should do on a battle-field. There were two of these. The first was the appointment of Godolphin to be Lord Treasurer and, as we should now say, Prime Minister. On this Marlborough had from the first been resolved. Against him stood Rochester with the whole Tory Party at his back. To the political world the matter seemed long in suspense.

Godolphin had proved his devotion in the days when Anne was under the scowl of "Mr Caliban," when Sarah was barred from the farthest limits of the Court, and Marlborough was in the Tower. He had been Anne's friend when Rochester would not even carry her letter to Queen Mary. Godolphin had always obstructed with the power of his office every attempt of William and Mary to reduce the Parliamentary grant by which the Cockpit household was sustained. Like the Churchills, Godolphin had not been driven in terror from Princess Anne's home and circle by the ban of the ruling Court. Like Marlborough, he had taught the future Queen a great deal about public affairs. Above all, he was an old friend. In the Queen's eye, therefore, Godolphin was of a different order altogether from the proudest dukes and greatest party leaders of the day. He was dignified in her mind by a title far above the common nobility. He was "Mr. Montgomery." She had conceived and bestowed this honour herself from her own heart, without the aid of the College of Heralds or the forms of the English Constitution. Historians have fallen into tangled arguments through failing to understand the intense responses of Anne's warm heart and cunning mind.

Sidney Godolphin as Lord Treasurer suited Marlborough and fitted his purposes as neatly and as smoothly as Cadogan or Cardonnel in their respective posts. It is curious how he had the very man he needed close at hand, fully qualified, joined to him by a proved political attachment, and lately by a family bond. This is in no way to disparage the great independent position of Lord Godolphin. We have traced his life across three reigns of a quarter of a century. He has nearly always been a Minister and usually in charge of the finances. He was a master of all the secrets of State, and no one understood the high administration so well as he. None had his knowledge, and few his easy, suave, adaptable competence, or his calm, even temper. He was as perfectly in tune with the movement of parties and events at this moment as personally with the Queen and Marlborough.

A new sovereign was to be crowned: most of the Ministers of the late King were out of favour with her. Not so Godolphin. He had been turned out of office barely a year before King William's death. He represented just in time the incoming Tory tide. There must have been a great dexterity, and there must have also been an enormous fund of serviceableness. We remember Charles II's pithy description of him —"never in the way, never out of the way." Thus all the turns and surprises of party politics and changes of rulers left Godolphin eminently agreeable to every Administration and sovereign. He had held the Treasury as one of Charles II's "chits." He had voted for excluding the Duke of York from the throne; he had been that King's Minister. He had accompanied him in unreproached loyalty almost to the beach. He had been one of King William's principal assistants, while making no secret of his sentimental devotion to the exiled Mary of Modena. He was never able to mount more comfortably into the saddle than upon the accession of Anne. Yet the bridging of all these gulfs did not seem a masterpiece of calculation. Each transaction had been smooth and natural, almost inevitable. Nor did he display at any time any keen appetite for office. He had resigned several times, and more often still had threatened to do so. He always had to be pressed to resume official service, and invariably declined with almost invincible obstinacy every post which was sure to be forced on him.

His life, though immersed in public business, was gay and debonair. Incorruptible, scrupulous to the last degree where public money was concerned, simple and frugal in his habits of living, he was renowned both as a gambler and a sportsman. Although constant to the memory of his wife,

74

he had been known upon occasion to write love-poems on the cards at gaming-tables. He is described as a slim little man, stiff and awkward, with an abstracted glance, who moved with what appeared to be a dreamy detachment through the Court and the Council. In his home he was inaccessible. When he emerged into society he parried political questions with remarks about the weather. He was never really contented except at Newmarket. He is the unchallenged father of English horse-breeding. If all his lifetime of Ministerial work were blotted out, his fame would be secure. Up till a certain point in the history of war we often read of the defeated king or commander escaping from the battlefield on his 'fleet Arab steed.' After Godolphin had lived, it is usually 'his English thoroughbred.' He it was who imported the immortal stallion, the Godolphin Arabian, who was "allowed to have refreshed the English blood more than any foreign horse yet imported," and brought into being a race of horses never previously known to man, more cherished and admired than all other quadrupeds in the human story.

> Who would not praise Patritio's high desert?
> His hand unstain'd, his uncorrupted heart,
> His comprehensive head? all intr'sts weigh'd,
> All Europe sav'd, yet Britain not betray'd?
> He thanks you not; his pride was in piquette,
> Newmarket fame, and judgment at a bett.[1]

Godolphin, of course, made his habitual objections. He did not wish to take office—there were so many other more amusing things to do. Of all offices the one he would least like was the care of the finances. How well he knew that arduous and thankless task! Surely after all these years he might be spared. He pressed this resistance to so sharp a point that we cannot tell at this distance of time, in spite of all research, with any certainty whether he wished to have the place or not. Certainly Marlborough had to use all his various influences to persuade him. The Captain-General declared in repeated letters that he

[1] Pope, *Epistle to Cobham.*

would not attempt to conduct the war and direct the armies unless Godolphin were Lord Treasurer. No one else could he trust. With no one else would he enter the struggle. He knew and foresaw many of the obstacles he would have to overcome before he could ever reach the enemy. He knew the Queen; he knew the Dutch; he knew the German Princes; he knew the English Parliament. Unless he could count on the Lord Treasurer to pay the British troops and their hired contingents, to pay for the supplies in the theatre of war and the munitions from home, he would not mount his horse. Sufficiently pushed, Godolphin yielded with dignity and on the best of terms, and thus in due course was opened the historic Marlborough-Godolphin Administration which through six years of general war led England and Europe triumphantly.

The burden of adjusting the minor offices fell upon Godolphin, and his letters to Harley will command sympathy.

> I never took such pains in my life to satisfy anybody as Sir Ch. M[usgrave] in every thing from the first moment I spoke to him, but it's pretty hard to follow humours so changeable and uncertain. He would not be in the Ordnance, and when it was too late then he would be. At first he would not be a Teller because it was a sinecure, and afterwards when he had kissed the Queen's hand for it, he would not take it because it was not Mr. Palmes's [vacancy]. . . . I wish with all my heart that four or five of these gentlemen that are so sharp set upon other people's places had mine amongst them to stay their stomachs.[1]

Here is a rebuke to Harley's dressed-up letter-writing:

> At first when I saw your hand upon the outside of the enclosed letter it gave me a great deal of satisfaction to think you had forgiven that torrent of impertinence [irrelevance] which dropped from me last night, but when I came to read it I concluded it was an old letter which must have been mislaid by some neglect of my servants.[2]

Marlborough had one other thought about the formation of the Government; and he urged the Queen to call

[1] May 28, 1702, Portland Papers. *H.M.C.*, iv, 39.
[2] May 21, 1702, *ibid*.

THE GODOLPHIN ARABIAN

From a print at Windsor Castle. By permission of His Majesty the King

Shrewsbury to her side. Here was the great Whig who would establish the national character of the Government. Since the Fenwick Trial eight years before the Duke of Shrewsbury had escaped from every form of public duty. He had confronted all appeals of King William with his health, affected by the hunting fall, and with his peace of mind, destroyed by worry and the prickings of conscience. He had for some years withdrawn from England and settled himself in Rome, where Italian skies, cosmopolitan society, and an ecclesiastical atmosphere soothed his nervous, super-sensitive nature. Shrewsbury was the other big figure which Marlborough required for his arrangements at home. Their established connexion, the anxieties they had both felt about their relations with Saint-Germains, Shrewsbury's vague but vast and durable prestige in English politics, all made his coming into the Government in any office he would like—even the lightest—appropriate and important. Shrewsbury was the Whig he wanted. No partisan could impugn his orthodoxy. No aristocrat could surpass his magnificence. But here Marlborough failed, and his failure condemned him to less good arrangements at home. He had to do without Shrewsbury. Shrewsbury, with many expressions of goodwill, excused himself behind several lines of personal fortification. He preferred an elegant dalliance by the Tiber, and soon fell in love with a widow—an Italian lady of experienced charm—whom he met by its banks. The fact that, although on the friendliest terms with Marlborough, he would not come home and do any work was untoward.

The Queen conceived that she knew as much as anyone about the Church of England, of which she was the supreme head, and was resolved to protect and rule it according to her lights. Godolphin was now undisputed master of the public finances. The armies and the Grand Alliance fell evidently into Marlborough's sphere. But there remained Parliament, and especially the House of Commons, with which the Cockpit must establish a direct relationship. It is noteworthy that the elective assembly was already recognized as the dominant factor in the State. Without its goodwill, or at least its compliance, the authority of the Crown, the cohesion of the allies, and, of course, finance and war would all fall in helpless futility. Who was to manage the House of Commons? Who was to provide this indispensable foundation for the whole action of England? The Crown had inherited from King William at least a hundred members on whom for one cause or another reliance could be placed. These, added to the Tory strength, gave a working majority in this Whig Parliament; and the Whigs themselves could be counted on for the war. There was therefore a considerable accord upon the national issue. But the quarrel of the two parties proceeded all the more fiercely in the numerous fields that still remained open for political combat. Each watched vigilantly for the chance to discredit, trip up, or strike down the other. However, the Tory Party was not all one. Its fervent "Highflyers" were too extravagant for a large number of country gentlemen and moderates, some of whom were in the hands of the Government, but most of them entirely independent. They looked beyond the Tory chiefs in the Cabinet, to Robert Harley, the Speaker and also, as we should say, Leader of the House. To him resorted many of the Whigs in their new distress. There was a great body of members around the Speaker who admired his cautious good sense and moderate views, and were associated with him in all the day-to-day work of Parliament.

Harley was a man of the middle. He represented at this time moderation in its most crafty and efficient form. He was a monument of common sense surrounded by dodges. It had not always been so. Only four years before he had been the leader of the most violent Tory follies against King William. He had voiced the passions of the squires to disband the Army, and establish a Land Bank in opposition to the Bank of England. He said jocularly of himself that it was always his practice "to howl with the wolves, and if his friends wished it, to call black white and white black." Still, he was a man of the middle. He was a Nonconformist who had become a mouthpiece of Anglicanism, without

78

repudiating his original sect. He was a Tory leader who had begun as a Whig and still preserved friendly Whig connexions. He was a strident pacifist and disarmament-monger who now thought that there was much to be said for vigorous participation in the European war. He understood the House of Commons from every angle. At thirty-nine he had been chosen Speaker and in a sense Leader of the House. The Tories considered him their future candidate, and the Whigs would rather have him than any other Tory.

But Harley embodied much more than the contradictions of his career; he was a man of broad and solid ability. He was no seeker for small or near prizes. In vain had William cast the Ministerial bait before him. He seemed with strange shrewdness to seek to represent the central opinion of the Commons without losing contact with the main body of the Tory Party. We may picture him in the Chair hearing confidences from both sides, persuading the one to concede and the other to forbear; and giving when asked advice which suited his general purpose, withal preserving agreeable relations in every quarter. In his desire to dwell at the hub of Parliamentary opinion he had necessarily to use much artifice. He spoke slowly, "with serpentine convolutions, numerous hypotheses, and long involved periods." He performed prodigies of dark and oracular utterance. It was remarked that the broken and often obscure style of his official letters corresponded with his ambiguous speech. Even his caligraphy conformed. Just as he stuttered and stammered in speaking, so in writing he used to slur and entangle the lines.

No greater disservice can be done to his memory than to read his letters. There is a personal awkwardness about them and a scent of lamp-oil, redolent even after two hundred years. None of the eminent men in England in or out of office wrote quite this kind of letter either to their betters or their clients. It was said of Robert Harley that if he desired anything for himself or another he preferred to knock at the back door even of his closest acquaintance rather than go straight up to the front. For no particular reason but simply out of habit or preference he would take tortuous and secret alleys rather than the street. His supporters said that in managing the parties he would "burrow like a mole and used with great skill a dozen petty underground sources of information"—only regretting there was not a thirteenth.

His frequently disconcerted opponents dubbed him trickster and sharper. They said that his political creed reached its pinnacle in the conviction that power, fortune, and influence were identical with enjoyment. When the factions of the day rose to such extravagant heights a man in a central position needed to protect himself from their fury by an entire scaly apparatus of ruse and ambiguity. That Harley was false to every cause and every man was in a certain sense true; but he was not false to himself, nor to his persistent purpose of steering a middle course for England between many alternating extravagant attitudes and perils. At this juncture he presents himself in his youthful prime as at once the most massive and most artful Parliamentary figure.

Harley was the man whom Marlborough and Godolphin needed in 1702. Here was the means by which they would form a direct contact of their own with the House of Commons. Here was the expert who could advise them upon what that House would or would not do in any situation. Here was the agent who heard everything, and could sway decisions. From the very beginning both these super-Ministers saw in Harley the means of making themselves independent of the ordinary party channels. Rochester and Nottingham might pose and fulminate in the Lords, but Harley could cover a very large body of sober Tory and Whig opinion. It may be said that Marlborough and Harley had this in common, that in their different spheres they deflected and deceived enemies or wild people into courses which kept England safe. It was certainly upon this basis that they came together.

We have seen Marlborough's relations with Harley growing steadily in the last years of King William, and now strong and ripe. Harley had already an admiration for Marlborough, and was well content to be drawn by him into the elevated circle around the Queen and into the majestic chaos of Europe. He knew, however, that all his value depended on his ability to control or at least sway the Commons and to induce the Tory Party to follow paths of sanity and patriotism. He knew that to lose his influence with these forces would destroy his means alike of service and ambition. He was no simpleton to have his head turned by the courtesy or glitter of the governing group. The advice which he gave to them about the House of Commons, welcome or unwelcome, was expert, and he gave no undertakings which he did not believe he could make good. He so bore himself that it was the Court who courted him. We have only to read his correspondence with Marlborough and the voluminous letters which Godolphin, who understood him and his task even more thoroughly than Marlborough, wrote him week after week to see the importance attached to him and the consideration and regard with which he was treated.

From his unique Parliamentary position Harley soon became, though not actually in the Government, superior in importance to any of the ordinary great office-holders, and Marlborough and Godolphin reached out to him across the Tory Ministers and drew him into their private confidences. Harley was not joined in the Cockpit by those deep ties of personal friendship or family connexion which bound the rest; but he soon became an independent and almost indispensable partner. His own central following in the House of Commons could henceforward feel themselves more closely associated with the conduct of the State through the Speaker working with the great Ministers than by their regular party chiefs in office. For all the toilsome discharge of business Marlborough, Godolphin, and Harley were gradually to become a triumvirate, and were so described by their contemporaries.

We may suppose that the Queen and Marlborough delayed the announcement of Godolphin's appointment until the Tory Ministry was complete. Rochester was allowed to indulge his hopes to the very end. Another great issue had to be settled before they could afford to render him desperate. By solemn pact Marlborough, with the Queen's authority, had bound England, simultaneously with the Empire and the States-General, to declare war upon France on May 4/15. This secret was in England known only to these two and Godolphin. But now May was at hand. The new Cabinet must be confronted with the decisions of supreme power. Not only must the question of peace or war be settled, but also the kind of war England must wage. Was she to be an ally, playing a full part upon the Continent, or was she to be an associated Power, joined, indeed, to the confederacy against France, but limiting her exertions to picking up what she could overseas on the outskirts of the struggle? Here the collision between Marlborough and Rochester was direct. Rochester seemed to have made much headway with the Queen. He was leading her steadily forward on Tory and party courses. He felt strong enough to meet Marlborough foursquare upon the issue that England must intervene as only an auxiliary.

But Marlborough was found armed with an argument which was judged conclusive in those times. He remarked that by the commands of the Queen, following upon the resolves of Parliament, he had procured the assent of the allies to the additional article denouncing the claim of the pretended Prince of Wales. Here, then, was a major purpose of exclusively English interest to which the other partners in the Grand Alliance had agreed reluctantly at English insistence. England was therefore formally involved as a principal, and must contribute her whole power to the common cause. This contention cut the ground from under the Tory chiefs; for it was they, as we have seen, who in the hope of shattering King William's plan by disgusting the Emperor had brought forward this additional article and made it a test of faith at home and abroad. We now see, a month after, the explanation of Marlborough's vehemence to the Grand Pensionary and Count Goes at The Hague. There is no doubt he looked ahead.

The new Tory Cabinet seem to have been quelled or even rallied by this deployment of their former party demands.

Behind lay the growing realization that the Queen, if really forced to choose, would throw her whole weight upon the side of Marlborough and Godolphin. In the end the Queen was not troubled with the dispute. It was agreed that England should throw her whole weight into the war.

On May 4, at one o'clock in the afternoon, the King-at-Arms rode out from the Queen's palace splendidly adorned and surrounded by the heralds and the guards. From St James's he went by way of Charing Cross and the Strand to the City, where he proclaimed the declaration of war against France to the clash of cymbals and the blare of trumpets. His challenge to Louis XIV was everywhere cheered by the masses and the poorest citizens, the genius of whose race had taught them that their freedom and the greatness of their country were at stake. Two days later, all being now committed to the struggle, Godolphin received the White Staff of Lord Treasurer, and Rochester saw himself finally relegated to his Irish Viceroyalty.

CHAPTER IV

THE TORY FERMENT

(1702, August)

THERE was an extraordinary soreness among the Tories
at this time. All the prosperity which seemed to be
coming to them in the new reign in no way mollified their
general wrath. They could not forgive—they could not even
forget—the dissolution of 1701. We can see what a mistake
William had made in dissolving the Tory Parliament and yet
keeping his Tory Ministry until the elections were over. By
this he had fallen between both stools. He had forgotten
Machiavelli's sombre remark that "men can resent small
injuries, but not graver ones." The Tory Party had been
mortally offended by his action, while the Whigs on whom he
was counting had only half a chance. This was the kind of
error, heating to men's minds and obvious to all politicians,
from which Marlborough and Godolphin had struggled almost
passionately to save him. It had left King William in the
final year of his life in one of the most uncomfortable positions
of his reign.

His last act with his Whig Ministers had been to affix his
stamp—he could no longer sign his name—to the Abjuration
Bill. This measure which passed triumphantly through
Parliament expressed the immediate reaction of the nation
against Louis XIV's recognition of the Pretender. It declared
the whole exiled house permanently deprived of royal rights.
Now, here was a grave matter. Although in the mood
of the hour the Tories had found it a difficult proposal to
dispute, they resented it bitterly. Since the beginning of
William's reign and as the result of the combination of the
two great parties against James II, the question of principle
about the succession had slumbered under a mask of
"national emergency" which enabled every High Tory to
serve loyally a *de facto* Parliamentary King. But the Abjura-
84

tion Act cut at the very root of the whole Tory conception of legitimacy and Divine Right. The fact that this had been thrust down their throats upon an impulse of anger at Louis's intrusion left them only the more outraged.

Moreover, these Tories, still unappeased, felt themselves morally in the ascendant. All the themes for which they stood were in tune with the popular mood. In our modern politics we see how hard lines of division can be drawn between different shades of the same opinion. Thus Socialists have an affinity and sentiment for Communists, but make a frontier against them and fight them vigorously. Something similar to these relations ruled between the irreconcilable Jacobites and the constitutional Tory Party with Queen Anne at its head. And it is also to be remarked in those days, as in these, that when the mood of the nation changes all the groups and parties of the Right or of the Left suffer or prosper together. The victory of the moderates on either side carries with it a new impulse to the passions and ideals of their own extremists.

With the death of William and with the accession of a Tory Stuart Queen, Jacobite sentiment, which lay low and deep throughout England, and stirred in so many hearts and consciences, surged forward and became the fashion and temper of the hour. Even in his lifetime, according to Burnet, a certain Dr Binckes had preached a sermon before the Convocation "in which he drew a parallel between King Charles's sufferings and those of our Saviour, and," says the Bishop, "in some very indecent expressions gave the preference to the former."[1] These emotions found their expression, curiously enough, in loyalty to the new monarch, who in her own person and in the most effective manner barred the return of the lawful Prince, and but for the warming-pan— now much battered—made a mockery of all the theories of Divine Right. However, an indifference to logic where it is likely to lead to serious trouble is one of the strongest of English characteristics. Here at last was a sovereign of Stuart blood, of Tory inclinations, and happily a fervent adherent

1 Burnet, v, 16.

of the Church of England. All Tory England was ready to make the best of that. Many Non-Jurors, reconciled by the arrival of an undoubted Stuart upon the throne, were willing to be rallied. The mass of the Tory Party, laity and clergy, felt that this was not only a way out of their difficulties, but at least a partial vindication of their principles. Anyhow, Queen Anne was an immense improvement upon a foreign Calvinist King, imported by the Whigs.

At this moment in our history, therefore, all the Tory forces, from those who regarded Anne regretfully as a usurper to those who acclaimed her as a supreme blessing vouchsafed by heaven, swelled together in an incongruous yet not unexplainable harmony. Throughout every circle and degree Toryism was bitter and aggressive; while the Whigs, for their part, were thrown into the embarrassing position of being roughly assaulted by the Government whose main policy on the greatest issues of the age—Europe and the war—was their own.

We have therefore this Tory Party, so intractable and unyielding in character, so unreasoning and narrow in outlook, equally conscious in the highest degree of their grievances and of their power. This is the first great political fact in the reign of Queen Anne. By the Acts passed on the morrow of the Fenwick Plot, Parliament was prudently no longer dissolved on the demise of the Crown, but continued automatically for six months and no more. Whig hopes that the House of Commons elected in 1701 would be allowed to run its normal course never had any foundation. The law prescribed and the Queen desired a dissolution. In the late summer there must be a general election, and the Tories, already possessed of office, eagerly looked forward to over-throwing their Whig antagonists, who stoutly prepared for resistance. In this delectable sport nearly all the time and the thought of England was occupied without much regard being paid to the impending general clash of arms in Europe.

Nowadays a Government is usually an expression of the previous general election; but in this nascent phase of our Parliamentary institutions the Crown first gathered certain Ministers and interests around it, and then tried by every means in its power to procure a House of Commons which would support its general policy. The weight of the Crown and the Government was formidable at the elections. Lord-Lieutenants, magistrates, sheriffs, squires, and parsons influenced, and frequently over-influenced, both the gathering and the counting of the votes. To all this there was added the deep loyalty of the people to the sovereign, and the reluctance of the ordinary elector to cast a vote against the policy of his lawful ruler. Thus the Government of the day, enjoying the fresh flush of royal favour, had a marked advantage at the polls. The character of the Ministry made it unmistakably plain that the Queen wanted a Tory Parliament. The Tories were seen to be favoured; the Whigs were obviously under a cloud. Moreover, this inclination of the royal will corresponded with the natural sentiment in favour of change and against the agents of the late unpopular King.

The party fight shaped itself as the dying Parliament drew towards its end. The parties girded at each other, and marshalled the points of malice and prejudice upon which they relied at the impending trial of strength. Sir Edward Seymour remarked from the Ministerial bench that the Queen's generosity showed "that she was wholly English at heart. Governments have been known from which such help could not have been expected even in the greatest calamity." Lord Spencer, the old Sunderland's son and Marlborough's son-in-law, made the telling and even decisive rejoinder, "That King William had not an English heart can be said by none save those who have a French one." This turned the tables with a vengeance. Every Jacobite, every pacifist, every isolationist in the Tory ranks felt himself smitten. The "English heart" topic was dropped as a counter in the House of Commons' debates.

Another shape taken by the party fight was the attempt by Rochester to oust all minor Whig officials.

It was generally believed that the Earl of Rochester and his party were for severe methods, and for a more entire change, to be carried quite through all subaltern appointments; but that the Lord Godolphin and the Earl of Marlborough were for more moderate proceedings.[1]

The Tories in the House of Commons, with the encouragement of their representatives in the Cabinet, sought to envelop all the transactions of William's reign with the taint of corruption and fraud. In these days many new fortunes seemed to be made and great estates acquired without sufficient explanation. The Tories were the champions of peace, of parsimony, and of financial purity in public life. With the favour of the Crown and its Ministers they pursued the Whig members of King William's Governments. The Earl of Ranelagh was accused of peculation, and immense expectations were aroused of the exposures which the Parliamentary inquiry would make. In fact, however, though irregularities had occurred, the inquisition yielded very much less than was feared, or, should we say, hoped.

Another incident throws a revealing light upon the Queen's party bias. A story was set on foot that the late King and his Ministers had deliberately planned—"conspired," it had now become—to bring in the Electoral Prince of Hanover and exclude Princess Anne from the throne. It was further alleged that the assent of the Emperor and the Dutch Republic to the plan had actually been procured. These ideas had certainly been mooted, and we remember how Marlborough had said, "If ever they attempt it, we would walk over their bellies."[2] Now everything stood in a different light. Nothing could be more damaging to the Whigs than the suggestion that they had sought to stand between the 'English-hearted' Queen, for whom there was so much enthusiasm, and her lawful right. And, of course, it could be suggested that as an essential feature Anne must have become a prisoner of State in the Tower. The Whigs denied these aspersions with vehemence. The Earl of Carlisle, Deputy-Hereditary Marshal of England, and as a Lord of the Treasury one of the remaining Whig Ministers, demanded an immediate inquiry. Five Lords, of whom Marlborough was one, were commanded

1 Burnet, v, 12.   2 *Cf.* Vol. II, p. 253.

by the Queen to "visit the late king's papers" and "to bring her such of them as related to alliances or to the succession of the Crown." The five lords reported that, having searched the King's papers, they had found nothing to justify such accusations; and the House of Lords, where the Whigs commanded a majority, proceeded to stigmatize the authors of scandalous untruths, which, they said, besmirched the memory of a great King and exposed his servants and friends to national opprobrium. They sent a deputation, of whom Lord Carlisle was one, to the Queen. Anne received their address. But after the deputation withdrew she directed an equerry to recall Lord Carlisle. She then observed, "I have to inform you that I intend to make other arrangements about the Treasury." In these terms, on this occasion, and in this connexion, another of the Whigs was dismissed. Thus the Queen seemed to show herself no friend to those who had been injured by what was admitted to be lying rumour. Her frowns were reserved for those who had protested against it, and were still to suffer from it. Burnet says:

> When the falsehood of those calumnies was apparent, then it was given out, with an unusual confidence, that no such reports had been ever set about; though the contrary was evident, and the thing was boldly asserted . . .: so that a peculiar measure of assurance was necessary, to face down a thing, which they [the Tories] had taken such pains to infuse into the minds of the credulous vulgar, all England over.[1]

In Marlborough's absence at The Hague, Rochester, venerable, furious, absentee from Ireland, wove the Queen into Tory electioneering. On May 25 she dismissed King William's Parliament with the blistering passage, "I shall be very careful to preserve and maintain the Act of Toleration and to set the minds of all my people at quiet. My own principles must always keep me entirely firm to the interests and religion of the Church of England, *and will incline me to countenance those who have the truest zeal to support it.*"[2] To the Whigs this was a declaration of war upon them by the Sovereign. All

1 Burnet, v, 15–16.   2 Boyer, i. 42.

the popularity and prestige of the new Queen Anne, with her English heart, were to be marshalled at the hustings against them. At the same time their Tory opponents before the election proclaimed a measure against Occasional Conformity which would make every Dissenter a political outlaw. What had they done, the Whigs exclaimed, to be treated as public enemies? They were the force which had made the Revolution of 1688. They were the men who by the Act of Settlement had placed the Queen upon the throne. They were the traditional champions against the Jacobitism and Popery which everybody condemned, or affected to condemn. They were the party which earnestly supported the war Lord Marlborough had gone abroad to wage. And the Whigs were half the nation! Wherein had their conduct failed the Queen and Constitution? The future and the freedom of England rested in their midst. Why, then, was their loyalty so spurned? Because, said they, there was some dark intrigue to bring in the pretended Prince of Wales and subjugate England to Rome and France. But the Tories replied that the Whigs were all republicans and atheists at heart, who paid lip-service to the Crown in order to devour it, and took the Holy Sacrament to qualify for positions from which they could the better destroy, not only the Church of England, but all faith of man in God. On these agreeable platforms Whigs and Tories proceeded to the polls.

However, the fibre of both parties was tough. The election of August 1702 was no landslide. Just as the Tories had come through the election of February 1701 much better than they themselves expected in the circumstances, so now the Whigs made a stubborn fight and were perhaps not more than a hundred behind the Tories in the first Parliament of Queen Anne. Harley, the Tory leader, was again elected Speaker; this time unanimously. His Parliamentary gifts and ascendancy commended him to the House as a whole. His moderation comforted the Whigs. His party colouring just held the Tories. Across the gulfs of a Tory majority and Government and the disfavour of the Crown the Whigs could regard him as a link with Marlborough and Godolphin, the national Ministers above the ebb and flow of party. For the rest they remained effective, weighty—almost half the nation—organized with a grip inconceivable to-day. Moreover, they were still entrenched in strong positions both in Church and State.

Although in William's reign there had been Tory Governments and moderate or pliable Tory Ministers, the whole bias of the Crown had been to secure the ascendancy of the Whigs in the peerage, in the Church, and in the Judiciary. There was a Whig majority in the House of Lords. The judges had been chosen as King William's men. The bishops were nearly all Whigs and Broad Churchmen. Joined with the Whig nobles, they dominated the Upper House of Convocation. These advantages at the summit were reproduced in a lesser degree throughout the kingdom in many aspects of local life, and determined Whigs were found stubbornly rooted in every kind of parochial and municipal office. Thus the victorious and elated Tories, with, as they could claim, the favour of the Crown, the will of the electors, and the mood of the times on their side, found themselves confronted with a solid array ready to encounter them at every point.

The first Parliament of the new reign was therefore the scene and occasion of a fierce and not unevenly matched struggle between the nominees of the old reign and the aspirants of the new. If the Tories had a majority in the Commons the Whigs ruled in the Lords. If the rank and file of the Church of England priesthood (recruited from what were then the virtually religious seminaries of Oxford and Cambridge) were ardent Tories, rank High Churchmen, and in many cases, if the truth were known, Jacobites and Divine Right men at heart, the bishops and the Upper House of Convocation were Latitudinarians. If the country squires, "the gentlemen of England," as they called themselves, were predominantly Tory, against them rose the new expanding power of the City, with its far-spreading mercantile and financial interests, ardent for the Whigs and the war. Thus conflict showed itself simultaneously between Whigs and Tories, between Churchmen and Dissenters, between Lords and Commons, between the bishops and their clergy, and between agriculture and commerce. Nor could these conditions be readily altered. Vacancies occurred rarely in the Bench of Bishops or among the judges. The peerage was permanent and irremovable. Even minor Whig functionaries and notables, backed by all the wealth, learning, and activity of a great party, could not be evicted without some reason. If these positions were to be captured some method must be found. And here the Tory Party had the inspiration of the Occasional Conformity Bill.

During the whole of the reign Church politics was the strongest theme at home. The cry "The Church in danger" represented all the sentiments, principles, prejudices, interests, and tactics of Toryism. There had been a time, not long before, when the great Halifax had written his "Letter to a Dissenter" to show how much Church and Chapel had in common against Rome. But once Popery was no more a menace, High Church Tories were free to turn their full antagonism against Dissent. They saw in Ireland William's late favouring of Presbyterians. They saw a Presbyterian Church established in Scotland. Above all, they saw Dissenters holding many positions of power in England. All these religious animosities revived and grew monstrously. They enabled the Tories to make a resolute solid set against the Whigs, and put the Whigs in a great difficulty and disadvantage, especially as they were bound to support the war.

Under the laws of England as they had been administered in King William's reign no attempt had been made to persecute Nonconformists for worshipping as they pleased, and a very wide measure of practical toleration existed for the people. Even Papists were not molested, if they behaved discreetly. But where the holding of public office was concerned it was argued that no one ought to be trusted to enforce the laws who disagreed with them on grounds of conscience. Office-holders of all kinds from the highest Minister to the smallest revenue officer—Lord-Lieutenant, magistrates, all who would be concerned with elections, every one who sat in either House, the heads of all colleges and universities, nearly every one charged with the education of youth—all these must by law be communicant members of the Church of England. The Corporation Act and the Test Act prescribed that no one could hold any of these key-posts without taking the sacrament according to Anglican rites. But the wealthy, influential Dissenters who formed so valuable a part of the Whig forces, who by their standing, substance, and capacity were qualified for public office, were not so easily to be ejected or shut out from power by the manœuvres of their political and religious opponents. With the full assent of Whig and Nonconformist opinion, they had been accustomed by King William's goodwill to turn the flank of the Test Act by taking the Anglican sacrament as required by law, and thereafter continuing in their Dissenting tabernacles. This attitude of compromise was accepted by their co-religionists and party friends, who were fully alive to the importance of their having a share in the public functions, which again were so helpful in all elections.

Here, then, was a widespread practice, enjoined by the custom of a decade, which the law could not punish—nay, which conformed most strictly to its letter. The practice ran in high places: and here again lay the strength of the Whigs. Even Harley, or at least his family, were only Occasional Conformers; and the Queen's husband, Prince George, had his private Lutheran chapel in the palace, and partook of the Anglican sacrament but once a year.

The Tories, on the wave of Jacobite, Stuart, and Church emotion evoked by the accession of Queen Anne, and not unmindful of the vacancies which would be created, determined to bring this fraudulent abuse, as they regarded it, to an end. One can hardly conceive an issue better adapted to make a quarrel. Genuine religious feeling was outraged at the spectacle of prominent, well-established men by hundreds publicly taking the sacrament in a form which they were known to dislike. Party politicians were infuriated at their keeping by so paltry a device the offices which they sought for themselves or their friends. The whole Tory Party thought the practice wicked, blasphemous, deceitful, an outrage upon the body and blood of Christ, and also extremely inconvenient at election times. The Whigs rejoined that there was and ought to be toleration in the realm, if not among Christians, at least among Protestants; and that no country, least of all one so grievously threatened, could afford to deprive itself of the aid of large and powerful classes of loyal, well-to-do, and God-fearing citizens: that no sovereign should divorce herself from so great a body of her subjects and ban them from all share in her service. Then the religious leaders of Nonconformity came forward declaring that there was no irreverence or dishonour in a Dissenter taking the Anglican sacrament, while at the same time preferring for his ordinary devotions to enter the House of the Lord or to come to His Table in his own way. The Anglican sacrament, they declared, was not in their eyes inherently wrong or obnoxious. They understood, respected, and in large measure shared the feelings of those to whom it was most dear. No question of faith or even of doctrine arose which should utterly sunder Christian men. It was a matter of mode, outlook, and temperament which our advancing civilization should comprehend. And here they were endorsed by William's Broad Church bishops—Burnet and the rest—and by the Archbishop of Canterbury himself. Thus a great volume of practical good sense and high spiritual authority, marshalled and sustained by the Whig nobles, met the Tory demand front to front.

But the dominant party was not to be easily denied, and their pertinacious, passionate, ruthless exertions to root out Occasional Conformity and punish those guilty of it, far outstripping the world war and Marlborough's victories, became during the opening years of Queen Anne's reign the main issue and topic of English political life.

After the Church the second great party cleavage of the reign was upon the character of the war. We have already seen this brought to an issue in the Cabinet. For many genera-

tions, even down to our own day, there have been two sets of
opinions about the kind of wars that England should wage:
the first for playing a great and direct part on the Continent;
the second for using our island position and naval power to
gather trade and possessions overseas. The difference showed
itself very plainly in King Charles's reign in the dispute about
whether we should retain Dunkirk or Tangier—a bridgehead
on the Continent or a gateway to the Mediterranean. Neither
party has adhered throughout its history to one view. Whigs
and Tories have exchanged sides several times as the compulsion of events led the Government of the day into particular
action and the Opposition gravitated towards the contrary
group of ideas.

But these two conceptions of war seemed quite distinct;
and at this time the Tories obstinately championed the policy
that if we were drawn into a war we should go as little to the
Continent, send as few troops, fight as near to the coast as
possible, and endeavour to secure territory and traffic across
the oceans. Whigs, on the contrary, dwelt upon the theory
familiar to us as the doctrine of "the decisive theatre," and
sought, with the largest army that could be maintained, to
bring the war to an end by a thrust at the heart of France,
the supreme military antagonist, arguing that thereafter all
the rest would be added unto them.

It should be noticed that the Tories favoured the
popular idea that the Navy should be the stronger and
the Army stinted. This gave them a good constitutional
position as against the Whigs, who, though equally opposed
to a standing army, had to have one if they wished to fight
on the mainland. Here was a new cause of confusion. As
the reign of Anne continued these opinions organized
themselves, to a degree almost unbelievable, in hard-and-fast
party principles about the kind of strategy and operations
which should be adopted. The Tories were prone to judge
every action not so much by whether it was successful as by
whether it was in accordance with their party doctrine.
Thus taking a town near the coast was more to be applauded
than taking one farther inland. Thus an action at sea was

preferable to one ashore. The Tory policy leaned to operations against Spain and the liquidation of the Spanish colonies as a prize of war, and to the entry of the Mediterranean with all the exploitation of trade in the East that would come with the command of the sea. Marlborough's march to Blenheim was therefore, as we shall find, the greatest violation of Tory principles which could be conceived. Even dazzling success could hardly redeem such a departure from the orthodox and conventional party method of waging war.

Marlborough throughout his campaigns was bound, apart from military facts and the enemy, to consider the character of any operation by the effect it would have on Tory opinion in the House of Commons. Both parties could use powerful and capacious arguments in support of their dogmas, and neither hesitated to turn the fortunes and accidents of the war to its special account. From this it followed again that not only were victories in the field or afloat classified as Whig and Tory victories, but the officers concerned in specific operations became coloured with the party hue. Generals and admirals were encouraged to have strong party affiliations, and each faction had its favourites whom it praised and defended through thick and thin. Indeed, neither side in Parliament hesitated to foment rivalries and jealousies among the commanders and to set one against another, or against their commander-in-chief. From this again we see how vital it was to Marlborough that he should have Godolphin at the Treasury; otherwise he might find his strategy in the face of the enemy hamstrung by money being granted for one operation and refused for another. It was equally necessary to him that no one serving under his command should be appointed except by and through his authority. The slightest weakening of the principle that he alone governed all promotions and appointments would in the party commotion have thrown the whole of his forces and of his plans into disorder.

CHAPTER V

THE STRUCTURE OF THE WAR

(1701–1712)

ALTHOUGH Eugene's brilliant campaign in Italy had opened the War of the Spanish Succession in 1701, no shot had been fired in the northern theatre. In Flanders, upon the Rhine, and upon the Moselle armies had assembled, and each of the great combatants was busy securing smaller allies. Louis XIV had, as we have seen, acquired partial control of the Archbishopric of Cologne and the Bishopric of Liége at the same time as he had occupied the Belgian fortresses.[1] The first overt act of the Germanic states was the coercion of the Duke of Brunswick-Wolfenbüttel. This prince was a mere figurehead whose younger brother had collected in his name, but with French gold, an army of twelve thousand mercenaries, and was forming a league of French supporters in North Germany. The Elector of Hanover at length intervened. During the night of March 20 the younger brother was driven out by Hanoverian troops, and the mercenaries agreed to serve henceforth under the Emperor. This was the first war news which reached Queen Anne after her accession.

Marlborough had arranged that on May 4/15 war should be simultaneously declared upon France by England, the States-General, and the Empire. This event finally reassured the Dutch, who hitherto, despite Marlborough's firm assertions, had feared that their island ally intended only to act as an accessory—i.e., to pick up what was good for herself at the expense of friend and foe. The causes of England's quarrel were set forth in a proclamation which is a model of forceful historical compression. Its conclusion should be noted.

We henceforth strictly forbid the holding of any correspondence or communication with France or Spain or their subjects. But because there are remaining in our Kingdoms many of the

[1] Vol. I, p. 262.

subjects of France and Spain, We do declare our Royal intention to be, that all the subjects of France and Spain, who shall demean themselves dutifully towards us, shall be safe in their persons and estates.[1]

This passage will jar the modern mind. We see how strong was the structure of Christendom in these times and with what restraints even warring nations acted. Of course, nowadays, with the many improvements that have been made in international morals and behaviour, all enemy subjects, even those whose countries were only technically involved, even those who had lived all their lives in England, and the English women who had married them, would, as in every other state based on an educated democracy, be treated within twenty-four hours as malignant foes, flung into internment camps, and their private property stolen to assist the expenses of the war. In the twentieth century mankind has shaken itself free from all those illogical, old-world prejudices, and achieved the highest efficiency of brutal, ruthless war.

We shall see that the same kind of archaic conduct ruled in the field. After the fury of battle was spent both sides, and especially the victors, laboured to rescue the wounded, instead of leaving them to perish inch by inch in agony in No Man's Land. If in their poverty they stripped the dead of their clothing, they also exchanged prisoners with meticulous accounting. The opposing generals paid each other every compliment and courtesy which did not hamper their operations, and in the winter season issued passports to prominent officers to traverse hostile territory on their shortest routes home. Although the great causes in dispute were stated with a robust vigour and precision which we have now lost, no hatred, apart from military antagonism, was countenanced among the troops. All was governed by strict rules of war, into which bad temper was not often permitted to enter. The main acceptances of a polite civilization still reigned across the lines of opposing armies, and mob violence and mechanical propaganda had not yet been admitted to the adjustment of international disputes.

[1] Boyer, i, 31.

Since from this time forward military affairs must play a main part in our story, the reader should survey the whole scope of the war, and consider the governing conditions under which it was fought. As in the recent world war, two great European countries, one much weaker than the other, found themselves lapped about and almost encircled by a numerous alliance of which England was the mainspring, and by the sea, of which she was already the mistress. The kingdoms of France and Spain were in a central position in 1702 similar to that of Germany and Austria in 1914. They had the advantage of interior lines and could strike outward in various directions. They could throw their weight now against this opponent, now against that. All their fortunes depended upon an army, incomparable in power, numbers, organization, and repute, and upon the authority of its War Lord. Spain throughout followed the guidance of Louis XIV in the same subordination that in our days Austria observed to Germany. Louis XIV, like the Kaiser William II and his general staff, at the beginning could choose for each campaign where the decisive theatre should lie. He could perfect his plans in secrecy, and execute them without any domestic hindrance. The allies, so loosely and precariously joined together, among whom communication was slow and slender, were liable to be struck down one after the other.

The command of the sea rested throughout in the hands of England and Holland. Queen Anne had above two hundred ships of war—half of them of over fifty guns and "fit to lie in the line"—manned by forty or fifty thousand sailors and marines. To these the Dutch joined three ships to every English five. The French were scarcely half of this combined strength. They never attempted seriously to dispute the Narrow Seas or the Channel. Their frigates and privateers maintained themselves upon the oceans; but for the rest their aim was to preserve the control of the Mediterranean. Until the allies could alter this King Louis was only partially enveloped, and still had the advantage of striking where he chose. On the other hand, the fact of having to defend simultaneously so many ports and potential landing-places from amphibious attack was a serious drain on French man-power.

A prevailing purpose of Marlborough's strategy was to secure the command of the Mediterranean. But this did not depend upon ships alone. Cadiz, Gibraltar, Barcelona, Toulon, Genoa, Naples, and Port Mahon, all the great fortified harbours of the inland sea and its approaches, were held by the Two Crowns, and Lisbon was neutral. The battleships

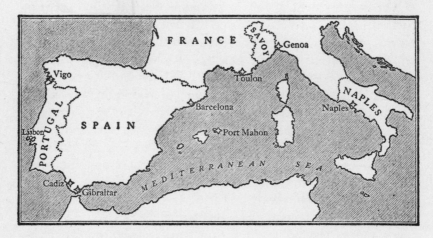

MEDITERRANEAN NAVAL BASES

of those days, dependent only upon the winds for movement, could keep the sea for five or six months, or more; but the dangers of crossing the Bay of Biscay and entering the mouth of the English Channel amid the winter gales were fearful; and without fresh meat, green vegetables, and intervals of repose ashore the mortality among the sailors was grievous. It was little use sending the fleet to the Mediterranean only for June and July. A secure harbour and well-equipped dockyard, where the ships could be careened, repaired, and replenished, and where the crews could be eased and refreshed, were indispensable. The search for this dockyard dominated the policy of the Cabinet and of the Admiralty. Although temporary resting-places were found by diplomacy at Lisbon in 1703 and by the conquests of Gibraltar and Barcelona in 1704 and 1705, it was not until 1708, after the Italian theatre had ceased to count, that a secure, well-equipped base for the fleet was established at Port Mahon, in the island of Minorca. Meanwhile year by year the Cabinet forced the Admiralty and the naval commanders to run undue risks by going out early and coming home late in the season, and much suffering and loss of ships and life followed therefrom.

The employment of the Navy was as usual divided between furthering the main purposes of the war and trade protection. Naval opinion and the whole mercantile interest wished to set trade protection first; but this was not the view of the Government, nor of Parliament. Whigs and Tories alike wished the fleet to be used as a part of the main war-effort. Marlborough directly, and through his brother, Admiral Churchill, at the Admiralty, pressed in this direction; and certainly in the War of the Spanish Succession the energies of the fleet were devoted to fighting purposes and the main war-plans in a far higher degree than ever before or since. Sir George Rooke, the Admiral of the Fleet, was the chief opponent of this view. He resisted at every stage and by every means the policy of trying to dominate the Mediterranean. Arrogant, crafty, obstinately entangled in his own tackle, and afflicted with persistent ill-health, he saw no prize worth the risk and trouble in securing an overseas base on the Iberian Peninsula; still less was he attracted by the prospect of such a base being used to draw the main fleet into the Mediterranean. The Tory Admiral was a sluggish, wary man whose imagination had no room for great designs, and who was forced by circumstances and accident into the achievements which have rendered him famous. Shovell, Fairborne, Leake, Norris, and others were far more daring, vigorous admirals, and lent themselves more readily to the wishes of the Executive and the general purposes of the war.

If the allies were to rid themselves of the peril of being attacked in detail they must wrest the initiative from Louis XIV, and by dominant action at one point or another rivet the attention of the central mass. The paths by which

France could be invaded were not so numerous as might appear. Roads were few and bad, and in the absence of railways all the natural obstacles of forests, mountains, and barren regions asserted their full power. Armies of from sixty to a hundred thousand men could only live by moving constantly through fertile lands or where their supplies could be brought them by fresh or salt water. The great rivers were the railways of this war. The control of the long, uninterrupted course of rivers and canals enabled armies to operate in their full power, drawing their food and ammunition easily to them week by week and moving their siege trains. But for this very reason every river and canal, especially the confluences and junctions, was barred by strong, elaborate fortresses, each of which had to be separately captured. The value of every fortress and the cost of taking it in time, life, and money were measured with high exactness on both sides; two months for this, a month for that; a fortnight for a small place, and three or four days for a mere castle. Thus the rivers represented the lines of railways, and the stations on them were forts barring all traffic to those who held them not.

The shipping resources of the two Maritime Powers, relatively large though they were, their harbours, quays, and port accommodation, were never sufficient to make the invasion of France possible by any sea-borne army likely to overcome so mighty and war-like a state. Raids and diversions of all kinds could be considered in their place, but our ancestors never believed that a grand and decisive stroke would be launched upon France from the sea.

There were, however, three or four practicable lines of invasion open to the allies. In the south there was the Riviera road. An army might work its way slowly from Italy into France along the coast, being fed and helped by its ships from port to port. This was a plan which several times attracted Prince Eugene. However, the invader would enter France at an immense distance from Paris, and in provinces the loss of which, though fertile, would not affect the war-making strength of Louis XIV. From the Mediterranean northward for more than three hundred miles France

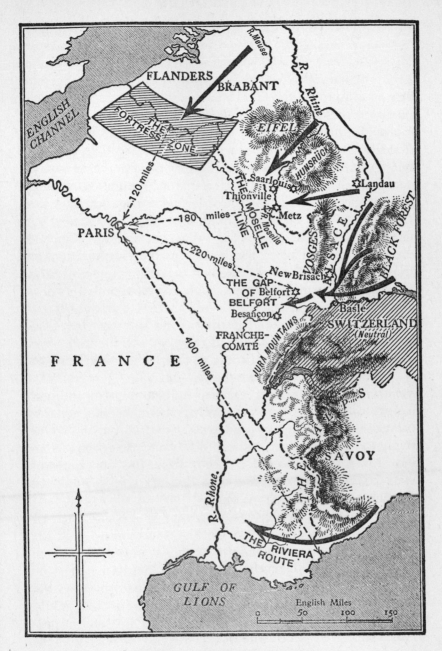

FRANCE: PATHS OF INVASION

103

was protected by the enormous confusion of the Alps and the robust neutrality of the Swiss. A second line of invasion was offered in the gap between the Jura Mountains in the north of Switzerland and the southern spurs of the Vosges. This road was obstructed by a French fortress system of some strength comprising New Brisach, constructed by Vauban, Belfort, Besançon, and other strong places. North of this gap again France was protected for another hundred miles by the triple obstacles of the Black Forest, itself almost a mountain-range, the Rhine, and the Vosges Mountains, one behind the other. The third route was through Northern Alsace or along the Moselle, converging on the French fortress group Saarlouis, Thionville, and Metz. This was generally believed to be the surest and most deadly, and, if Marlborough had found it possible to marshal the effective strength of Germany behind him, it was the pathway he would certainly have made his own.

Lastly there were the plains of Flanders, fertile, populous, intersected by their great and magnificent rivers and canals, offering every facility to the movements of the largest armies and enabling the two Maritime Powers to act in the closest harmony. But this area was covered by immense systems of fortification. More than thirty large fortresses of the first class, complete from outworks to citadel, and perhaps fifty fortified towns and strongholds, the work of two generations, formed artificial barriers between France and Holland. At the time when Marlborough's campaign began nearly all these fortress-towns were in the hands of France. All the fortresses of the Spanish Netherlands had, as we have seen, been seized by Louis XIV in 1701. All the fortresses on the Meuse and Rhine, with one remarkable exception, had passed to the French by the seduction of the priestly rulers of Cologne and Liége. Thus the Dutch began the war deprived of virtually the whole of their barrier and of all the strong places they had held in the time of King William. They had a few fortresses like Nimwegen and Bergen-op-Zoom in their own land, but for the rest they must rely solely upon the manhood of their armies.

ADMIRAL GEORGE CHURCHILL
Sir Godfrey Kneller
By permission of the Trustees of the National Maritime Museum, Greenwich

The exception was Maestricht. This very large fortress on the Meuse lay in an enclave of Dutch territory. It had not been affected either by the transfer of the Spanish Netherlands or by that of the Bishoprics of Cologne and Liége. It was a fortress of the first order, of historic fame and modernized defences. Within its earthworks the Dutch had gathered immense supplies, very considerable stores, and a trustworthy garrison of no less than fourteen thousand men. The French, on the other hand, had as their second line the great fortresses within the French frontier, and thus enjoyed both their own defences and those which should properly have belonged to their opponents. Thus at the outset of the new war the French had the control of the Scheldt and all its tributaries, of the Meuse (excepting Maestricht), and of long stretches of the Rhine and the Upper Rhine. Finally, Louis had constructed in 1701 a continuous line of fortifications along a seventy-miles crescent from Antwerp to Namur. These "Lines of Brabant" had been sited under Vauban's supervision by the best French engineers; and entrenchments, palisades, and inundations, all vigilantly watched, offered an unbroken defensive position, on any sector of which the French field army could confront an assailant from the north.

During 1701 the attitude of the Germanic princes was ill-defined. They were taking precautions and raising forces; but they were for the most part indisposed either to succour the Emperor, as their antiquated feudal fealty required, or to declare war upon France. In these circumstances the Margrave of Baden, whose domains around Rastadt, between the Upper Rhine and the Neckar, were very near the conflagration, was a personage of high importance. At the head of the Imperial armies he had gained several notable victories over the Turks in bygone years. He was reputed an accomplished soldier, and was certainly a man of proved physical courage. As a ruling prince he was prepared to lead troops of his own against the French. It was natural, therefore, that he should receive the command of whatever

Imperial armies should be assembled to defend Germany. He thus appears at the outset of the war as the first general of the Empire.

During the autumn and winter of 1701 the Margrave busied himself with the defence of the Black Forest and the valley of the Upper Rhine. He aroused considerable enthusiasm among the German populations threatened by French invasion, especially in the circles of Swabia and Franconia. He organized local militias, supported by the inhabitants of the towns and villages, to aid the regular troops which were gradually coming into the field. For further protection he constructed a number of fortified lines barring the least difficult tracks through the Black Forest. But the most important strategic task which he accomplished was the creation of the celebrated Lines of Stollhofen. These fortifications ran from the river to the wooded mountains, and barred a French advance from the Strasburg bridgeheads down the Rhine valley on the right bank of the river. They covered a front of about nine miles from a strong star-fort opposite Fort Louis, through Stollhofen and Bühl to the castle of Windeck on the wooded heights. These lines were of great strength, and took full advantage of the marshes and other obstacles. In places they were continuous, and protected by deep, broad ditches filled with water. The system seems to have been extremely well conceived for its purpose. During the whole of the war the French never felt themselves strong enough to attempt the crossing of the Rhine below the Lines of Stollhofen. The project was frequently discussed; but the risks which an invading army would run during, and still more after, the passage of the broad, rapid river, proved in practice a complete deterrent. So also were the mountains and forests on which the left of the lines rested. A frontal attack upon the fortifications, if they were adequately garrisoned, seemed a hazardous and certainly a very costly major operation. It was not until 1707 that Marshal Villars captured them by a brilliant and almost bloodless surprise. Thus the Lines of Stollhofen played a most serviceable part throughout the early critical years of the war, and their

106

construction must be regarded as a military measure of rare discrimination and of the highest value.

In nearly every great war there is some new mechanical feature introduced the early understanding of which confers

THE LINES OF STOLLHOFEN

important advantages. Military opinion is naturally rigid. Men held in the grip of discipline, moving perilously from fact to fact and staking their lives at every step, are nearly always opposed to new ideas. For more than forty years the flintlock had been in actual use in Europe. Its superiority over the matchlock, with its fuse and delayed, uncertain discharge, was only very gradually recognized. As early as 1660 the English Guards had the flintlock. The Dutch haltingly followed this example. The French were the most conservative of all. During the campaigns of King William the flintlock was gaining acceptance and displacing the matchlock in all the armies, but last of all in the French. Nevertheless the difference between the two patterns of musket, though, as we might think, slight and feeble, carried with it for those who had the seeing eye a decisive change in infantry tactics and in the rôle of infantry upon the battlefield. This change was facilitated by the invention of a ring-bayonet which was fastened around the muzzle of the musket instead of blocking it by being screwed inside it. The infantry soldier by this device—which he owed to General Mackay's reflections upon Killiecrankie—became at once pikeman and musketeer. At the same time the improved fire of the flintlock made the function of musketeer increasingly important. Infantry armed with the flintlock and the ring-bayonet could develop a volley-fire of a destructiveness both to horse and foot hitherto unknown. During King William's wars these conditions already existed, but they were not consciously applied by any of the combatants.

Marlborough used this new fact. When he became Commander-in-Chief his root conception of infantry was not a thing that stood, but a thing that fired. The flintlock was by now universally adopted in the armies of the Sea Powers, and to a very large extent in Germany and the Empire. All Marlborough's training of infantry was directed to developing fire. He used frequently to parade large bodies of infantry and practise them in firing. Whereas a French company fired rank by rank, Marlborough's troops fired platoon by platoon, thus assuring the control of the officer commanding the platoon over the volley and the reloading. Fire discipline was already one of the established bases of his thought. All his handling of infantry was governed by the desire to develop precise, regular volley-firing by platoons, and to deploy lines of infantry each company unit of which should be capable of self-sustained, steady fire. Such units while they kept their ranks could not only hold their own against cavalry, but inflict great damage upon them if they came too close. Moreover, brought front to front within sixty or seventy yards of the hostile foot, they could give more hurt than they received. Infantry organized, trained, and deployed for fire could not long be brought in close contact with infantry organized for stability without experiencing a sensible advantage. After half an hour of conflict the other side would look much more ragged than they. This comprehension of the fire-power of infantry was a definite characteristic of Marlborough's tactics. He did not invent or discover it. It had grown unperceived. He saw it and applied it.

The armies of Louis XIV had for two generations held the professional primacy of Europe, but perhaps for that very reason they had been less capable of progress. Turenne long before had sought to develop infantry fire. In spite of the inferior firearms of his day, he tried to make some use of infantry in action other than merely to stand in solid blocks in particular positions. He even experimented with individual skirmishers, and certainly he wished to claim for infantry a higher position upon the battlefields of the seventeenth century. But Turenne's training only covered the troops under his immediate eye, and in the rest of the French Army in the third quarter of the seventeenth century every regiment did what its colonel thought best. Louvois as War Minister imposed uniformity from on high; the whole Army should practise the same drill. He enforced this with the authority of the barrack-square. Fortunately from our point of view, the valuable element of uniformity was not combined with the true choice.

Thus when the world war began again French commanders had a distinctly lower view of the capacities of infantry than Marlborough or those who served under him. They adopted the flintlock tardily. Even as late as the beginning of William's campaigns the French orders were to break up flintlocks captured in the field. Not until 1700 was the flintlock definitely authorized in France, and its adoption was not complete for some years. It follows from this that the French infantry formations remained five or six ranks deep, while Marlborough favoured a depth of three or four. Their tactical regulations for 1703 still spoke of "le combat à la pique et au mousquet." This phrase reveals how imperfectly the significance of the flintlock, the ring bayonet, and fire tactics were realized in the French Army. They learned in a hard school, but they learned slowly. Once the armies were brought in contact the English and Dutch infantry felt themselves superior to the French, and this accounted for their trust in themselves and for Marlborough's trust in them.

Moreover, the French conceptions arising from these slightly distorted data rated the infantry too low and did not assign them their full scope in the battle. Louis XIV taught his Marshals that infantry attacks were useless and that cavalry was the decisive arm; whereas we always see Marlborough's infantry used with the cavalry and made to play their part with mobile cannon at every stage in the general attack.

Neither in the use of cavalry did the armies of Louis XIV excel. They placed an undue emphasis upon the long horse-pistol, and trained their squadrons to deliver from the halt volleys rank after rank at opposing cavalry, using the sword rather when they came to the mêlée. Certainly one may say that pistol and sword counted equally with the French cavalry. Very different were Marlborough's regulations. With the infantry he relied more on fire and less on steel than the French. With the cavalry he relied entirely upon steel. He did not, indeed, discard the pistol utterly, but he only allowed his cavalry *three pistol-rounds per man for the whole campaign,* the idea being that the pistol was the weapon for individual emergency or foraging duty. The sword and the shock of a mass of horsemen were the factors on which Marlborough counted. His cavalry were trained to manœuvre, to approach the enemy slowly and in close order, and then to ride upon them at a heavy trot in the teeth of their pistol-fire. This was justified by the fact that, although the musketry-fire of well-trained infantry could break cavalry, the pistol-fire of horsemen was no defence against a resolute charge.

It would be a mistake to assign decisive qualities to the differences in the tactics of the opposing armies which have been set forth here. There was no contrast of black and white, but only of various shades of grey. The hostile troops were often so closely engaged and the war went on so long that the armies learned from one another continually. Yet one can see a certain superiority of method from the very beginning of the new war, which asserted itself on several great occasions and no doubt at many other times which were not noticed.

Nevertheless these were still the great days of cavalry, and from a quarter to a third of the men in each army were horse soldiers. A wide expanse of flat or gently undulating country was required for a trial of strength. Marlborough's battles were all fought on fronts of four or five miles, whereas Waterloo filled but three. To find again such large fields we have to come down to the nineteenth century, with its Gettysburg and Gravelotte. The armies of Marlborough's time could usually refuse battle by retiring within "inclosures" or by remaining in rough, scrubby, broken ground. A smooth plain was also necessary for the infantry. It is difficult for a modern officer, with his ideas of individual foot soldiers working and scrambling separately or in small groups across or through any kind of country, and feeling the safer the more it is accidented, to realize what tiny obstacles were serious to the infantry of this period. Most of these historic features would hardly be noticed by a tourist in his walk. But the infantry of Marlborough and Louis XIV depended for their existence in battle upon keeping close and perfect order. Although their fire-power was growing, they must still depend largely upon their strict array and their bayonets, while all around, close at hand, often within hailing distance, moved the flashing squadrons which upon the slightest disorder could crumple them almost instantaneously into bloody and fatal confusion. Thus passing even a small hedge or ditch, which unarmed men could easily jump or perhaps step over, was in the presence of the enemy a most anxious business, and every movement, even of a hundred

111

yards, had to be judiciously foreseen as to the ground and timed as to the enemy.

It would, however, be a mistake to infer that battles under these conditions were slow conflicts of feeble forces. On the contrary, they were far more sudden and intense than those of the Great War. Instead of struggles lasting for several weeks along fronts of seventy or eighty miles, all was brought into a small compass and a single day. Sometimes two hundred thousand men fought for an afternoon in a space no larger than the London parks put together, and left the ground literally carpeted with a quarter of their number, and in places heaped with maimed or slaughtered men. The destiny of nations flowed with the blood from their brief collision. The spectacle of one of the battlefields of Marlborough, Frederick, or Napoleon was for these reasons incomparably more gruesome than any equal sector of the recent fronts in France or Flanders.

We do not think that the warriors of our own time, unsurpassed in contempt of death or endurance of strain, would have regarded these old battles as a light ordeal. Instead of creeping forward from one crater to another or crouching low in their trenches under the blind hail of death and amid its shocking explosions, Marlborough's men and their brave, well-trained opponents marched up to each other shoulder to shoulder, three, four, or six ranks deep, and then slowly and mechanically fired volley after volley into each other at duelling distance until the weaker wavered and broke. This was the moment when the falcon cavalry darted in and hacked and slashed the flying men without mercy. Keeping an exact, rigid formation under the utmost trial, filling promptly all the gaps which at every discharge opened in the ranks, repeating at command, platoon by platoon, or rank by rank, the numerous unhurried motions of loading and firing—these were the tests to which our forbears were not unequal. In prolonged severe fighting the survivors of a regiment often stood for hours knee-deep amid the bodies of comrades writhing or for ever still. In their ears rang the hideous chorus of the screams

112

and groans of a pain which no anæsthetic would ever soothe.

Here we must make a digression which may illuminate for the lay reader not one but many operations of war. Accounts of battles and campaigns almost invariably describe the *qualitative* character of the manœuvres without reference to their *quantitative* side. For instance, we read that this battle was won by turning the enemy's flank, and that by breaking his centre; that this army retreated because its line of supply was threatened; or that that advanced boldly, although its communications were cut, and in turn assailed those of its opponent. Where, then, is the secret of victory? It looks at first sight so simple to say "turn the flank," "pierce the centre," or "cut the communications." But apparently none of these processes work by themselves. All are liable to be countered by other equally obvious and desirable movements. Thus the text-books on war too often merely show certain relations of the fronts and flanks of armies which have been as often favourable to one side as to the other. In truth, all these relations, though suggestive to a student, are meaningless apart from their *quantitative* data. Circumstances alone decide whether a correct conventional manœuvre is right or wrong. The circumstances include all the factors which are at work at the time; the numbers and quality of the troops and their morale, their weapons, their confidence in their leaders, the character of the country, the condition of the roads, time, and the weather: and behind these the politics of their states, the special interests which each army has to guard, together with many other complications. And it is the true comprehension at any given moment of the dynamic sum of all these constantly shifting forces that constitutes military genius.

The problem can seldom be calculated on paper alone, and never copied from examples of the past. Its highest solution must be evolved from the eye and brain and soul of a single man, which from hour to hour are making subconsciously all the unweighable adjustments, no doubt with many errors, but with an ultimate practical accuracy. Thus while nothing is more easy than to assign reasons for success or failure by describing the movements, it is between more or less equal opponents impossible to reveal the real secret of either. That is why the campaigns of the greatest commanders often seem so simple that one wonders why the other fellow did not do as well. That is why critics can write so cogently, and yet successful performers are so rare. Almost any intelligent scribe can draw up a lucid and logical treatise full of laboriously ascertained facts and technical phrases on a particular war situation. But the great captains of history, as has been said, seem to move their armies about "as easily as they ride their horses from place to place." Nothing but genius, the dæmon in man, can answer the riddles of war, and genius, though it may be armed, cannot be acquired, either by reading or experience. In default of genius nations have to make war as best they can, and since that quality is much rarer than the largest and purest diamonds, most wars are mainly tales of muddle. But when from time to time it flashes upon the scene, order and design with a sense almost of infallibility draw out from hazard and confusion. "The mere aspirant after a type of character only shows his hopeless inferiority when the natural orator or fighter or lover comes along."[1]

The task of the commander in Marlborough's wars was direct. There were no higher formations like divisions and corps. Even the brigade was an improvization adopted for the campaign. The armies were often divided into wings. There were for each wing generals of cavalry and infantry. Each, like the Chief, was assisted by lieutenant-generals. These high executive officers were available either to carry out particular tasks assigned to them often in the heat of action, or to see that the main plan, with which they were made acquainted, was carried out. The control of the battle was maintained on each side by eight or ten superior officers who had no permanent commands of their own, and were virtually the general staff officers of modern times, working in a faithful subordination. It was with and through these

1 William James, *The Varieties of Religious Experience.*

114

that the commander-in-chief acted, and it is astonishing how smoothly and effectually the troops were often handled and great changes of plan and formation effected even in the stress of action.

In the midst of the scene of carnage, with its drifting smoke-clouds, scurrying fugitives, and brightly coloured lines, squares, and oblongs of men, he sat his horse, often in the hottest fire, holding in his mind the position and fortunes of every unit in his army from minute to minute and giving his orders aloud. We must picture him in those days when the Signal Corps was non-existent, attended not only by three or four generals of high rank, but by at least twenty young officers specially trained and specially mounted, men who were capable of following the event with intelligent eyes, who watched the field incessantly, and who knew where to find the subordinate commanders, their brigades and regiments. For short distances or less important orders the runners we see in the tapestries with their long brass-headed staves of authority were used. Thus in the space of four or five hours perhaps thirty or forty thousand men were killed or wounded on the two sides, and another fearful but glorious name was inscribed in the annals of war.

All this was quite different from the trials of our latter-day generals. We will not belittle them, but they were the trials of mind and spirit working in calm surroundings, often beyond even the sound of the cannonade. There are no physical disturbances: there is no danger: there is no hurry. The generalissimo of an army of two million men, already for ten days in desperate battle, has little or nothing to do except to keep himself fit and cool. His life is not different, except in its glory, from that of a painstaking, punctual public official, and far less agitating than that of a Cabinet Minister who must face an angry Chamber on the one hand or an offended party upon the other. There is no need for the modern commander to wear boots and breeches: he will never ride a horse except for the purposes of health. In the height of his largest battles, when twenty thousand men are falling every day, time will hang heavy on his hands. The heads of a dozen departments will from hour to hour discreetly lay significant sheets of paper on his desk. At intervals his staff will move the flags upon his map, or perhaps one evening the Chief of the Staff himself will draw a blue line or a brown line or make a strong arrow upon it. His hardest trials are reduced to great simplicity. "Advance," "Hold," or "Retreat." "There are but ten divisions left in reserve: shall we give three to-day to the beseeching, clamouring battle-zone, or keep them back till to-morrow or the day after? Shall we send them in trains to the north or to the south?" His personal encounters are limited to an unpleasant conversation with an army commander who must be dismissed, an awkward explanation to a harassed Cabinet, or an interview with a representative of the neutral Press. Time is measured at least by days and often by weeks. There is nearly always leisure for a conference even in the gravest crises. It is not true that the old battle has merely been raised to a gigantic scale. In the process of enlargement the sublime function of military genius—perhaps happily—has been destroyed for ever.

But in the times of which we tell the great commander proved in the day of battle that he possessed a combination of mental, moral, and physical qualities adapted to action which were so lifted above the common run as to seem almost godlike. His appearance, his serenity, his piercing eye, his gestures, the tones of his voice—nay, the beat of his heart—diffused a harmony upon all around him. Every word he spoke was decisive. Victory often depended upon whether he rode half a mile this way or that. At any moment a cannon-shot or a cavalry inrush might lay him with thousands of his soldiers a mangled bundle on the sod. That age has vanished for ever. Other trials are reserved for the human spirit. New and vaguer problems overtop such minds as are available. But let us not pretend that modern achievements can be compared, except by million-tongued propaganda, with the personal feats which the very few great captains of the world performed.

CHAPTER VI

THE HEATHS OF PEER

(1702, Summer)

QUEEN ANNE'S Cabinet under Marlborough's impulsion formed immediately resolute war plans by land and sea for the opening campaign. Marlborough would go to the Low Countries—it was hoped in command of the armies of the Sea Powers, or at least of all the troops in English pay—and would strive by every means to obtain a major decision in the field. Sir George Rooke and the Duke of Ormonde would conduct a large naval and military expedition to capture Cadiz. From this base it would be possible, certainly in the following year, to take Minorca and thus dominate the Mediterranean. Meanwhile, in 1702, after the capture of Cadiz, the fleet was to cruise along the Riviera coasts for as long as possible in the summer months and bring brief but possibly important aid to Prince Eugene. That Marlborough had resolved on this plan of naval action from the moment that he took power and while the Cabinet was still only partially formed is proved by the following letter.

Marlborough to Godolphin

THE HAGUE
April 4

I do not doubt they [the Dutch] will come into the project of Cadiz; and when we are masters of it, I believe they will be of opinion that part of the fleet may go with six or seven thousand men as high as Naples, but not stay above three weeks. *The time this squadron is in the Straits, the rest of the men must be employed in fortifying Cadiz.*

A further thought here is that before the fleet shall return home they should seize upon Corunna, and leave a garrison there if the place be tenable. In order to know that it is, the Queen would send a good engineer by the packet-boat to Corunna.

117

What I now write arises from a conversation I had with the Secretary of the Admiralty last Sunday, before I had your directions.[1]

To both these bold designs violent opposition arose from all concerned. We shall see presently the impediments to the campaign on land, but the obstruction of some of the high authorities in the Cabinet and of Sir George Rooke to the naval expedition was vehement. In 1701 under King William, who had a deep comprehension of Mediterranean naval strategy and its relation to the general war, he had written, "I must repeat my opinion that no service can balance the hazard of bringing our great ships home in the winter" (*i.e.,* keeping them out so late that they would have to cross the Bay and enter the mouth of the English Channel in the winter). He now incited the merchants to cry out that the Channel would be at the mercy of the French. He persuaded Sir Cloudesley Shovell, who was to be in charge of the Channel, to complain that his force was inadequate. All this resistance and the arguments which sustained it were beaten down by the leading men in the Cabinet, and the main Anglo-Dutch fleet in overwhelming superiority to the enemy sailed for the coast of Spain and the attack on Cadiz at the end of July. They carried besides marines eight thousand soldiers under the Duke of Ormonde, and were thus capable of seizing this all-important harbour by an amphibious descent.

For the year 1702 Louis had decided to set his strongest army against Holland. He knew the divisions and uncertainty into which the Republic had been thrown by the death of King William. He believed that the links which joined it to England had been at the least gravely weakened. He counted upon a period of hesitation and loss of contact which, if turned to good account by military action,

---

[1] Alfred Morrison Papers, *H.M.C.,* Report IX, Part II, 464.

might break the Dutch and scare off the English. The prejudices of the Tories against heavy war on the Continent and their sympathy with Jacobite sentiment were well known at Versailles, and indeed throughout Europe. Their preponderance in Queen Anne's Administration was widely accepted as opening a period of English detachment from the main struggle. It was quite natural for friend and foe to reckon without Marlborough. The Courts and chancelleries knew Sarah, and had made a study of her relations with the new Queen. They regarded Marlborough as a favoured Court personage, able no doubt, and busy with intrigue, but owing his influence entirely to the Queen's affection for his wife. True, he had also been in the previous year King William's man, but it was well known that William managed all great business very closely himself. How could foreigners measure the real relations of the Cockpit group? How could they know what Marlborough was or foresee what he would become?

According to the treaties of the Grand Alliance, the Emperor should have ranged ninety thousand troops out of his quota of a hundred and twenty thousand in the field against the French. Actually he was unable by midsummer to place more than forty thousand in Italy under the command of Prince Eugene, and could only muster twenty thousand upon the Rhine under the Margrave Prince Louis of Baden. The Imperial forces had been weakened by an insurrection which had broken out in Hungary, and also by the unfriendly and already almost menacing attitude of the Elector of Bavaria. We shall deal hereafter with both these vexatious developments.

The evident failure of the Empire to make any serious concentration upon the Upper Rhine led the French to leave that theatre in suspense while they used their principal armies against Eugene in Italy, and against the formidable Anglo-Dutch forces which were now on a war footing in the Netherlands. Two Marshals of France, Villeroy and Vendôme, with sixty thousand men, were assigned to the Italian theatre. Marshal Boufflers, with sixty thousand men, comprising the first army of France, confronted the Sea Powers in the Low Countries. Marshal Catinat, with twenty thousand men, watched the Margrave about the confluence of the Neckar with the Rhine, and guarded Alsace. By the beginning of June both sides had placed about two hundred thousand men upon the fighting fronts, with large and growing establishments in the rear.

In all prudence the French should first have blotted out the Maestricht enclave as well as the neighbouring small patch of Dutch territory around Jülich. Maestricht cut the navigation of the Meuse, and spoiled the main line for the supply of armies invading Holland. But it was possible by convoys from the province of Brabant and from Cologne, and by forming large magazines in Venloo and Ruremonde, to carry the tide of war to the north, leaving Maestricht isolated behind it, to be submerged later on. And of course, if their forward plans had succeeded and the Dutch armies had been beaten and the homelands of Holland invaded, the life of Maestricht was severely limited. Therefore the Great King and the French High Command did not hesitate to place their main army, as soon as the campaigning season began, within twenty miles of Nimwegen in the narrowing tongue-tip of Cleves, which divides the valleys of the Meuse and the Rhine. This was a plan which would answer best, if everything went well. Marshal Boufflers, having Tallard, the former Ambassador in London, as his lieutenant, lay therefore at Xanten with the French northern army. He was based on two long stretches of the Rhine and the Meuse, along which he held all the fortresses, except only Maestricht. From this position Boufflers began to negotiate with the Elector-King of Brandenburg-Prussia, offering him the whole terirtory of Cologne and Liége if he would abandon the allies and lay Holland open to invasion. The Elector, newly recognized as King 'in' Prussia by the Emperor and, at Marlborough's insistence, by Queen Anne, played with the envoys, gathered his troops, but also kept the Dutch on tenterhooks.

The Dutch, with Marlborough's approval, but before the

question of command had been settled, had begun the campaign of 1702 by laying siege in the middle of April to the fortress of Kaiserswerth, a place "mean but well fortified."[1] Rheinberg, some fifteen miles to the north of it, was out of

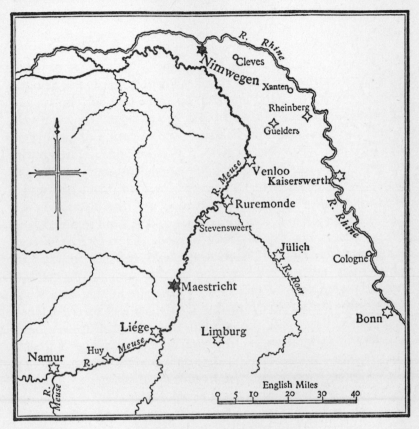

FORTRESSES OF THE MEUSE AND RHINE, EARLY IN 1702[2]

cannon-shot of the river and no effective barrier upon navigation. The fall of Kaiserswerth, therefore, would open the Rhine at least as far as Cologne. Moreover, this movement would be encouraging to the German allies and the Empire,

1 T. Brodrick, *A Compleat History of the Late War* (1713), p 11.
2 All places not shown in the small plans will be found in the general map, facing p. 256, vol, IV,

with whom it would put the Dutch in closer relation.
The French were watched by the Earl of Athlone, better
known to us as Ginkel, with a weaker allied force at Cranenburg, while the allied besieging force made its way to
Kaiserswerth, keeping the broad Rhine between them and
the French.

As soon as the investment of Kaiserswerth began Boufflers
detached Tallard with thirteen thousand men to hamper the
siege, even if he could not relieve the place. Tallard did

THE SIEGE OF KAISERSWERTH

not feel able to cross the
river in the face of the
Allies, nor was it thought
wise to make this direct
assault upon the German
Reich. Although he can-
nonaded and harassed
their camps, Tallard was
not able to prevent the
regular progress of the
siege. Early in May the
Duke of Burgundy had
arrived at Xanten to
'learn the art of war'
under Boufflers, and as-
sumed nominal command
of the French army. The presence of a Prince of the Blood
was held to require special exertions from all. Boufflers therefore on June 10, while Kaiserswerth was still holding out, suddenly and swiftly advanced in two columns through Cleves
and Gennep to cop[1] Ginkel. The experienced Dutch soldier
was nearly caught. His own information was late and faulty.
At the last moment he was saved by a warning message
from the Prussian King and by an instant precipitate retreat
through the night. At dawn the French cavalry pincers almost
closed upon him; but by barely a single mile and half an
hour he escaped, and his breathless troops, for whom an

1 We plead that this admirable word, used as early as 1704, should take its place
in the English language without any further reproach of slang.

122

English brigade was the rearguard, turned to bay beneath the fortress guns of Nimwegen.[1] Even these might not have been available for their protection. The governor of the town was suspected of being suborned by the French, and it was the burghers alone who armed and manned the batteries after breaking into the arsenal in which the pieces and their ammunition lay. Berwick thought that if a battle had been fought on the glacis of Nimwegen the French might have entered the town pell-mell with the routed Dutch. But the cannon which the burghers had dragged to the ramparts during the night and morning now began to fire in large numbers and with effect upon the pursuers. Boufflers hesitated and, narrowly baulked, eventually drew off and posted himself near Gennep. This episode deeply alarmed the Dutch in their disturbed political condition. Indeed, they might well have abandoned the siege of Kaiserswerth if that place had not fortunately capitulated on June 15.

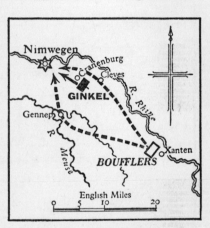

THE CRANENBURG PINCERS

Marlborough had reached the Dutch capital on May 26 to find every one in distress and everything in dispute. The supreme command was still unsettled. In June the Prussian King arrived to press somewhat half-heartedly his claim. There is little doubt that Heinsius and his colleagues meant by now to have Marlborough; but the actual announcement was embarrassing. In these circumstances they requested him to remain at The Hague as long as Frederick I was there.[2] Ginkel's narrow escape and the growing public danger forced the decision. Nimwegen, the key of the

---

1 See Lord Cutts' account (Portland Papers, *H.M.C.*, iv, 40) and Cardonnel's comments and corrections in Add. MSS., 28918, ff. 13–18.
2 Cardonnel to Aglionby, June 21; S.P., 84/225.

Rhine delta and the gateway into Holland, had obviously been in dire peril for some hours. This was no time for compliments to royalty. The foreign princely candidates, including the Prussian King, had all been ruled out by Queen Anne's opposition. The Dutch, with the French bayonets glistening at their very throats, were sure that Queen Anne's husband would not do. Indeed, since May they had made it clear that for their part they would never consent. Still they hesitated, and the tension on the front grew. On June 30 Marlborough, judging the moment opportune, announced that he must leave for Nimwegen, presumably to command the British troops and those in English pay.[1] This apparently clinched the matter; for when he started for the front the next day he was in possession of a patent which conferred on him the title of Deputy Captain-General of the Republic. Cardonnel wrote to say, "The States have given directions to all their Generals and other officers to obey my Lord Marlborough as their General."[2] On July 3 there is a letter of Marlborough's from Nimwegen thanking the Dutch for their decision.[3] Thus we may say that from the beginning of July 1702 Marlborough assumed command of all the Dutch, British, and hired German forces and became the principal general of the Grand Alliance. This post, with its authority varying according to events and the different signatory Powers, he held continuously till the end of 1711. It was never in his power to give orders which covered the whole field of the war, and in many quarters and conjunctures his command was disputed, divided, or merely nominal. But for these ten years he was by loyal assent or tacit recognition the leading general of all the armies of Europe leagued against France. His own discretion and frequent submissions, combined with the shattering military events which he produced, preserved to him, if often only in a ghostlike form, a vague but majestic primacy. He could at no time have asserted a claim to be Generalissimo without widespread

1 Stanhope to Hedges, June 30; S. P., 84/224, f. 68.
2 *Dispatches*, i, 4.
3 Letter to Fagel, *ibid.*, p. 5.

repudiation; but there was never an allied demand for anyone else.

The Dutch, when at last they gave Marlborough the command of their armies and to enforce their authority paid him a salary of ten thousand pounds a year, had very definite intentions about the kind of warfare he should wage. They thought he was the best man for the command, and, indeed, the only one who could hold it. But their confidence did not go so far as letting him fight a battle. By the Constitution of the Republic two members of the Government were bound to accompany their Captain-General throughout his operations, and no important action could be fought or town besieged without their assent. They had even sent their deputies to King William's headquarters. They now provided Marlborough with mentors and censors in the Baron Heyden and Mynheer Geldermalsen. All the Dutch generals looked to the two Dutch Deputies, and Marlborough had to fight his first campaign as well as he could within the limits which they prescribed. We shall relate how this system hampered and frustrated Marlborough's plans. But it must not be supposed that this arose from the personal timidity of the Deputies. They had definite instructions from the Dutch Government that no battle was to be risked that could possibly be avoided, and that prudence and moderation should rule both strategy and tactics. Marlborough's endeavour was to persuade them to depart from their instructions, and how he tempted and inspired them will presently be seen. Geldermalsen, a Zeelander and a former Ambassador to England, soon succumbed to Marlborough's arts, and stood up vigorously for the rights of the English general, even against his own fellow-countrymen.

When the news of Marlborough's appointment as Commander-in-Chief reached the camps, indignation rose high among the Dutch generals at their supersession. Ginkel had to the last contended for the command upon alternate days. Opdam, Overkirk, and Slangenberg deemed their military records and experience superior to those of this foreigner. He had, they argued, never grounded himself in the theory of war by professional study. Court favour, diplomatic influence, political intrigue, a chain of accidents, the mutually destructive claims of better men, had given him the coveted distinction. There was truth in much of this; but there was other truth besides.

Upon his arrival at Nimwegen Marlborough at first remained in considerable seclusion. He sat through the councils of war silent and observant. He took his great position sedately. To Godolphin, who wrote his congratulations, he replied, "The station I am now in . . . would have been a great deal more agreeable to me if it could have been had without dispute and a little less trouble; but patience will overcome all things." He treated Ginkel and the other Dutch generals with equal respect and reserve. He seems to have spoken more intimately to the captains of the foreign mercenary contingents. These soon gained the impression that the new Commander-in-Chief did not approve of the cautious methods of making war which reigned in the allied camp. He seemed dissatisfied with the idea of passively protecting the frontier, and possibly capturing some Belgian fortress in the course of the campaign. He was reported to hold strange doctrines about war. England was not attracted by small warfare or limited objects. It was not this town nor that which she sought. The annihilation of the French army in a great battle and the humbling of Louis XIV in the open field were the purposes which had brought the English troops to the Netherlands. He would not agree to be responsible to the Queen if the allied army tethered itself at the gates of Nimwegen, and allowed the enemy to live at its side on friendly soil between the Meuse and the Rhine. He had not been a week at headquarters before it was known that he was demanding drastic decisions from the Dutch Government.

Marlborough to Godolphin

DUCKENBERG
July 13, 1702

I am ashamed to write from this camp, for we ought to have marched from hence three or four days ago; but the fears the

Dutch have for Nimwegen and the Rhine created such difficulties when we were to take a resolution that we were forced to send to The Hague, and the States would not come to any resolution, but have made it more difficult, by leaving it to the general officers, at the same time recommending, in the first place, the safety of the Rhine and Nimwegen. . . . If the fear of Nimwegen and the Rhine had not hindered us from marching into Brabant, they [the enemy] must then have had the disadvantage of governing themselves by our motions, whereas we are now obliged to mind them.[1]

His attitude caused excitement in the camp and perturbation at The Hague. Heinsius felt so insecure in his authority, and all parties in Holland were in such lively alarm, that it was only with extreme difficulty that they could be persuaded to entertain any offensive operation. They clung to the strong army which now stood between them and the enemy, and sought to prevent any movement which would uncover Nimwegen. They could not bear to "lose sight of the Army." But Geldermalsen supported Marlborough. He wrote to Heinsius on July 9:

I must beg you in the name of God to be so good as to work unceasingly for a resolve to do something effective; for without action all is lost. . . . Mylord Marlborough cannot but be in lively distress to see himself at the head of the stronger army tied to the gates of a town or subsisting with the enemy upon allied soil. It will be difficult to justify such manœuvres to England, and there they will accuse the weakness of our Government.[2]

The discussions were protracted both in the capital and in the camp. Meanwhile Marlborough was drawing in reinforcements from every quarter, and by July 6 had concentrated in front of Nimwegen at Duckenberg an army which, though somewhat smaller than the French, gave him the assurance that he was master. He held a grand review, and sixty thousand well-trained soldiers, equipped and furnished in every way and led by experienced or veteran officers, paraded before him. On the 15th he marched with

1 Coxe, i, 171.   2 Von Noorden, i, 260.

his whole force directly towards the enemy and camped upon the Meuse about Grave. Here only seven miles separated the two armies. He found time to write to Sarah.

John to Sarah

July 17, 1702

We have now very hot weather, which I hope will ripen the fruit at St Albans. When you are there, pray think how happy I should be walking alone with you. No ambition can make me amends for being from you. If it were not impertinent, I should desire you in every letter to give my humble duty to the Queen, for I do serve her with all my heart and soul. I am on horseback or answering letters all day long; for besides the business of the army, I have letters from The Hague, and all places where her Majesty has any Ministers. So that if it were not for my zeal for her service, I should certainly desert, for you know of all things I do not love writing.[1]

The ostensible object of the advance had been the siege of Rheinberg, but Marlborough intended, once the army was in motion, to substitute a larger design. The challenging movement of the army and its magnificent appearance freed the troops from the sense of weakness and irresolution by which they had been oppressed while they huddled around Nimwegen. His perfect self-confidence, although he was for the first time at the head of a great army, spread itself throughout the ranks. But the Dutch generals were stubborn, and their Government quaked. It took Marlborough a fortnight to persuade them to the next move. It may be that if he had had a free hand he would have marched directly into Brabant and towards Antwerp. But he knew the States-General would never allow their provinces to be, as they would have declared, exposed. There was, however, another plan which offered remarkable advantages. Marlborough saw the rickety foundations beneath the bold, aggressive position which Boufflers had assumed.

Sixty miles behind the menacing French front lay Maestricht, strong and unsubdued, with its ample supplies,

1 Coxe, i, 172.

beckoning its friends from the north. The advance of a strong army towards Maestricht would immediately bring Boufflers hurrying back to Brabant and to a safer line of communications. He would have to abandon the Meuse and its three French fortresses of Venloo, Stevensweert, and Ruremonde, or— fight and win a battle. Without alarming the Dutch by dwelling unduly on this second possibility, Marlborough pressed for permission to march south from Nimwegen. Even for this limited movement he had a wearying struggle. He had to persuade not only generals who, like Ginkel, resented his command, but a crowd of anxious Dutch functionaries and magnates. He took a number of these upon a reconnaissance towards Boufflers' camp, and, pointing to the long lines of French tents, remarked, "I shall soon rid you of these troublesome neighbours."

As the Rheinberg project faded from the lateness of the siege material, and as delay threatened to sink into futility, Marlborough made an offer to the States which, while it allayed their fears, increased his and their dangers. He offered to divide the army. Geldermalsen was speeding to and fro between headquarters and The Hague. "Should we follow what he thinks to be best," wrote Marlborough to Godolphin on July 20,

> I think the French may have it in their power to beat us. But to comply as far as I can, I have this night proposed to them the leaving twenty squadrons of horse, and eighteen battalions of foot, to entrench themselves before Nimwegen, and to pass the Meuse with the rest of the army, or to march with the whole towards Cleves, in order to get between Venloo and the French, if possible, so as to be able to attack them.[1]

At length after the loss of ten precious days his patience and the sense of confidence he inspired around him prevailed. The Dutch still disbelieved that the march he proposed would have the result of forcing Boufflers to retire, but they consented to the experiment. At the last minute a disappointment occurred. The Prussian and Hanoverian contingents had arrived with orders that they were not on any account to

1 Coxe, i, 173.

cross the Meuse. "In that case," said Marlborough, "they need not have come at all." When this remonstrance, combined with the recent recognition which Marlborough had procured from Queen Anne of the Great Elector as King in Prussia, reached Berlin it was effective. At last on July 26 Marlborough, having thrown his three bridges under pretence of seeking forage, crossed to the left bank of the Meuse with about fifty thousand men, including the English. That night and on the following days he marched steadily southward.

MARLBOROUGH STRIKES SOUTH

On the 31st he captured a small frontier garrison and three hundred men in the castle of Gravensbrück, and reached Lille Saint-Hubert the same night. Here he halted, having covered forty miles. What would the enemy do?

They did what Marlborough had promised. The results were immediate. He obliged the enemy, in Captain Parker's homely words, "to quit their camp and dance after him."[1] He gained the initiative. From the very first moment that Boufflers saw his movement he broke up his camp near Cleves, marched with all speed back to Ruremonde, and summoned Tallard's detachments to join the main army. On the 28th he was at Ruremonde, waiting anxiously for Tallard to draw closer. The danger of his position on the Meuse, with hostile Maestricht behind him, was apparent the moment it was tested. He must form contact again with his true base in Brabant. But to do this he had to march round Marlborough's front. Says Parker, "We were just between

1 Parker, *Memoirs*, p. 79.

them and home and they had no way homeward but by marching over a heath which was within half a league of our camp."[1]

On the 30th Boufflers, seeing no other chance open, turned westward and began his perilous march. The reader will see from the diagram that the two armies were now approaching each other almost at right angles and that a serious battle might be fought. Boufflers was at a grave disadvantage, because he had, in slipping past, to expose during the whole day his right flank to Marlborough's downward spear-thrust. He had to make a flank march across the front of an army which he must presume would attack him in the midst of that awkward manœuvre. He could not know what troops, if any, Marlborough had been obliged to leave behind to soothe the Dutch. There might well be seventy thousand men on top of Boufflers when he was most ill-arranged to receive them. Moreover Maestricht, that hostile fortress with its large garrison, was already obtruding itself upon his movements. The gap between Marlborough's army and Maestricht was now only twenty miles. Boufflers decided to run the risk. Meanwhile Marlborough was joined by the English artillery, escorted by two battalions and comprising thirty-four cannon and four "Hawbitzers," or half the artillery of the army.

We can see from the letter which he wrote to Godolphin upon the morning of the 30th how crucially the relations of the two armies were defined.

Marlborough to Godolphin

CAMP NEAR HAMONT
July 30, 1702

. . . I might have less time [to write] to-morrow since our march will in all likelihood that day be governed by the motion of the French army. For if they march from Weert, where we take their camp now to be, we shall endeavour to make their march uneasy [*i.e.*, attack them]. If they stay in their camp, which it is generally believed they will not, we shall then post ourselves between them and the Demer. Our marches have already had the effect desired, which was their repassing the Meuse,

1 *Ibid.*, p. 80.

which had we done sooner had been much better. But the very extravagant fears all Holland had for Nimwegen and the passage of the Rhine had like to have spoiled all the campaign. I hope now we shall oblige them to quit the Meuse by which we shall be able to besiege Venloo, and make the [our] army for the rest of the campaign subsist in their country. *If they would venture anything this summer, it ought to be this day: for our march is upon an open heath and we are weaker by sixteen regiments of foot than we shall be three days hence.* I am just getting on horseback to begin the march, and my letter is dated from the place where we are to camp to-night. The French are nearer to it than we are, but I do not think they will venture [*i.e.*, fight]. But by this march they must own that we do not avoid meeting them. In my next I shall be able to tell you what party [*i.e.*, *parti* = decision] they have taken; for they must resolve either to quit the Meuse or abandon Brabant.[1]

There is an air of suppressed excitement about this matter-of-fact letter, and one feels that the writer, about to mount his horse and hoping in a few hours to command in his first great battle, wished to leave some record of his mood and situation. It was an impulse to which he rarely yielded. We have only one or two instances when he seems to look at himself and his background in a mirror. We may measure the tenseness of the business from this fact. Actually the climax was delayed.

Marlborough had from the beginning intended to bring matters to a point where both the French, in spite of their disadvantage, and the Dutch, in spite of their misgivings, would be compelled to fight. Once on the move and in contact with the enemy he began to assert his authority. "From day to day," said Geldermalsen, "he makes it the more felt that he is Commander here; whereas at Nimwegen he sought to do nothing that was not decided by the generals."[2] He hoped that once the Dutch were presented with a rare war-chance of taking the enemy at a marked disadvantage he would be able to swing them into the battle. But he reckoned vainly. On the night of August 1, at Little

1 Partly in Coxe (wrongly transcribed), i, 175.
2 To Heinsius, August 1, 1702; von Noorden, i, 261.

Bruegel, he saw that the moment had come. He exposed to the Dutch Deputies his intention to attack Boufflers with his whole army the next day. We do not know how long he wrestled with them: in the end they agreed. All the baggage was sent back, and the allied army was set in battle array. Dawn broke, and Marlborough was on horseback, meaning to order a general attack upon the French, the heads of whose columns were to be seen approaching from the southward, about to cross his front. But then ensued a painful scene. The Deputies had given their consent: the decisive commands were about to be issued: and now they withdrew it. They were conscious of their weak position. They did not dictate —they besought him not to put the army of the Republic upon the cast of the die. He might have been right about the strategy, but no one could tell whether he would be victorious in a battle. There was the risk of defeat and the certainty of heavy loss. Besides, they had now heard what he had known the day before, that Tallard was close behind Boufflers and that the enemy's army was thus superior in numbers. They implored him to let them off their over-night resolve.

Anyone acquainted with war will realize that this was a very hard trial for a general. But the armies of a coalition cannot be handled like those of a single state. Swallowing his feelings, the Commander-in-Chief bowed to their appeals. There should be no battle: but he exacted a condition. They must, he said, ride out with him to see what might have happened. They did so, and beheld during the whole of the morning of the 2nd the French army, in imposing numbers but considerable disorder, streaming across their front with their whole flank exposed. As this spectacle told its own tale, the Deputies admitted that a grand opportunity had been lost. But another immediately recurred. After their long march the French were forced to camp on the night of August 2 at Zonhoven, still in a most dangerous position. Marlborough, hopeful that his demonstration in the morning would win him freedom to give the necessary orders, again urged an attack the next day. Again the Deputies could not bring themselves to do such violence to their instructions.

133

Upon the opportunity we have confirmation from the other side. Berwick, with his military instinct, measured the position as well as Marlborough.

> The Earl of Marlborough proposed to march up to us, by passing the defile of Peer, by which a battle on the heaths would have been unavoidable; but the Deputies of the States-General would never consent to this, any more than to attack us in our camp at Sonoven. This was very fortunate for us; for we were posted in such a manner that we should have been beaten without being able to stir, our left being very high, and our right sunk into a *cul-de-sac* between two rivulets.[1]

The retreat of Boufflers from the Meuse had enabled Marlborough to draw six thousand men, nine battalions, to his army from the troops extorted from him to cover Nimwegen. When these joined him he was again definitely the stronger. But the veto on battles continued. Thus Boufflers, so recently aggressive and menacing, was able to make his escape into Brabant. He had lost no battle, but he had abandoned the whole Meuse with its fortresses and two out of the three areas which he had been told by Louis XIV it was his duty to guard. Here was the first crux of Marlborough's campaign of 1702.

Amid these trials he found relief in writing to Sarah about all sorts of things, great and small. * "We do not march to-morrow so that I have written to Lord Churchill [his son]. If you do not like it, send me such a letter as you would have me write." Apparently the children were in Sarah's special department, or perhaps this was in answer to his son's request to be allowed to go to the wars. "This afternoon is the only time I have had to myself this seven or eight days, and I have employed it in writing to you and my dear Children for I have no mind to go to bed. . . ." "You say nothing to me," he complained, "how the Election went at St Albans, nor how my garden is, which I have not forgot. . . . I do beg of you not to be uneasy that you have not sent me the accounts, for I had much rather never have them, than that you should do it at a time when it might be troublesome to

1 *Memoirs*, i, 170.

you." He asked Sarah whether anything could be done for one of his assistants—Courant. "It is not reasonable to expect the Queen should remember her intentions of doing something for [him], instead of letting him be page of the backstairs; but since he had the honour of being in the poor Duke's family [the late Duke of Gloucester] I desire you would some way know if anything be done for him; for his being with me should not be the occasion of his being the only one not provided for." He deals at length with the time of the meeting of Parliament. It would be "very much for her Majesty's interest in the country if they meet early in October, so that everybody might see that the new Parliament as well as her Majesty are zealous for the Common Cause. . . . Till that be seen the Empire will not do as they ought." He hopes that timely notice will be given to the Members and Peers, so that they will not settle down for the autumn in their country estates. He thinks Ministers are foolish in going to their country houses and hoping for a quiet holiday when Parliament will inevitably be summoned soon. He urges, "If this matter be not resolved quickly and notice given, I am afraid you will find Sunderland, and a great many of his friends, not consider, or not know, the great advantage it would be to the Queen, and the Common Cause, to have them meet early, but [will] consider only their own conveniency of staying in their countries and so be against the meeting." He says that "76" (? Harley) will be disappointed if he imagines that he can go to his country house and yet be back in time for the meeting of Parliament.

In all these desultory fragments two sentences break in at different points which show us what was really in his mind. *"These last three or four days have been very uneasy, I having been obliged to take more pains than I am well able to endure."* And, later, *"Pray give my humble duty to the Queen. I was in hopes the day before yesterday I might have done her some service."*[1]

The second disappointment arose in the following manner. Louis was shocked at the loss of the Meuse and the occupation

1 This letter is dated August 3. It was plainly not finished for some days. The underlining is Marlborough's.

by his enemies of the large territories of Spanish Guelderland and the Bishopric of Liége. He had not been accustomed to such treatment. He sent insistent instructions to his grandson, the Duke of Burgundy, to show greater vigour, and above all to make sure that Venloo and the other now isolated fortresses on the Meuse were not captured. Marlborough, with what the confederates called "the grand army," still lay in the heaths about Peer, and their supply was an intricate business. They could not use the Meuse because of the untaken French fortresses. They had to subsist either upon stores drawn from the immense magazines of Maestricht or by convoys from Nimwegen and Bois-le-Duc, which latter place the English soldiers, anticipating modes which they used in the Great War, quaintly called "Boilduck."

Boufflers, animated by Berwick and spurred by the King, tried to interrupt Marlborough's communications with the north. Accordingly, on August 9 and 10 he marched to Riethoven, sending Berwick forward to Eindhoven. Now this movement was not at all objectionable to Marlborough. On the contrary, he saw in it another opportunity of drawing the French and enticing the Dutch Deputies to where they would have to fight. So he played the second phase of this double game the goal of which was battle.

It happened that an important convoy, probably of seven or eight hundred wagons containing both bread and treasure, was moving under the escort of Lord Albemarle—William's friend, the young Keppel—down from "Boilduck" to the army. Boufflers and Berwick in their new positions were well placed to intercept it. Marlborough, facing about at Hamont, sent the Dutch general Opdam, of whom more (and little good) hereafter, with six thousand men to Helmond to bring in Albemarle and his convoy safely. We can see without doubt that he meant to use both Opdam and the convoy as glittering baits of different sizes and character to provoke a general action. On the morning of August 16 the convoy had nearly joined Opdam, and Berwick was about to fall on both. Boufflers was hurrying forward with his main army; but just as Berwick was about to fall on Opdam—in

136

fact, only a mile separated the forces—Boufflers learned that
Marlborough with his whole army was advancing rapidly on
his own flank. The Marshal thereupon recalled Berwick,
who was indignant at being baulked, and countermarched
himself with rapidity out of harm's way. The hook had been
shown too soon. Marlborough withdrew south for another
cast, and once again he used Opdam as the bait. He kept
Opdam and his tempting
detachment just far
enough behind him to
attract the French.

Boufflers, with his back
towards Holland, now
followed for three days,
Marlborough retreating
towards France. Where
armies are equal the gen-
eral who is retiring can
always turn and fight,
and as he can choose the
moment, so he can choose
the ground. For three
days the French had the
exhilaration of apparent-
ly driving the enemy be-
fore them and away from

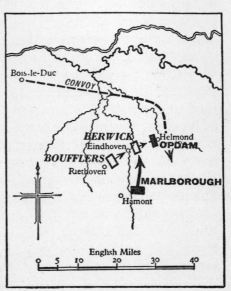

THE SECOND THRUST

his home and his communications. On the afternoon of the
third day they began to emerge from difficult country on to
the Heath of Helchteren, a wide expanse well suited to the
action of cavalry, in which arm Marlborough was superior.
Here they saw the allied army suddenly drawn up in full array
and evidently about to strike. Now even the Dutch Deputies
were converted. Any plain man could see the advantage they
would have in attacking the French while they were but half-
debouched from defiles, scrub, and morasses. They gave their
assents, and the Commander-in-Chief, so called, issued his
orders. The cannonade opened from both artilleries, and
several hundred men were stricken in each of the armies.

137

At five o'clock Opdam on the right, reinforced to ten thousand men, was ordered to begin the battle by attacking the French left, whose difficulties and disarray could be plainly seen. But after the Dutch Deputies the Dutch generals. Opdam, alleging the state of the ground, consumed three vital hours without making any appreciable movement. The advance of the rest of the army depended upon Opdam. Night fell and under its cover the French were able to complete their deployment.

The next day, the 24th, although the battle would have been much more even, Marlborough still wished to engage. But now it was the Deputies who jibbed. They could see the advantages which might have been seized yesterday, but to-day the issue seemed balanced. Surely it was wiser to wait till to-morrow. If Boufflers attacked he must be encountered; but if he did not attack the matter could be reconsidered on the morrow. "To-morrow," said Marlborough, "Monsieur de Boufflers will be gone." And so he was. "The French lofty army," wrote Sergeant Millner, "immediately withdrew from their attempt and fell backward."[1] A pursuit by the English cavalry yielded only minor advantages. Here was the second crisis of the campaign. Here was the second lost opportunity.

We owe to Ailesbury a glimpse of Marlborough on one of these days which seems to bring him near to us. The Earl had asked to visit Marlborough at the front in order to press for leave to go to England on his private affairs. Marlborough had replied that he had better not, "and you may guess the reason," he said in a letter. He had described himself as "set round with a company of officers that he knew were my enemies." So Ailesbury sent his secretary, one Mr West, with a letter. The secretary found Marlborough under cannon-fire, "standing in the middle of a circle of generals. The bombardment was to celebrate St Louis's day." The secretary, guided by a companion, approached. Marlborough recognized him, and, turning aside from his staff, said, "Mr West, my humble service

1 Millner, *Journal*, p. 26.

to my lord. You see I cannot write now, but I will send an express to Aix." He added a warning that the spot was dangerous. Mr West bowed and withdrew with his companion a short distance. There was a long whistle and another horrid sound; Mr West's companion had had his head sheared off. The secretary thereupon considered his mission at an end; "not being used," says Ailesbury, "to such hot work, no doubt he was severely affrighted."[1] The day of St Louis is August 25, and Ailesbury explicitly cites the year as 1702. We may therefore fix this incident during the contact of the armies around Helchteren.

Marlborough repressed his wrath at the obstructions by which he was hampered. It has been said of him that he had so many plans all thought out in his mind, and could change so easily from one to the other, that he suffered less by the frustration of his combinations than would a general whose heart was set on some particular scheme. He always felt that if he was not allowed to win one way, he could find another. Still, these were torturing experiences.

He wrote to Godolphin from Helchteren on August 27:

> I have but too much reason to complain that the ten thousand men upon our right did not march as soon as I sent the orders, which if they had, I believe we should have had a very easy victory, for their whole left was in disorder. However, I have thought it much for her Majesty's service to take no notice of it, as you see by my letter to the States. But my Lord Rivers, and almost all the general officers of the right, were with me when I sent the orders, so that notwithstanding the care I take to hinder it, they do talk. . . .
> . . . Venloo will be invested to-morrow. . . .
> I am in so ill humour that I will not trouble you, nor dare I trust myself to write more; but believe this truth, that I honour and love you, my lady Marlborough, and my children, and would die for the Queen.[2]

One thing, however, was beyond endurance. He could not bear that his kinsman Berwick, whose merit he divined, and Marshal Boufflers should suppose that he had himself

1 Ailesbury, *Memoirs*, ii, 535.   2 Coxe, i, 180–181.

thrown away glorious chances and shrunk from carrying his combinations to the point of battle. His professional pride and instinct asserted themselves above all things. We have the strange spectacle of a Commander-in-Chief apologizing to his antagonists for not attacking them upon two occasions when they knew he would have been technically right to put all to the test. He actually sent a trumpet with letters to Boufflers and Berwick to assure them with compliments that the failure in coming to battle was none of his fault. There is no doubt from their movements at many crucial passages in this and the next campaign that they believed him. Whether his candour was wise or not can never be decided. It is certainly curious.

CHAPTER VII

THE FORTRESSES OF THE MEUSE

(1702, Autumn)

MARLBOROUGH was forced to recognize for the time being that even under the most favourable circumstances he would not be allowed to fight a battle. No one can measure the internal stresses of the general who has to conduct war against an equal enemy under such paralysing control. All that Frederick the Great and Napoleon have taught us in war shows how far the methods of Marlborough were in advance of his time. For the last forty years Flanders had been the scene of campaigns which, though hard-fought, had no purpose but the capture or relief of one or the other of its many fortresses, no prize that was not geographical. It almost seemed that Governments and their commanders avoided the destruction of their enemy, were content to let the process run on, exercising the generals on both sides in methodical sieges, the correct management of magazines, and other text-book performances, and repaying the over-taxed public with fresh exciting news from the front. Turenne alone, and only occasionally, aimed at the battle as the true solution. The idea of seeking a battle under favourable conditions and shattering the enemy's main force by fighting was the military commonplace of the nineteenth century, and was carried to fearful lengths in the twentieth. But now Marlborough must reconcile himself to the conventional warfare of the end of the seventeenth century. He must content himself with parades, manœuvres, the sieges of fortresses, and the control of foraging areas. This was not his kind of war. But if it was the only one permitted, he would make it serve. The fortresses on the Meuse were within his grasp. But in this project he had already encountered many disappointments.

141

Marlborough to Godolphin

EVERBEECK
August 21, 1702

* It is now eight days since we made the detachment for Venloo, and last night we received a letter from Monsrs Geldermalsen and Cohorn from the Grave which says that for want of powder and other necessaries they can't begin the siege till the beginning of the next month. Notwithstanding the great conveniency and desire the States have to have Venloo, yet their Government at this time is so very negligent that I am afraid at last [in the end] they will not be able to attack it by which all the frute of this campaign will be lost. I have written very pressing letters to The Hague and have endeavoured to make them sensible how scandalous it would be if this siege should miscarry for want of necessary preparations. They promised that everything should be ready by the 2nd of this month old style [August 13]. What I say of Venloo and the Dutch you will see is fit only to be known by the Queen and [the] Prince; for a friendship with these people is absolutely necessary for the common cause and her Majesty's service, and I am in hope that the prudence of the Pensioner this winter may order matters so that their parties may unite, and then there can be no doubt but everything will go better.

I received two days ago the enclosed letter from M. Schmettau, the King of Prussia's Plenipotentiary at The Hague, by which you will see how much that King is pleased with her Majesty's having allowed the ceremonial he so much desired. It has already had the good effect that we could not have made the siege without his troops which we could not have had if he had not been pleased with this thing; for upon the assurance of it he gave orders to the Baron Heyden to obey whatever orders I should give him during this campaign, and accordingly he has passed the Rhine with the troops under his command, and has assured me that he shall invest Venloo on that side of the Meuse whatever day I shall direct him. At the same time he has made difficulty of being commanded at the siege by my Lord Athlone [Ginkel], which is the reason of the States sending for the Prince of Saarbrook to command, . . . for with him he can't dispute. . . .

The convoy from Boilduck which we have been so long expecting joined us yesterday so that we shall march to-morrow and continue our march next day towards Diest for till all things are ready for the investing Venloo, we are at liberty of marching where we please, and by this march we shall make their convoys very uneasy, or oblige their army to march out of the mairie of Boilduck.

All authorities were agreed upon the siege of Venloo. The Dutch and the French attached equal importance to it; and Marlborough himself had perforce to describe it as the "frute of this campaign." Venloo was much the strongest of the three fortresses which the French held on the Meuse north of Maestricht. The same strategic events which would decide the fate of Venloo would probably involve Rure-monde and Stevensweert. On August 29 Venloo was regularly invested by the Prince of Nassau-Saarbrück, reinforced by Opdam to a total of 32 battalions and 36 squad-rons. Marlborough, with the rest of his army of about forty-five thousand men, took post at Asche. Here he covered Maes-

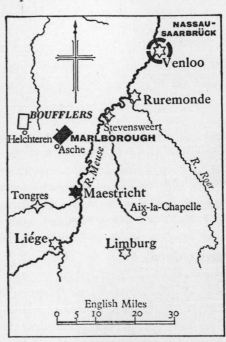

MARLBOROUGH COVERS THE SIEGE
OF VENLOO

tricht and could, if need be, draw supplies from it for a time. Here he was on the flank of any effort by Boufflers to relieve Venloo. Once again the value of Maestricht became evident. Marlborough could afford some risk to his communications with Holland because of the fortress and its exceptional supplies, but Boufflers, moving north past Marlborough's right, would run the gravest risks both of battle and interception. If alternatively he recrossed to the right bank of the Meuse and sought to rescue its fortresses

143

by a turning movement through Limburg and Aix-la-Chapelle, he would expose the whole of Brabant to immediate invasion. One has only to study the map to admire the choice of Asche for all purposes.

Louis XIV now wrote to Burgundy urging him with royal and family insistence to face the hazards and try to relieve Venloo. Burgundy used all his influence, but a council of war decided obstinately and rightly that, having regard to the position of Marlborough's army, the difficulties of supply were too great; and the generals could only suggest as a consolation and diversion the siege of Hulst, a small Dutch town on the other side of the theatre between Antwerp and Ostend.

Thus a fortnight passed. The siege of Venloo at first went very slowly. Marlborough's secret letters, as we have seen, complain of the Dutch. For weeks preparation had been ordered for this deeply desired event; but after the investment had been made everything was late. The arrival of the heavy batteries and their munitions, the opening of the trenches by civilian labour, and all the necessary sapping and mining, were many days behind the schedule prepared and counted upon for this operation. Cohorn as the expert engineer, the specialist in sieges, was soon in quarrel with the Dutch generals, each party blaming the other for the delay. Now that so many allied troops were at the siege Marlborough was a good deal weaker than Boufflers. He had to watch him from hour to hour, and be always ready to fight. On September 13 Boufflers moved to Tongres, where he was but ten miles from Liége, and Marlborough, moving south, placed himself between him and Maestricht. Here he was well supplied both from the north and from the district.

Marlborough to Godolphin

ASCHE
Aug. 31, 1702

I thank God we have now the finest weather that can be desired, which makes me very impatient to hear of the cannon being arrived at Venloo, which place was invested last Monday; but they can make no great progress till they have their artillery.

England, that is famous for negligence, should any they employ be guilty of half what I see here, it would be impossible for them to avoid being justly torn to pieces by the Parliament.[1]

Marlborough to Godolphin

ASCHE
September 7, 1702

They make so many difficulties at the siege of Venloo, that to-morrow there go from this army five battalions and five squadrons, notwithstanding we have notice that the business of Flanders is over, and that their [the enemy's] detachment will join them this day. And it is said that part of the troops with the Marquis of Bedmar have also orders to join the army. I have also intelligence from Venloo, that orders are come there for the baking of bread for the army. If all this be true, I shall be of your mind, that they will attempt something. If so, pray God give us success, and the sooner they attempt the better, their army being much sicker than ours. If they come to us now, we shall have 15 battalions and 28 squadrons less than we had, when we were last in presence with them. However our men are in so good heart, that I dare say we shall beat them.[2]

Marlborough to Godolphin

SUTENDAL
Sept. 14, 1702

* Your going to the Bath has been the reason of my having none from you by the last post which came here yesterday. The French army having marched three days, which has brought them to the Camp of Tongres, has obliged us to come to this place, for the securing our bread from Maestricht, as also for the conveniency of having our forage from the Spanish Geldre on the other side of the Meuse. . . . The trenches at Venloo having been opened last Monday, I hope a fortnight more may finish that business, after which the fate of Ruremond will depend upon the goodness of the season, which may make my stay in the field a fortnight longer than otherwise it would be. That I may do all that is in my power for the complying with your desires of my being early in England, I am pressing all that I can that we might from this Army make a detachment of eight battalions and ten squadrons,

1 Coxe, i, 182.　　　　2 *Ibid.,* i, 183.

145

with which Lt. G. Shults offers to undertake the siege of Stevensweert, which can only be attacked in a dry season as this is.
The difficulty is not because the French are so near us, for our
camp may be made very strong; but we can't do it but by having
the cannon and mortars, and all other things necessary from the
garrison of Maestricht, which can't be done but by the States'
order. You will see in the map the situation of this place being
between Ruremond and Maestricht makes it very necessary that
we should have it. It is not to be imagined the backwardness
and sloth of these people, even for that which is for their own
good.

On September 18 a surprising feat of arms was performed
at Venloo. The Royal Regiment of Ireland, later the 18th,
with two English battalions, had been ordered as one of the
processes in the siege to clear the glacis of Fort St Michael
and drive the enemy from the covered way. However,
Lord Cutts assembled the officers and told them that he
assigned no limit to their attack. If they could get farther,
all the better. This unusual order produced astonishing
results. The Anglo-Irish brigade rushed forward, and,
having chased the enemy from the covered way, followed
them over the drawbridge and across the open ditch so closely
that "the loose planks were not slipped" and the whole
crowd arrived together on the actual ramparts of the fort.
By more good luck the governor had omitted to mow the
grass, and all the redcoats scrambled up the steep slope by
hand and foot, mingled with the flying French, and tumbled
pell-mell into the interior of the fort, where after some
slaughter the whole garrison of fifteen hundred men surrendered to fewer assailants. Thus was the mad escapade
rewarded by astounding success. Our diarists of the Royal
Irish were indignant.

Had not several unexpected accidents occurred in the affair,
hardly a man of us would have escaped being either killed,
drowned, or taken, . . . but success . . . crowned the event
which got the Lord Cutts great applause of which he boasted all
his life after, though neither he nor any of the noblemen stirred
one foot out of the trenches till we were masters of it, except the

146

young Earl of Huntingdon, who stole out of the trenches from them and kept up with the foremost.[1]

The loss of Fort St Michael broke the spirit of the defence, and preparations were pressed forward for the final attack. On September 22 the news arrived that the fortress of Landau, far off in Germany, had been taken by Prince Louis of Baden. A joy-fire of musketry and of all the cannon was ordered in celebration of this event. The defenders of Venloo, not knowing the reason of these loud explosions, deemed them the prelude of the assault. They therefore displayed white flags, beat a parley, and forthwith capitulated. Altogether we had much good fortune in the siege of Venloo.[2]

Marlborough to Godolphin

SUTENDAL
September 28, 1702

The very ill weather gives too reasonable an excuse that the sieges do not go so fast as could be wished. However, I think there is no doubt but we shall have them. That of Stevensweert I hope we shall have by the beginning of the next week; and as soon as we have those troops again with us, I shall do my utmost with the Deputies and my lord of Athlone, that we may march between Liége and Tongres, which will oblige the marshal Boufflers to take his party off defending Tongres, or retreating behind his lines. I think he will do the last, but my lord of Athlone is of another opinion; so that he would stay till the siege of Ruremond is over, that those troops might also join us. My fears are that if we stay till that siege be finished, the ways will be so very ill that we shall not be able to carry our cannon with us, and then I am sure what we call our left wing [*i.e.*, those always against fighting] will not go, for they begin to say that they ought to be contented with what has already been done. If the French be not obliged to quit Tongres, they will have it in their power to bombard Maestricht any time this winter; besides, it will give them the advantage of quartering a very great body of troops on this side of their lines.[3]

1 Richard Kane, *Campaigns*, second edition (1847), p. 39. This gentleman volunteer had been wounded a few weeks before at the siege of Kaiserswerth, and as he could hardly stand he paid two soldiers to carry and drag him forward, which they did.
2 See particularly Captain Parker's account, p. 74.
3 Coxe, i, 186–187.

147

Cardonnel to Ellis

SUTENDAL
October 2, 1702

By my next I hope to send you the like good news from Ruremond, where we reckon Mr Cohorn is more nice than wise. He is losing time there as he did before Venloo, and will not begin till he has everything ready to a tittle, though it may be half the preparations might do the business; for we reckon Stevensweert must be the strongest of the two. We do not question however to be masters of the place in four or five days after we begin. And all this good fortune I may venture to say is entirely owing to my Lord Marlborough's good conduct. For if his excellency had not been very firm in his resolutions, against not only the Dutch generals, but even the States themselves, the alarm in Flanders had carried good part of our troops that way, and entirely defeated our designs upon the Maes this campaign. I think you need no further proof of what I allege than the enclosed copy of a letter to Mons. Geldermalsen.[1]

These were days of strain for Marlborough. He had 55 battalions and 110 squadrons against Boufflers' 70 battalions and 86 squadrons. He might any day, almost at any hour, be forced to fight a battle at considerable odds; but he was better placed than Boufflers to receive supplies or to manœuvre. Thus days grew into weeks, and weeks passed while the two armies stood bristling at each other—the stronger seeking a chance to strike, the weaker always offering baffling propositions. Meanwhile, by Marlborough's orders, the captors of Venloo had advanced up the Meuse towards him. They took Stevensweert in four days and Ruremonde in nine. By October 7 Marlborough had the whole line of the Meuse clear behind him, and was about to be joined by a force which would make him much stronger than Boufflers. The Marshal and his officers had foreseen with dread this new situation. Evidently Liége itself was in the gravest danger. Already, in the third week of September, Boufflers had inspected the fortress and reinforced the citadel. But as he also feared for Bonn, which might

---

1 Add. MSS., 28918, f. 77. Coxe dates this letter wrongly, and states it was written to Harley. Ellis was an Under-Secretary.

CADOGAN AND MARLBOROUGH

By permission of Earl Cadogan

alternatively be attacked, he felt bound to detach Tallard to strengthen it. Boufflers's only uncertainty now was what further punishment he would receive. "The King," writes Berwick, "seeing the ill turn affairs took in this campaign, recalled the Duke of Burgundy from the army to save him the mortification of being merely a spectator of the Earl of Marlborough's victories."[1] The Royal Duke made no difficulties. Indeed, he may himself have invited the recall. Anyhow he quitted his pretended command of the army in deep disgust.

Marlborough's letters show that he would formerly have been content with clearing the Meuse up to Maestricht. October was now a third spent, and it was deemed hard service to keep the troops in the field so late. But now a new favourable prospect opened before him. He tried again to win the Dutch consent to a battle to break up the French army. The Council of War again refused, and would go no further than the siege of Liége. This was certainly far bigger "frute" than Venloo, and would crown the campaign. Liége was the only remaining passage by which the French garrisons on the Rhine, at Rheinberg, Düsseldorf, Cologne, and Bonn, could be rapidly aided or rescued. The Dutch Government, knowing the importance the French attached to Liége and what a large part it played in their affairs on the Rhine, feared that an advance on that place would lead to a battle. All had gone so well without incurring that awful risk and expense. Why jeopardize it? Why not take their profits and settle into winter quarters? But here was this English commander who was able to transform everything at his touch, who seemed as he moved to and fro about the countryside invariably to impose his will on the formidable French; here was this unproved man, whom they had with such difficulty withheld from fighting battles which he declared he could win (and perhaps he could—no one could tell), who now wanted more. Still, their generals were all in favour of the siege. Their own hearts were cheered by everything that had happened. How gloriously different was their

1 *Memoirs*, i, 179.

situation in October from what it had been in June! Their confidence had grown. Marlborough got leave to move.

At this time we must note the comment of Deputy Geldermalsen, written at the time, which shows the stresses. "It is impossible to describe the scorn with which he [Marlborough] judges Lord Athlone, his irresolutions, his weakness of opening himself to nobodies, and following their advice in the teeth of decisions definitely taken."[1] This is the first of several evidences of Marlborough's vehement and fierce behaviour behind the scenes, which were the counterpart of his inexhaustible patience in public.

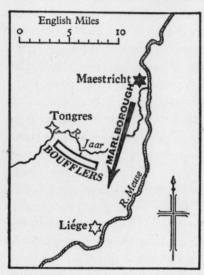

MARLBOROUGH MOVES ON
LIÉGE

English Miles
0   5   10

Maestricht

Tongres

R. Jaar

BOUFFLERS

MARLBOROUGH

R. Meuse

Liége

Boufflers had orders from Paris on no account to allow Liége to fall into the hands of the allies. Easy to say: but he was now definitely weaker than Marlborough. He therefore sent reinforcements into Liége and withdrew behind the Jaar stream, a tributary of the Meuse, fortifying himself at Tongres and hoping by threatening Marlborough's right to cover Liége and also to prevent a movement into Brabant, should that be Marlborough's purpose.

Marlborough received permission to act on the 12th. At midnight precisely on the 13th he marched all night to the southward, crossing the Jaar before dawn between Boufflers and the Meuse. He could now besiege Liége; but he wanted to attack Boufflers. The proposed battle was, of course, vetoed, and the siege of Liége began. Boufflers, feeling his rôle exhausted, withdrew behind the Lines of Brabant. The burghers of Liége opened the gates

[1] To Heinsius, October 14; von Noorden, i, 265.

of the town to the allies, and the siege was confined to the citadel and to the Chartreuse fort, a detached work of considerable strength. These were stern operations. The full bombardment of the citadel began on the 20th, and by the 22nd the destruction of both ramparts and magazines was such that the engineers reported that the breach was fit to be stormed. Marlborough offered the governor honourable terms for immediate surrender. M. de Violaine replied that "it would be time to think of that six weeks after." Whereupon, on the afternoon of the 23rd, the British troops headed the general assault. Without firing a musket till they came to the closest quarters, the allies pierced the counterscarp and the covered way, passed the ditch, mounted the breach, and took the place "by dint of sword." The governor was taken prisoner in the breach. His officers beat a parley, "but the victorious allies, being already in the place, would hear none of it, and had killed all they met, if the French had not thrown down their arms and begged quarter, which they obtained."[1] Captain Parker says, however, "Our men gave no quarter for some time so that the greater part of the garrison was cut to pieces."[2] The British alone lost above five hundred killed and wounded, or perhaps one-sixth of their numbers engaged, and the troops were slow to pause. Important treasures in money and valuable stores were captured or partly pillaged before the soldiers could be calmed. More than one-third of the defenders were destroyed. The rest of the eight thousand men were given 'quarter at discretion.'

The three battalions defending the Chartreuse had been eyewitnesses of the fate of the citadel. Nevertheless their commander resolved to abide the bombardment. It took six days to carry the heavy batteries across the river and plant them opposite the Chartreuse. Then, after four hours' bombardment, the garrison begged for terms. They were refused the honours of war (drums beating, flags flying, bullet in the teeth, etc.), but accorded 'honourable terms,' and marched out disarmed, "with their hands in their

1 Lediard, i, 190.   2 Parker, p. 75.

pockets." This episode cost the French in all nearly ten thousand soldiers, and in those days soldiers were hard to come by and valuable.

Some of Marlborough's unpublished letters to Godolphin reveal the rigour of the fighting.

BEFORE LIÉGE
Oct. 16, 1702

* Our march upon Thursday night gave so great alarm to the French that they marched a-Friday morning early, and abandoned Tongres with such haste that they have left all their wheelbarrows, shovels, pickaxes, and everything else with which they have been fortifying that place for above this month. They are now encamped near Landes, about seven leagues from this town. We had possession of the gates of this place a-Saturday night, and we have now three English, and three Dutch battalions in the place; the French have eight battalions in the citadel and four in the Chartreuse. The difficulty of getting the cannon up these hills, is the occasion of our not opening the trenches till to-morrow night. The Chartreuse, being on the other side of the Meuse, is not to be attacked till the Citadel is taken. However I hope in a fortnight's time we may be masters of the whole; if it please God we have fair weather. . . .

I believe this may find you at Newmarket and if Lord Churchill be with you, you will let him know that I hope to see him by the end of this month, for my stay at The Hague will be very short. . . .

Marlborough to Godolphin
BEFORE LIÉGE
October 23, 1702

I wrote to you this morning in haste, and gave you an account that the counterscarp of the citadel was to be attacked, which was done this afternoon. After the French were beaten out of the counterscarp, our men attacked the breach, and after a resistance of half an hour they carried it. The governor was taken in the breach by an English lieutenant, which shows that the Queen's subjects were the first upon the breach. This has been an action of much vigour, so that it is impossible to say too much of the bravery that was shown by all the officers and soldiers. The governor and great numbers of their officers are already brought to my quarters.[1]

1 Coxe, i, 189–190.

THE FORTRESSES OF THE MEUSE

Marlborough to Godolphin

LIÉGE
Oct. 26, 1702

* Before this can come to you her Majesty must have opened the Parl: in which I wish her with all my heart and soul good success. The weather beginning to be bad makes the removal of the cannon go on very slowly, so that I am afraid we shall not have our batteries ready [for the Chartreuse] till Saturday morning. As soon as the French had the news of the citadel being taken they decamped, having first demolished St Tron[d]. We have put a garrison into Tongres, and if it had not been thus late in the season, (but [for] that we might have hoped for ten days good weather), I think they could not have hinder'd us from taking Huy. I am now giving the necessary orders to the 40,000 men paid by H.M. for their winter quarters, so that I hope by this day senight I may begin my journey towards The Hague.

We are taking methods that those that remain of the eight regiments taken in the citadel, shall not do us much hurt the next campaign; and if that of the Chartreuse stays till the breach is made, they will not be better used than their companions. But I believe they will not stay the utmost extremity, as you will see by the enclosed letter of Marshal Boufflers, [here follows one of the few touches of humour in which Marlborough ever indulged] which was brought me last Saturday by a spy of his, which I gained some time ago, so that he has had an opportunity ever since of cheating us both.

In your next you will be pleased to let me receive all your commands of what I am to do at The Hague.

Marlborough to Godolphin

LIÉGE
Oct. 30, 1702

* Since my last I have had none from you, so that I shall trouble you with nothing but what we are a-doing here. As soon as our cannon and bombs began to fire yesterday at the Chartreuse, they hung out a flag; and last night the capitulations were signed. Cardonnel sends them to the Secretary. We are in possession of a gate, and they march out to-morrow. I hope all necessary orders may be given, that I may march out with the army a-Thursday; for we must repass the Jaar before we divide. I reckon a-Saturday, the troops will be able to march to their several quarters, and then I shall begin my journey for The Hague, lying the first night at Ruremond.

Then follows an explanation of the treatment meted to the survivors of the garrison.

I hope the measures that are taken for what remains of the eight battalions taken in the citadel will make them incapable of doing much hurt the next campaign. 1733 were sent for Holland last Saturday, and 166 officers will be sent thither upon Wednesday next.

These strokes, one upon the other, establishing beyond question the victory of the allies in the northern theatre, were watched with a kindling enthusiasm by the famous general who fought in the south. From the scene of his disputed victory at Luzzara Prince Eugene wrote to Marlborough the first extant letter in their correspondence.

FROM THE CAMP NEAR LUZZARA
October 2, 1702

* MILORD,

I feel the more deeply honoured by Your Excellency's letter of yesterday[1] assuring me that you interest yourself in the affairs of this country since I have long desired to become acquainted with a man who fills with such dignity the command of an army only accustomed to obey one of the greatest kings in the world. I do not doubt that the campaign will end in your quarter as fortunately as it has begun; as for the affairs of this country the superiority of the enemy prevents advantage being taken of the recent action: it is to be hoped that the situation will change and this army will soon be placed in a state to act offensively. I await with impatience news from the land where you are, being interested in glory above all men.[2]

1 *Dispatches*, i, 30.
2 The following is the original form of this letter:

"DU CAMP PREST DE LUZZARA
"*ce 2 Oct^{bre} 1702*

* MILORD,

"L'honneur que vous m'avez hier voulu faire de m'assurer par la lettre que V.E. m'at fait l'honneur de m'écrire que vous vous interessé aux affaires de ce pais m'est d'autant plus sensible qu'il y at longtemp que je souhaitais d'estre connu d'un homme qui remplit si dignement le commandement d'une armée qui n'etait accoutumé d'obeir qua un des plus grands rois de la terre. Je ne doute pas que la campagne

The strategic consequences of the capture of Liége were of higher importance than the heavy losses of the enemy. The French had been expelled from the Meuse and the lower Rhine.

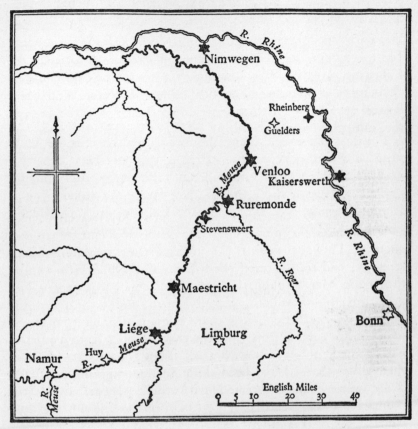

FORTRESSES OF THE MEUSE AND RHINE, END OF 1702

The Archbishopric of Cologne and the Bishopric of Liége had been recovered from their hands. Already by the end of the

ne finirat dans vos quartiers aussi heureusement qu'elle at commencé, quant aux affaires de ce pais la superiorité des ennemis empesche de profiter des avantages de la derniere action il faut esperer que les conjonctures changeront et qu'en peu de temp on mettrat cette armée en estat d'agir offensivement. J'atens avec impatience des nouvelles du pais ou vous este, m'interessant plusque personne a la gloire.

De V.E.
　　　　　　　　tres humble et tres obeissant serviteur,
　　　　　　　　　　　　　　Eugene de Savoye"

Marlborough's answer is in the *Dispatches*, i, 52.

campaign an ally of the Great King, the priestly Elector of Cologne, was wandering through the Netherlands without territory, army, or revenue. The navigation of the two great rivers was now open to the allies, and to the allies only. Their garrisons occupied Kaiserswerth, Venloo, Ruremonde, Stevensweert, Maestricht, and Liége. Marlborough arranged for the winter siege of Rheinberg, which fell eventually on February 9, 1703. The new campaign could be begun under favourable conditions. The first army of France had been powerless to prevent these losses. To the French the end of the campaign was an intense relief. "We in the camp on the Mehaigne," wrote Berwick, "heard this with great content; for in the mood to let everything slide in which we found ourselves any further operations of the enemy would not have met with any resistance on our side." What a testimony to the dominance which Marlborough had asserted upon the minds as well as the movements of the enemy! This new man, those sure marches, that compelling strategy, had transformed the scene. The Dutch, who when they gave Marlborough the command were crouching in the deep anxiety of valiant, puzzled men under the guns of Nimwegen, were now, less than five months later, masters of a territory many times greater than all that King William had gained in eight campaigns. They no doubt plumed themselves that all had been done without fighting a battle. They were equally satisfied with their general and with themselves. The least contented man in the allied army was Marlborough. He might rejoice at what had been gained, but he also knew what had been lost. He had not been allowed to strike one of those crashing blows in the field which he believed would have given him the necessary control of the war, and might have led swiftly to its victorious end. He had not been allowed to make war, but only to play military chess. Undoubtedly he had won the game.

In the first week of November the armies, except the troops besieging Rheinberg, dispersed into winter quarters, and their commander set out upon his journey for England, home, and the political crisis. And now we must describe the hazardous adventure which befell him.

Much the best way to The Hague was to be towed down the Meuse. On November 2 the Commander-in-Chief embarked in a 'yacht' at Maestricht. He had with him the two Dutch Deputies, General Opdam, some personal attendants, and an escort of twenty-five men. He joined Cohorn, who travelled in a larger boat with a guard of sixty soldiers, at Ruremonde. It was arranged that fifty horsemen should reconnoitre the country, and keep pace along the banks with the vessels by day and protect them at night. These seemed ample precautions against any French raiding parties which might be abroad. But after passing Venloo, where a new cavalry escort took charge, various accidents occurred. The larger

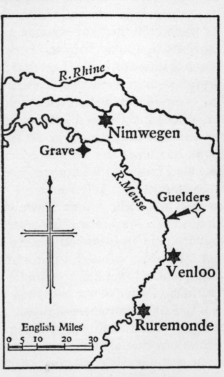

THE GUELDERS AMBUSCADE

boat outstripped the smaller, and the cavalry escort were forced by the lie of the land to quit the river-bank. The French still held the fortified and marsh-protected town of Guelders, far behind the allied front. A trap was laid for persons of high consequence descending the river from the armies, and above all for the Commander-in-Chief. The lieutenant chosen for this service had special knowledge of the country. He was an Irish deserter from the Dutch service named Farewell, who had fled from Maestricht under accusation of conspiring to burn the magazines. He had

157

taken refuge in Guelders, and had been accepted as a partisan leader by the French. In the darkness of the night this desperate man led his troop with stealth to that point on the river where the cavalry escort would be forced to diverge. They pounced upon the 'yacht,' drew it to the bank by the tow-rope, fired a volley, and threw a bouquet of hand-grenades on board. Before any resistance could be set up they had Marlborough, Opdam, and his two colleagues in their hands.

Catastrophe! Here Fortune sported with Destiny, and many great tales might have perished unborn. However, the raiders proceeded according to the customs of war. They knew the two Deputies; but all the Dutchmen had passes signed by the Duke of Burgundy to free them from annoyance on their voyage. The lieutenant knew Opdam, and said at once that he had "stood sentry a hundred times over his tent." Marlborough had no pass; not caring to be beholden to his enemies, he had trusted to his escort. But Fortune was at heart his faithful friend. While the Deputies' papers were being scrutinized in the lantern-light of the cabin one of his secretaries, or clerks rather, Stephen Gell, slipped into his hand a pass accorded to his brother, General Churchill, which had not been used. This was one of the situations for which Marlborough's gifts were well suited. With perfect calm and in the most natural manner he tendered the pass to the leader of the raiders.

A prolonged parley followed. All British historians tell us that the lieutenant did not know Marlborough's face, and Marlborough in his letter of November 8, probably to Hedges, says, "I have desired Mr Cardonnel to send you a particular account of my having been in the power of a French party near five hours, but I thank God they did not know me but took me for Lieutenant-General Churchill. . . ." The validity of the passport was argued at length. No one knows what was said on either side. It seems that the lieutenant chose at last to release Marlborough upon the pass which was made out for his brother Churchill, which was out of date and did not cover transit by water; or alternatively he allowed this English general, evidently of the highest rank, to count as one of the two servants or secretaries allowed upon the pass of Field Deputy Geldermalsen. It is certain that he and his men took all the money and plate out of the vessel because it was not mentioned in the passports, carried off the crew, the cook, and the escort of twenty-five soldiers as prisoners of war, and allowed the three gentlemen and their servants to continue their journey by water. The yacht floated on down the stream and soon overtook Cohorn and his armed guard.

The question has been properly asked by all Continental inquirers whether the lieutenant was really so stupid. Surely some great inducement was held out to him to take this favourable view. Count Goes in his dispatch[1] says, "I think that the lieutenant did not sin through ignorance." Another commentator says this was one of the occasions when Milord Marlborough did not exercise his usual thrift. But if it had been only a question of money or material reward there was surely as much to be said on one side as on the other. The promises made to the lieutenant must have satisfied other desires which were dear to him. Although he had no difficulty in carrying his prisoners and their booty into Guelders, he did not himself accompany them. He vanished for a space, and when after two months he presented himself at The Hague he received a free pardon for his desertion, withdrawal of all earlier charges, and a captaincy in the Dutch service. Ailesbury says that had the French got hold of him, he would have been broken on the wheel.

While this long struggle for the heart of the lieutenant had been proceeding in the cabin of the yacht, what had happened to Marlborough's cavalry escort? They heard the firing and soon learned the facts. The officer in command seems to have become panic stricken. But perhaps he was told that any attempt at rescue would mean the immediate slaughter of the captives. He did nothing but report what had happened. The news, distorted, outsped the current of the river. By daybreak the alarm was general. Marlborough had been captured! He had been carried into Guelders! It would

[1] November 20; Klopp, x, 83.

have been easy, says Ailesbury, to have conveyed him on horseback through the disturbed country into France. The news was received in Paris on the morning of the 10th that Marlborough and the others, all named, were taken. Directions were at once given by Louis XIV that Marlborough was to be well treated. Confirmation arrived by a second messenger from Boufflers's headquarters. It was not till the 11th that a third messenger reported that the lieutenant had let the prisoners go by mistake.

The report reached the governors of Venloo and Nimwegen. Discarding the regulations for the defence of fortified places, both officers set out at once with their whole garrisons for Guelders. "Deliver him unharmed, or we will exterminate you." The governor hastened to surrender Marlborough's cook, and to offer the looted plate for ransom. During the 4th the news reached The Hague. The States-General assembled; they ordered all troops within reach to join the forces marching upon Guelders. They sent couriers as fast as men could ride to the Emperor at Vienna to warn him to hold Marshal Villeroy, who had been captured by Prince Eugene two months before, as a hostage for exchange. Villeroy was an intimate friend and favourite of Louis XIV. We cannot tell how the Great King would have chosen, but certainly much would have depended upon his choice. However, while horses galloped, and columns of soldiers marched, and the commander of Guelders found himself threatened by trumpet with appalling penalties, and with only the cook to offer, Marlborough and his party arrived peacefully in the evening at The Hague. When it was known he was safe and approaching the city a spasm of relief and joy shook all classes. The whole population was on the bank and in the streets to receive him. In those days the populace were sparingly admitted to great affairs. The spectacle of cheering, weeping, caressing crowds was one Marlborough had never seen before; nor did he see it again until twelve years later, when he returned from disgrace and exile and was acclaimed by the Londoners. Both the peril and the welcome made a deep impression

160

upon him: indeed, it is said he was moved to tears in the throng. "It was not without great difficulty he could get through them to his lodgings, to such a degree was he beloved, and of so high esteem was the name of Marlborough, with people of every condition."[1]

The letter written to Godolphin a few days later (November 9) describes not only the public emotion, but his own:

My room is full at this time, I being more welcome to them by an accident I had, of being taken by a French party. Till they saw me, they thought me a prisoner in France, so that I was not ashore one minute, before I had great crowds of the common people, some endeavouring to take me by the hands, and all crying out welcome. But that which moved me most was, to see a great many of both sexes cry for joy. I have been extremely obliged by the kind reception I have met with: for from five in the afternoon till after ten at night, there was a perpetual firing in the streets, which is their way of rejoicing.

He added in a broad thankfulness, "I pray God bless the Queen and her undertakings, for the liberty of Christendom depends upon it."[2]

The narrow escape also left its mark. He wrote to Godolphin:

THE HAGUE
November 24, 1702

* By my last letter you will have seen that I was in hopes to have left this place the next day, but now the wind seems to be [so] settled in the west, that I am out of all heart, for the wind must be fair four and twenty hours before I can stur to carry the men of war out, and my last accident makes me afraid of coming without them. . . .

Marlborough did not forget Stephen Gell. He gave him a pension of fifty pounds a year for life and secured him adequate employment in the Exchange of Prisoners Office for the whole of the war. The last letter of the five or six thousand printed in Murray's *Dispatches* is one written by Marlborough after his disgrace in 1712 to the Pensionary confiding the fortunes of "le sieur Gell" to his care.

1 Lediard, i, 198.   2 Coxe, i, 194.

While the campaign in Flanders prospered mixed fortunes had attended the naval operations. The great expedition which the Cabinet ordered had sailed at the end of July, and anchored off Cadiz on August 12/23. Sir Stafford Fairborne, according to Rooke's journal of August 14/25,

having proposed to the Admiral his forcing the harbour and destroying the eight French galleys which lay under the walls of Cadiz, he [the Admiral] called a council of flag officers to consider the same; but upon mature debate it was unanimously judged unreasonable and impracticable *to hazard any the least frigate* on such an attempt.

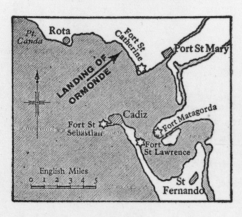

CADIZ

Fairborne maintained his opinion before the House of Lords Committee which subsequently inquired into the failure of the expedition. In two or three days a strong boom was placed across the entrance and ships were sunk in the channel by the enemy. What was hopeful before became impossible now. Sir George Rooke followed the temptation of the line of least resistance in landing the troops to capture the forts from the shore. Ormonde readily consented, and a prolonged series of desultory operations ensued, accompanied by pillage and sacrilege, tales of which spread far and wide throughout Spain. Meanwhile the defence grew continually stronger, and after a month it was decided to re-embark the soldiers and sail for home.

The ignominy was, however, relieved by a lucky windfall. As Rooke and Ormonde, on the worst of terms and each blaming the other, were returning disconsolately home, news was brought that the Spanish treasure fleet with the millions of the Indies aboard had run into Vigo Bay. Excited councils of war ensued. It was decided to raid the harbour. This was protected by a boom and batteries, behind which lay the enemy squadrons of forty-one vessels, including fifteen ships of the line. To reach them and their treasure it was necessary to break the boom and enter the long sleeve of a completely landlocked harbour under the heaviest fire from the shore. One writer has said of Rooke that "he swooped upon his prey and, with same spirit as at La Hogue, hacked through the boom, struck panic into his foes, and overwhelmed them in destruction;"[1] another that "he lay in his berth, ill of gout, far down the bay."[2] On October 12/23 Vice-Admiral Hopsonn in the *Torbay*, followed by all but the heaviest English and Dutch battleships, braved the fire of the batteries, crashed through

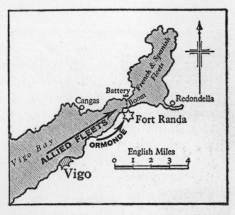

VIGO BAY

the boom, and penetrated the inner harbour. Here a fierce battle was fought with the French warships, while Ormonde with two thousand soldiers attacked the principal fort from the land. Whether the lure of gold or the sting of Cadiz or both inspired the leaders, at last they let loose their brave men, who fought with indomitable fury. By sundown they were masters of Vigo Bay. The entire enemy fleet was sunk, burned, or captured. Not one escaped. The treasures of the Indies were frantically carried inland by mules before the action; but enough remained for the victors to bear home a million sterling to sustain the Treasury and appease Parliament.

Although the edge was taken off the Cadiz fiasco by the brilliant event in Vigo Bay, the House of Lords insisted upon

1 Callender, *The Naval Side of British History*, p. 134.
2 Trevelyan, *England under Queen Anne*, i, 270. Certainly he took no active part in the execution of the plan.

a searching inquiry into the conduct of Rooke and Ormonde at Cadiz. As these two high officers were still in violent enmity, it seemed as if the inquiry might prove fruitful. Marlborough with his usual common sense pointed out to both parties through Godolphin how little they had to gain by blackening each other's records.

Marlborough to Godolphin

THE HAGUE
November 21

My letters tell me that the Duke of Ormond is governed by people that will incline him to accuse Sir George Rooke. By what I am told here, I should think it would be more for his grace's service, and all the rest of the officers, that the conduct at Cadiz should not be inquired into; for what can be said for staying 26 days at Port St Mary; for, if Cadiz was to be attacked, they should not have stayed there; and if the taking of Cadiz was not thought feasible, then they should not have lost time, but have re-embarked, to have attempted what [else] was in their instructions.[1]

Under these suggestive warnings the Admiral and the General made a fairly obdurate joint defence before the Committee. Nevertheless the Navy and its important expeditionary force had during 1702 produced no results which had the least influence upon the general strategy of the war. Had they shown at Cadiz one-half of the spirit of Vigo Bay, the Sea Powers would have been masters of the Mediterranean in 1703. With Cadiz in their hands it must have been easy to secure Minorca in the next stage; and the presence of the allied fleet off the Riviera and the Italian coasts would have altered in a sense favourable to the allies the character of every forthcoming political and military event in that theatre. Party men drew the moral that the Whig policy on land under Marlborough had succeeded, while the Tory policy at sea had failed, and their bickerings proceeded on this basis. But this does less than justice to the Cabinet, which under Marlborough's general guidance had both ashore and afloat pursued strategic aims which were true, farseeing, and in harmony.

[1] Coxe, i, 198.

CHAPTER VIII

THE OCCASIONAL CONFORMITY BILL

(1702–3, Winter)

QUEEN ANNE was overjoyed by all she heard from Europe. Here was the admirable Mr Freeman, long the unfailing friend and champion of "poor unfortunate, faithful Morley," of whom every one now at last spoke so well. Her chosen Captain and Minister had returned home with laurels from the wars very different from those which "Mr Caliban" had ever gained—he who had never even acknowledged our congratulations upon Namur. And what was Namur compared to Venloo, Ruremonde, Liége, and all the others; not to speak of the French being smitten and chased time after time; and both Houses of Parliament so pleased about it all? Nothing would content her but that he must be made Duke, and £5000 a year must be settled upon him and his descendants for ever. Thus only could he maintain the station she had accorded him. Surely the House of Commons would not object to that. And dear, beloved Mrs Freeman—how proud she ought to be of her lord! How the Queen wished she could do more for them! Thus in the goodness and gratitude of her heart thought Queen Anne. But both Sarah and the Parliament were a good deal cooler. Sarah manifested a violent opposition to the dukedom; and the Commons would have nothing to do with the perpetual grant. Both have left their reasons on record.

The Queen prepared her reward for Marlborough with all that love of a surprise with which a mother would surround a birthday present to her child. She contrived it with her Ministers in secret, and only on October 22 wrote to Sarah:

Lord Treasurer intends to send you a copy of the address

of the House of Lords which is to be given me to-morrow, and that gives me an opportunity of mentioning a thing to you that I did not intend to do yet. It is very uneasy to your poor unfortunate, faithful Morley to think that she has so very little in her power to show how truly sensible I am of all my lord Marlborough's kindness, especially at a time when he deserves all that a rich crown could give. But since there is nothing else at this time, I hope you will give me leave as soon as he comes to make him a duke. I know my dear Mrs Freeman does not care for anything of that kind nor am I satisfied with it, because it does not enough express the value I have for Mr Freeman, nor nothing ever can how passionately I am yours, my dear Mrs Freeman.[1]

In after-years Sarah described her feelings on receiving this gracious, charming letter—every sentence poised to enhance the gift—the like of which the highest in the land might covet in vain.

When I read the letter first . . . I let it drop out of my hand and was for some minutes like one that had received the news of a death of one of her dear friends. . . . I was so easy for [indifferent to] anything of that kind, having before [already] all that was any use, by which it is plain I have no great taste for grandeur.

According to her, all that mattered was to be a peer with a seat in the legislature. "I do think there is no advantage in going in at a door; and when a rule is settled, I like as well to follow five hundred as one." She proceeded to dwell upon the burdens of a dukedom, especially "in a family where there are many sons. Though at that time I had myself but one, yet I might have had more, and the next generation a great many."[2]

This might pass for affectation if it were not confirmed by facts. It is evident that she wrote at once to her husband urging him to refuse the dukedom. Her letter does not exist, but we can easily reconstruct her arguments from his reply. He, on the contrary, was greatly pleased.

1 Coxe, i, 202.   2 *Conduct*, p. 304.

THE OCCASIONAL CONFORMITY BILL

John to Sarah

You know I am very ill at compliments but I have a heart full of gratitude; therefore pray say all you can to the Queen for her extraordinary goodness to me. As you have let me have your thoughts as to the dukedom you shall have mine in short, . . . but be assured I shall have a mind to nothing but as it may be easy to you. I do agree with you that we ought not to wish for a greater title till we have a better estate. Your other objection is also very just that this promotion may bring great solicitations upon the Queen which I am sure I would not give occasion for. The Queen's goodness in being desirous to establish my family answers the first, since that may be done this winter; for I agree with you that it should be done before the title.[1]

Two days later he wrote again after having talked over Sarah's objections with the Pensionary, "believed to be a very judicious man" and "very much my friend." Heinsius was all for the dukedom. When Marlborough insisted that it would come better at the end of the war he replied that it was an act of justice which would do the Queen good with all the princes abroad, especially in Holland, where he hoped she would employ him as long as the war lasted. "He said," wrote Marlborough, "if it were not done now in the heat of everybody's being pleased with what I had done, it would at any other time be thought the effect of favour, which would not be so great an honour to my family nor to the Queen's service." Heinsius could have wished the Queen had bestowed the honour while Marlborough was actually with the army, just as the King of France had done for Villars. The argument that other families in England would press for the same title he brushed aside. If it were done at once, it would obviously be for war services. As for Sarah's point, which Marlborough repeated,

that I should make a worse figure in England by being a duke than as I am till I had the estate for it, he said the Queen's kindness was such that I need not doubt a fortune, and that whatever was

1 Coxe, i, 204.

done at this time for my fortune as well as the title would be quite without envy since all the people were pleased with what I had done.[1]

Finally Heinsius remarked "that it was not reasonable to expect ever to have so much success in any other campaign as in this," and ended "in begging me for the good of the common cause, the Queen's service and my own sake that I should think this a proper time of being distinguished." All these reasons are taken from the long report of his interview with the Pensionary which Marlborough laboriously wrote out for Sarah. Weighing the matter dispassionately, he ended by deciding that it was his duty to comply with the Queen's desires and his own.

How typical is all this of Marlborough's method and demeanour! What trouble he took to persuade his wife! Of course he knew beforehand the advice which Heinsius would give. Indeed, it was obviously for the general advantage that the Commander-in-Chief of a confederate army in which so many princes served as subordinates, whose opponents were the Blood Royal of France, should be raised to a high pinnacle. Marlborough's advancement was effective propaganda to proclaim the undoubted success of the campaign. Still, it was better these things should be said by the Pensionary. We do not think he cared too much about the titular rank. Certainly he cared less about the dukedom than about the income to support it, and did not mean to have the one without the other. But how much rather would he have been rewarded by that free, unfettered command of his army which none but he among the captains of history have been denied!

The new Parliament met on October 20, and the Lords congratulated the Queen. The Commons added that "the vigorous support of Your Majesty's Allies and the wonderful progress of Your Majesty's arms under the conduct of the Earl of Marlborough have signally retrieved the ancient honour and glory of the English nation." This affront to the memory of King William was intended by the Tories to

1 The Hague, November 17; Coxe, i, 204.

168

irritate the Whigs, and for this purpose was well devised. Accordingly the House divided on the word "retrieved," "all who had any favour at Court, or hoped for any, voting for it."[1] Only eighty Whigs could be mustered against the Tory majority. A solemn thanksgiving was appointed; and on November 12 the Queen, with Sarah at her side, and attended by both Houses of Parliament, proceeded in state to St Paul's amid the tumultuous acclamations of the London crowds. The Tories in the Commons had taken pains to couple Marlborough with Ormonde and Rooke. Thereby they sensibly reduced the value of their tribute, and, indeed, of their judgment, but at the same time they proclaimed their preference for naval expeditions rather than Continental warfare. These signs of a cool and critical temper towards Marlborough in the new Parliament were ignored by the Queen. Marlborough did not return from The Hague till November 28/December 9. Sarah went to meet him at Margate, and he came into London in strict privacy, avoiding all popular demonstrations. "Il se comporte d'une modestie distinguée."[2] He replied in a becoming manner to the thanks which Sir Edward Seymour at the head of a Committee tendered him in the name of the House of Commons. On December 2 the Queen declared her intention to make him a Duke.

A Government is naturally shy of proposing a grant of money to its leading member, who must, however indirectly, be involved in the advice given to the Sovereign. Godolphin's letters to Harley tell the tale in modern terms. On December 9 the Treasurer writes to the Speaker that Marlborough, having been given a grant by the Queen for the support of his dukedom during her life, had been encouraged by his friends "to think it will not be difficult at this time to get this latter grant confirmed by Act of Parliament to him and the heirs of his body." He asked the Speaker's advice as to the procedure, and added that Sir Edward Seymour had been "very gracious" to Marlborough in this matter.

1 N. Tindal, *The Continuation of Mr Rapin's History of England*, xv (iii of Continuation), 434.
2 *Correspondance politique, Angleterre*, t. 214, f. 357.

The next day he says that Marlborough has had some talk with Sir Christopher Musgrave, and great professions from him and Sir Edward Seymour, but "much warmer from the younger part of the House."[1] Thus it seemed that the Government was agreed and the House agreeable. The Queen sent her message to the Commons, announcing that she had granted the Duke of Marlborough and his heirs a pension of £5000 a year upon the revenues of the Post Office for the support of his title during her lifetime. "If," the message proceeded, "it had been in Her Majesty's power, she would have granted the same term in the pension as in the honour; and she hopes you will think it so reasonable in this case as to find some proper methods for doing it."

But here immediately began animated and unpleasant debates. Permanent alienations of the public revenue to individuals had long been one of the best targets of Tory attack. How bitterly had they inveighed against King William's grants to his Dutch favourites! Upon all the hustings of the recent elections they had denounced such practices. Must the new Parliament begin its life by so incongruous an act? This mood of the Commons was not lost upon Marlborough's colleagues, and the natural resistances of the assembly were stirred by an open division which at once appeared in the ranks of the Government. Seymour, who but two days before had been "very gracious," led the opposition; and the Tory veteran, Musgrave, Clerk of the Ordnance, Marlborough's direct subordinate, from whom he had had "great professions," dwelt in a sour-sweet speech upon the pay and allowances the Captain-General was already receiving from British and Dutch sources. These certainly amounted to £60,000 a year, and little imagination is required to understand the feelings which were excited among much poorer people.

By December 12 Godolphin was writing to Harley:

I cannot dissemble to you that I am very much concerned at the little success which I find the Queen's message is like to

1 Portland Papers, *H.M.C.*, iv, 53 *et seq.*

meet with in behalf of Lord Marlborough, especially since it [the opposition] comes chiefly from those of whom I thought we had deserved better. . . .[1]

He asked the Speaker for his "direction and help in what is fit to be done." Evidently the next day these two Parliamentarians had a long talk. It was certain that the Commons would not agree to the permanent grant, and the only question was how to withdraw the proposal without humiliating Marlborough, with whom all were so pleased, or distressing the Queen, to whom all were so loyal.

Marlborough was both vexed and surprised at the position into which he had too easily allowed himself to be drawn. He agreed with Godolphin and Harley that "the chief thing is to avoid a division in the House because the consequence of that will be . . . that men will look upon themselves to be listed."[2] This would have involved a disastrous crystallization. He therefore urged the Queen to "forgo her message on his behalf, since it might embarrass her affairs and be of ill consequence to the public." On December 15, therefore, the Queen informed the Commons that the Duke of Marlborough had declined her Message to them.

Although the question had thus fallen to the ground, the House hastened to set forth a reasoned statement of its view. Their language is instructive. They spoke of

the eminent services performed by the Duke of Marlborough, who has not only by his conduct of the army *retrieved* the ancient honour and glory of the English nation, but by his negotiations established an entire confidence and good correspondence between Your Majesty and the States-General, and therein vindicated the Gentlemen of England, who had, by the vile practices of designing men, been traduced, and industriously represented as false to Your Majesty's Allies, because they were true to the interest of their country.[3]

With "inexpressible grief" they recorded their dislike of making a precedent for the alienations of the revenue of the Crown, "which has been so much reduced by the exorbitant

---

[1] *Ibid.*   [2] *Ibid.*, 54.   [3] Lediard, i, 208.

171

grants of the last reign." In conclusion they praised what the Queen had already done for the Duke, and assured her that "whenever you shall think fit to reward such merit, it will be to the entire satisfaction of your people." The Queen returned a brief formal answer. She was deeply offended by the rebuff, and not at all inclined to forget it.

The Queen to Sarah

Wednesday, Dec. 16

I cannot be satisfied with myself, without doing something towards making up what has been so maliciously hindered in the Parliament, and therefore I desire my dear Mrs Freeman and Mr Freeman would be so kind as to accept of two thousand a year out of the privy purse, besides the grant of the five. This can draw no envy, for nobody need know it. Not that I would disown what I give to people that deserve, especially where it is impossible to reward the deserts, but you may keep it a secret or not, as you please. I beg my dear Mrs Freeman would never any way give me an answer to this; only comply with the desires of your poor unfortunate faithful Morley, that loves you most tenderly, and is with the sincerest passion imaginable yours . . .[1]

This generous offer was refused by the Marlboroughs: and the Queen eventually allowed it to lapse. Alas for the glitter of our story! Sarah in adversity fell below her standards in good fortune. We shall have presently to record with Archdeacon Coxe how nine years later in her bitterness she reclaimed this gift with arrears, and how the Queen paid every penny of it.

For the moment, however, this awkward episode was not discreditable to any of the parties concerned. Cardonnel, who was in close touch with Marlborough at home as well as abroad, thought that, although the Commons' refusal to comply with the Queen's message was "done with all the decency and respect imaginable," yet at present the Duke was "a little chagrined."[2] Marlborough had only accepted the dukedom in the belief that provision would be made for

1 Coxe, i, 208. 2 Cardonnel to Watkins, December 15; Add. MSS., 42176.

its maintenance. His emoluments as Commander-in-Chief might be swept away at any time by a cannon-ball, or by loss of favour or a demise of the Crown. The idea of a poor duke seemed ridiculous and unnatural to that age. It was one of the main objects of his life to found a family whose wealth and magnificence would long survive him down the generations. Nor did this seem a vain desire in a society where rank and property were so deeply ingrained and seemed secure and permanent. Grants of money to successful generals and admirals were, and are still, a recognized custom of the English people. The General and Admiral of the Great War each received from a Parliament of universal suffrage a capital sum equivalent to the grant proposed by Queen Anne for Marlborough.

Sympathy should not be withheld from the House of Commons. They had done their duty with proper independence and with every sign of respect. But Marlborough registered the impression that the Tory Members were unfriendly to him. Had they not coupled the disreputable or flashy performances of Rooke and Ormonde with what Europe admitted was a most remarkable campaign? The behaviour of the Tory Ministers and place-holders, who after committing themselves to the grant had turned their sails so swiftly to catch an unexpected hostile breeze, was a measure alike of their character and their sentiments. It would have been more agreeable to the Muse of History if Marlborough had refused all honours and rewards, and had met the addresses of the Commons by saying that owing to the heavy charges upon the public he had resolved to fight the next campaign on half-pay. But then he would not have been the Marlborough who gained the victories. For certain it is that this same matter-of-fact care for his own interests and desire to found a powerful family in an enduring State was an inherent part of his great deeds. He was a builder for England, for posterity, and for himself. No one of these purposes could be removed without impairing the others, and part of his genius lay in their almost constant harmony.

Queen Anne was at this time tenderly concerned about the position of her beloved husband. She would have liked to make him Commander-in-Chief of the Grand Alliance; but the Dutch would not agree. She had wished to invest him with regal dignity as her Consort; but Parliament showed plainly that this was not to be done. At least, then, she would make sure that he should not lack comforts if he lived beyond her span. One hundred thousand pounds a year was the income which she sought to have settled upon him for his life. She moved her Ministers to lay her wish before Parliament. The charge was heavy for those days, and under all the burdens of war. Yet the Commons made haste to gratify the Queen. They passed the necessary Bill virtually without opposition. But some one had mischievously slipped in a little clause which caused the Lords to "blow up."[1] in anger. This clause specially exempted Prince George of Denmark from an ambiguity in the Act of Succession designed to exclude "strangers, though naturalized," from English offices and peerages in the event of a Hanoverian prince becoming king. The proposed exemption of Prince George seemed to imply that all King William's peerages of "strangers, though naturalized," would lapse at the death of Anne. This roused the Whigs. The Lords, moreover, saw at once that this proviso wore the aspect of a tack. Here was an important political issue to be affected or defined by an irrelevant clause in a Money Bill. They saw themselves committed not only to its provisions, but, far more grievous, to recognizing the procedure of a tack.

Now, the peers of all parties in large majority had banded themselves together by solemn resolution to vote against any measure which contained a tack. Once let the rule be broken and their power was gone. When the Commons blandly explained that this provision about Prince George was only an additional mark of their loyalty to the Crown, the Peers replied in terms of scorn. It seemed certain that the Bill would be rejected by the Lords, and Queen Anne

1 Godolphin to Harley, Portland Papers, *H.M.C.*, iv, 54.

looked about her in lively distress. She did not weigh the constitutional question which was at stake. She only saw that her husband was being denied through a Whig faction in the Lords the justice which the Commons would do him. On this Marlborough and Godolphin joined with Rochester and Nottingham in using the whole influence and power of the Government and the Tory Party to procure compliance with the Royal will. All pulled together for the Queen to show who could pull the hardest. Thus the measure was carried as it stood.

Among those who protested against it was Marlborough's son-in-law, now Earl of Sunderland.[1] The rigid Whig purist did not hesitate to set himself in opposition in this very personal business of the Crown to the whole interest and policy of the Marlborough family, with which he was now linked. The Duke, who had originally been against the match, no doubt refrained from saying to his wife, "I told you so." But Sarah was transported with a fury, the reasons for which, though easy to discern, are not well explained in most history books. Night and day, in season and out of season, she was labouring to reconcile the Queen to the Whigs. Mrs Freeman was using every argument and persuasion which from a lifelong experience she knew would be effective upon Mrs Morley to convince her that the Whigs were just as good friends to the monarchy as the Tories. She knew already that at times she was straining her favour and her friendship, profound though these were; and now here, upon a point which would pierce the Queen to her very marrow, was this young prig and coxcomb, her own son-in-law, giving a contradiction to all she had said and undoing whatever she had achieved. And this when politics were so critical, when she could see the Tory faction in the Cabinet and in Parliament daily labouring to supplant her lord the Captain-General and his faithful friend the Treasurer in the confidence and affections of their Royal Mistress! She felt herself tripped up by the party in whose interests she was so magnificently striving, and by the man who, of

1 His father had died on September 8, 1702.

all others, should have considered her position and his own. Such experiences are annoying even to the most urbane.

However, the Bill was through, and its narrow escape made the Queen only the more grateful to her friends. But she had a long memory for those rancorous Whigs who, for all their professions about the war and the Protestant Succession, were really at heart the inveterate foes of Church and Crown. And among them all this young Lord Sunderland was the most obnoxious. How shamefully he had turned against Mr and Mrs Freeman, into whose family he had been admitted! But what could be expected from his breeding? How she had hated and feared his father in the years before the Revolution! What a disreputable, lying cheat his mother had been! The Queen remembered her character, as she had described it to her sister Mary fifteen years ago.[1] Why had Mrs Freeman and her husband let themselves be drawn into such a connexion? They were both too easy-going, too kind-hearted, too unsuspecting. The Queen felt she saw through the dangers and deceits of the world more deeply than they. The hostility which she felt henceforward towards Sunderland became of great political importance when in a few years she had to accept him as a Minister. Meanwhile she wrote her thanks to Sarah in the warmest terms.

I am sure the prince's bill passing after so much struggle is wholly owing to the pains you and Mr Freeman have taken, and I ought to say a great deal to both of you in return, but neither words nor actions can ever express the true sense Mr Morley and I have of your sincere kindness on this and all other occasions; and therefore I will not say any more on this subject, but that to my last moment your dear unfortunate faithful Morley will be most passionately and tenderly yours.[2]

Meanwhile the new Parliament was aglow with Church and Tory fervour. Dr Sacheverell, a young and vigorous Fellow of Magdalen, had preached an election sermon

1 See Vol. I, p. 238.　　2 Coxe, i, 210.

HENRY ST JOHN
National Portrait Gallery

which had inspired the political campaign. The majority were determined to root out the humbug of Occasional Conformity and at the same time possess themselves of many desirable places of influence and profit. In solemn conclaves, in ardent tavernings, the Members inflamed one another.

There were not wanting men to see in this burning question a path which might lead them far. Here a new actor, destined to play one of the decisive parts, makes his entry upon our stage. Henry St John had been elected as a Tory in 1701 to William's last Parliament. His father had been mulcted £16,000 for a pardon from Charles II for killing a Sir William Estcourt in a brawl in 1684, and bore besides a drunken, rakish reputation. But the fortunes of his house were still substantial, and Henry, after undergoing the usual treatment at Eton and on a foreign tour, arrived in London well furnished with money and representative of the family borough of Wootton Bassett. He reproduced his father's traits, and now at twenty-four was a roysterer and hard-drinker, who lived notoriously with a Miss Gumley, described as "the most expensive demirep in the kingdom." It was said that, impelled by liquor or a wager, he had run naked through the park. But he had besides other qualities of which his father had given no sign. He was from his earliest efforts a most brilliant Parliamentary speaker who always commanded the attention, if not the agreement, of the House of Commons. He had elevation of thought, breadth of view, and rare distinction in his use and comprehension of the English tongue. He also spoke French exceedingly well, and had read discursively but widely in English and European history. Clever, apt, and audacious in the highest degree, he was possessed by ambitions which no scruples were ever seen to hamper. He picked his early steps in politics shrewdly. He chose both a Patron and a Question. The Patron was Harley, and already in 1702 Henry St John by his charming, vivacious assiduity had personally ingratiated himself with that eminent politician. The Question was Occasional Conformity.

In association with the old and upright Bromley, Member for Oxford, who lent the needed element of gravity and piety to his proceedings, St John began in the opening session of Parliament to make an exposure of the *pro forma* communicant-Dissenters a leading Parliamentary issue. The Tory Party, in the temper with which it glowed, took fire. The controversy soon eclipsed all others. The Occasional Conformity Bill was first brought forward in the autumn of 1702. It sought to destroy the abuse by imposing fines on any public official who, having attended Anglican communion presumably for the purpose of qualifying for office, had afterwards reverted to his non-conformist manner of worship. The fines were so heavy as to be prohibitive, and the aid of the 'common informer' was invoked for their enforcement. This measure passed the Commons by a large majority, and was carried by an excited mob of two hundred Members to the Lords. Here the Bill encountered a small but resolute Whig majority, composed in part of King William's thirty peers and his Broad Church bishops.

An immediate conflict between the two Houses arose. Great stresses also showed themselves in the Cabinet and above it, which cast a revealing light upon the politics of the whole reign. The Queen was for the Bill. She felt that the utilizing of the sacrament for the purpose of gaining a place of profit or influence was a malpractice from which the Church she loved and deemed she understood so well should be protected. Her uncle Rochester, the Lord-Lieutenant of Ireland, who remained in London and would rather have been Lord Treasurer, felt both as a Churchman and as a "Highflyer" a strong and sincere indignation, which was in no way lulled by the vehement support which the Bill had gathered in the House of Commons. The two Secretaries of State, Nottingham and his colleague Hedges, and, of course, Sir Edward Seymour, with his West of England faction, were convinced that so just a proposal could not be resisted. It was true that it would obliterate their Whig opponents and give them mastery of the whole Government. But such considerations ought not, they judged, to weigh against a

178

principle which involved both righteousness and religion. Even if it cost them their Whig colleagues, the minor Ministers, they still felt bound to persevere. At the worst they could fill their places with men of their own party, and each was prepared to suggest substitutes, if need be. Such vicarious sacrifices were often made in those early days of our Parliamentary and Cabinet system.

So at the outset the Queen, the Commons, the dominant Tory Party, and the characteristic Tory Ministers—the men that the party could trust—were all hot for the Bill. Against it was the barest majority of the Whigs and bishops of the House of Lords. Out-of-doors such an act of hard, calculated aggression by one half of the nation upon the other spread consternation and anger in every shire and town.

This schism was deeply embarrassing to Marlborough and Godolphin. As Tories they found it difficult to repel the arguments for the Bill. Nor did they care to begin their administration by a quarrel with their own party in full career. They did not wish to distress or upset the Queen, nor to consume their influence in persuading her against her will on a Church question, above all others. But if England were to be rent and infuriated by the same kind of passions which had reduced her to impotence in the days of the Popish Plot, how was the war to be carried forward? The issue was for them both delicate and dangerous. In all the Cabinet discussions upon the Bill the strength of Rochester was at its height. He had his party and the majority of the House of Commons behind him. He had his Tory colleagues in a solid group. He had the genuine agreement and sympathy of the Queen. He saw in this measure a wedge, which as it was driven forward might estrange Marlborough and Godolphin from the Queen, and would certainly separate them from their party. They saw all this as well as he.

Marlborough, viewing the situation with military eye, had no intention of being brought to battle on ground which was so suited to his enemy. He and Godolphin therefore presented an oblique front to Rochester's formidable advance.

They avoided his thrust by a practice, which even in our own reformed days is not unknown, of affirming their support for the principle of a Bill while taking steps to get it killed behind the scenes. They shielded Nonconformity from political ruin and preserved the national strength from a mad injury by dissembling their opinions and tricking their party. In this lamentable course they were carefully advised by Mr Speaker Harley.

Sarah was, of course, violent against the Bill. All her Whig principles and free-thinking sentiments were roused. She felt and spoke about this attempt of the Church to persecute the Chapel, and of a party majority to capture the civic offices of their opponents under a religious pretence, very much as most people would do now, if such a project were mooted. Severe stresses must have arisen between her and the Queen, and between her and the High Tory Ministers. This handsome, domineering woman, in the very centre of affairs, with her caustic tongue, her wit, her candour, and her common sense, was in herself a portent of the Age of Reason, which had already dawned. When she heard that Marlborough and Godolphin intended to vote for the Bill her wrath was extreme. We can judge the pressure she put upon her husband by a remarkable letter which he wrote her at this time.[1]

John to Sarah

I do own a great deal of what you say is right, but I can by no means allow that all the Tory party are for King James, and consequently against the Queen; but [on] the contrary I think it is in Her power to make use of almost all, but some of the Heads, to the true interests of England, which I take to be the Protestant Succession, to the supporting of which, by the help of Almighty God, I will venture my last drop of blood. As you are the only body that could have given me happiness, I am the more concerned we should differ so much in opinions; but as I am firmly resolved never to assist any Jacobite whatsoever,

1 This letter is undated, but it was most probably written in January 1703, while Rochester was still a Minister and before the division on the second reading of the Occasional Conformity Bill in the House of Lords.

THE EARL OF NOTTINGHAM
By permission of W. Finch, Esq.

or any Tory that is for persecution, I must be careful not to do the thing in the World which my Lord Rochester would most desire to have me do; which is to give my Vote against this bill. But I do most solemnly promise that I will speak to nobody living to be for it, and to show you that I would do anything that were not a ruin to the Queen, and an absolute destruction to myself, to make you easy at this time. By what has been told me, the bill will certainly be thrown out unless my Lord Treasurer and I will both speak to people, and speak in the House, which I do assure you for myself I will not do.[1]

This letter gives us a vivid glimpse of the duel which was proceeding between Marlborough and Rochester, and of the tactics which Marlborough adopted to baffle his opponent. But it has another aspect which is revealing. Evidently Sarah, in her desire to prevent her husband from voting for a Bill which would cripple the Whigs and Dissenters, had reproached him with conduct which would endanger the Protestant succession and help the Jacobites. In fact the Bill raised no such issues, and Sarah in her exaggeration displayed herself as more anti-Jacobite than Queen Anne. She used this argument because she knew it the most effective means of dissuading Marlborough, and of appealing to his fundamental prejudices. He responded at once by the most emphatic repudiation of all such ideas. "I will venture my last drop of blood. . . . I am firmly resolved never to assist any Jacobite whatsoever."

Now, John and Sarah were as closely linked together as any pair have been. They wrote to each other with perfect frankness and confidence, and with no thought of making a record for the public or posterity. Here, then, we see their deep common abhorrence of Jacobitism in all its forms and their unswerving allegiance to the Protestant Succession. Marlborough had before leaving The Hague received the Jacobite Hooke, had treated him most courteously, had put his hand upon his shoulder, and sent him away charmed with fair words. But his true position and that of his wife is exposed in this letter. It is only another proof of the fact

1 Coxe, i, 297.

which we assert in this account, that Marlborough pursued throughout his whole life the aims of the Revolution of 1688, and fooled the Jacobites as regularly as he defeated the French.

Upon the second reading of the Occasional Conformity Bill in the House of Lords Marlborough and Godolphin marched with Rochester. The Queen's ardour can be measured from the fact that she compelled her husband, whom the Bill would have disqualified from public life, to vote for it. But as he filed into the Aye lobby the poor Prince, who suffered many vexations in his comfortable life, was heard to exclaim to the Whig teller, Wharton, of whom Queen Anne so sternly disapproved, "My heart is vid you." The second reading was carried only by twelve votes. Under the promptings of Wharton the Whigs in the Lords pursued sagacious tactics. They proposed to exempt municipal and county functionaries, and confine the Bill to Parliamentary and national office. Thus they became the champions of the many, while in no way weakening their own array. But the shrewder stroke was reserved. They carried an amendment, represented as a compromise, reducing the fines to levels where they no longer deterred. Wealthy Dissenters, having already paid something in conscience, would not find it impossible to pay a little more in cash. Thus Occasional Conformity would be brought within the means of any man of reasonable substance likely to be affected.

This expedient at once enraged and baffled the House of Commons. Here was an intrusion by the Lords into the domain of finance, over which the Commons were supreme. Here was the classic issue between the two Houses, and, as Wharton had shrewdly foreseen, the Tory majority in the Commons, halloaed on by the Whigs, set off in full cry after this potent constitutional red herring. They almost forgot that what they were hunting was Occasional Conformity. Moreover, it was noticed that the authority of the Government was not used in any whole-hearted way to push the measure. Quite a number of persons dependent upon the Government and many Tory notables associated with Marlborough were found absent from divisions to support it. A damp fog seemed to be cast upon it by the two Ministers who over-towered all others. In these commotions and divergences the first Occasional Conformity Bill went to ground safely in February 1703.

The time had now come to deal with Rochester. Rochester was the Queen's uncle. She agreed with him in Church and party. He was the lay head of the Church of England which the Queen loved. He was in many ways the leader of the Tory Party which she favoured, and which was master in her new Parliament. But, further, Rochester had a theme and policy covering the whole action of the State, religious and secular, in peace or war. At the beginning of 1702 and 1703 he published successive volumes of his father's *History of the Rebellion* with a tendentious introduction of his own. The merit of this work stands high in our literature. To Tory England in the first years of Anne it carried an inspiring message. The Church was the foundation of the Throne, and the Church and Throne united could alone secure the freedom, safety, and advance of Britain.

But none of this availed Rochester at all when once Marlborough, choosing his moment, finally decided they could work no more together. Many and grievous were the provocations which Rochester gave. He was jealous of Marlborough, and prepared to dispute his ascendancy: but he thought Godolphin was the more vulnerable. Against Godolphin, therefore, he marshalled his influence and his faction. He would pull him down. Godolphin gone, Marlborough would be alone. He did not hesitate to criticize and oppose unpopular measures of the Government of which he was a leading member or to reveal its secrets in damaging debate. He strove ever to increase his authority in both Houses of Parliament at the expense of the Ministry and of public business. When every effort to rally him had failed Marlborough resolved that he should go. Then was seen Anne's loyalty to the old Cockpit days. What use had her uncle been to her when Mr Caliban and her own sister had tried to chase Sarah from the Court, and when Sarah's lord was in the Tower? What had he done when she had wanted her letter carried to Queen Mary? He had failed her in her darkest hour, and he had failed her in order to curry favour with the ruler of the day. But that ruler was no more; and the Princess who had vainly sought his good offices in her distress was now the Queen. Who was he to set himself against her dear and faithful friends—friends who, even against their inclinations and better judgment, as she realized, had newly obliged her by voting for the principle of the Occasional Conformity Bill? Mrs Morley, Mr and Mrs Freeman, and Mr Montgomery, joined in familiar conclave, had no doubt that the dismissal of Rochester would add to their difficulties, of which they already felt the weight. But once Mr Freeman said that it was no good trying to work with him any more, and that he was less dangerous outside than in, the matter was settled.

Early in February 1703 Rochester was astonished by receiving the Queen's command to go to Dublin and discharge his duties as Lord-Lieutenant of Ireland. He took a week to measure forces, and then intimated that it was his higher duty to remain in London. Forthwith his resignation was demanded, with no choice but that of dismissal. He quitted the Queen's Government accordingly, and without a day's delay appeared at the head of the High Tories who sought to wreck it. For such a position his previous action and his ably expressed and sincerely held convictions had prepared him. This disciplinary act necessarily weakened the Government; but it made Nottingham, Hedges, and Seymour understand clearly where political power resided. Henceforward they felt that in their conflict with Marlborough and Godolphin their political resources might prove inadequate.

In the midst of these activities almost the greatest sorrow that can come to man fell upon Marlborough. His only surviving son was now sixteen. We remember him as a playmate of the poor little Duke of Gloucester. He had been at Eton and had already gone to Cambridge, where Dr Hare, afterwards celebrated as Marlborough's chaplain, whom

184

we shall often meet during his campaigns, and eventually Bishop of Chichester, guided him in religion, morals, and learning. "Notwithstanding his high birth, splendid prospects, and courtly education," observes Archdeacon Coxe ingenuously, "he set an example of affability, regularity, and steadiness, above his years." Life began early in those days, and this handsome, eager youth wanted, of course, to go with his father to the wars. Bred in a martial atmosphere, he was thrilled by camps and soldiers, and especially by reviews and processions. His father would have liked to have him with him at the front; but his mother thought he was too young. In those days an officer on the staff of the Commander-in-Chief must be frequently under fire, and might be required at any moment to ride with a message into the hottest of the fighting. Sarah could not bring herself to let him go so young—while still a child. Let him stay one more year at Cambridge and finish his studies. Thus was it settled. But Death knows where to keep his appointments.

During the autumn of 1702 Lord Blandford often came over from Cambridge to stay with Lord Godolphin close by at Newmarket, and apparently made the best impression upon the Treasurer. There was smallpox in the town, but Godolphin thought that he, "going into no house but mine, will I hope be more defended from it by air and riding, without any violent exercise, than he could possibly be anywhere else." Meanwhile the boy was making plans of his own to join the Army, and with a friend was intriguing for commissions in a cavalry regiment.

It was at the end of his long visit to Godolphin that the infection fell upon him. He had scarcely returned to Cambridge in February when he was struck down by virulent smallpox. Sarah was there as fast as horses could bear her, nursing him herself and invoking all that the medical knowledge of those days could do. The Queen hurried her own physicians into the royal coach and sent them posting to Cambridge. It was less than three years since the same scourge had carried off her own child. She wrote to Sarah:

185

Thursday morning

I writ two words to my dear Mrs Freeman yesterday, and could not help telling her again that I am truly afflicted for the melancholy account that is come again this morning of poor dear Lord Blandford. I pray God grant he may do well, and support you. And give me leave once more to beg you for Christ Jesus' sake to have a care of your dear precious self, and believe me with all the passion imaginable your poor unfortunate faithful Morley.[1]

"I wish," she added in another letter, "that the messenger who carries the medicines which my dear Mrs Freeman sends for could fly, that nothing may be wanting the moment there is any occasion."

Till all hope was abandoned John was kept away. He wrote to Sarah:

Thursday, 9 in the morning

I am so troubled at the sad condition this poor child seems to be in, that I know not what I do. I pray God to give you some comfort in this great affliction. If you think anything under heaven can be done, pray let me know it, or if you think my coming can be of the least use, let me know it. I beg I may hear as often as possible, for I have no thought but what is at Cambridge.

Medicines are sent by the doctors. I shall be impatient to the last degree till I hear from you.[2]

Thursday night

I wrote to you this morning, and was in hopes I should have heard again before this time, for I hope the doctors were with you early this morning. If we must be so unhappy as to lose this poor child, I pray God to enable us both to behave ourselves with that resignation which we ought to do. If this uneasiness which I now lie under should last long, I think I could not live. For God's sake, if there be any hope of recovery, let me know it.[3]

Shortly after writing these words he received his summons and, hurrying to Cambridge, arrived as his son expired. On the morning of Saturday, February 20, John and Sarah crept off to Holywell to endure their pangs. The Queen wrote:

1 Coxe, i, 218.   2 *Ibid.*, 220.   3 *Ibid.*

186

LORD BLANDFORD
Sir Godfrey Kneller
By permission of the Duke of Marlborough

THE OCCASIONAL CONFORMITY BILL

St James's
Tuesday night

It would have been a great satisfaction to your poor unfortunate faithful Morley, if you would have given me leave to come to St Albans, for the unfortunate ought to come to the unfortunate. But since you will not have me, I must content myself as well as I can, till I have the happiness of seeing you here. I know nothing worth writing; but if I did, I should not trouble you with it, being sure no sort of news can be agreeable to your dear, heavy heart. God Almighty bless and comfort my dear Mrs Freeman, and be assured I will live and die sincerely yours.[1]

This blow not only cut at the natural feelings of John and Sarah, but seemed to ruin their future. Both were dynasts. To gather wealth and fame and found a family to run on down the ages was their dear—indeed, their over-dear—ambition. Now it was ended. The Duke had to make a fresh will, leaving his already large properties to Sarah in trust for his eldest daughter's husband, Mr Godolphin, to whom he desired that his titles should pass. But he was already overdue at the front. The Dutch awaited him, and the armies were entering the field. He sailed for Holland with a leaden heart in the early days of March. The will, which had not yet been engrossed, was sent after him, and his letters show the anxiety which he felt when the packet-boat containing it was reported captured by a French privateer. To Ailesbury, whom he met at The Hague, he said, "I've lost what is so dear to me, it is fit for me to retire and not toil and labour for I know not who. My daughters are all married."[2] It was in this sombre mood that he began a most harassing campaign.

1 Coxe, i, 221.   2 Ailesbury, ii, 558.

CHAPTER IX

NEW COMBATANTS

(1702–1703)

The Northern War

ALTHOUGH the struggle against French domination involved all Central and Western Europe, Italy, Spain, and the New World, and may justly be called a world war, its bounds could still grow wider. During the whole of 1702 and 1703 what was called the Northern War had been waged by the Sweden of Charles XII to defend her Baltic provinces against the simultaneous attacks of Russia under Peter the Great and Poland, then united under Augustus II to the Electorate of Saxony. The course and episodes of this considerable conflict, rendered memorable by the martial genius of Charles XII, form a minor and companion theme of hate and destruction in the general sufferings of Christendom. The Northern War, the politics of the states engaged in it, and above all the erratic, formidable personality of the Swedish King, often impinged, as will be seen, upon Marlborough's task.

The reader will remember that at the close of the seventeenth century Sweden was by far the greatest of the northern Powers. Charles XI reigned not only in the homeland of Sweden, but over an empire which comprised all that we now describe as the Baltic States—Finland, Ingria (St Petersburg), Esthonia, Livonia (Latvia), and West Pomerania (Stralsund and Stettin). Although Swedish professional discipline and valour had met its match in the Prussians at Fehrbellin in 1675, the Swedish Army still dwelt in the glories of Gustavus Adolphus. In 1697 Charles XI had died, and the crown of Sweden passed, under a regency, to a youth not yet fifteen. The great possessions of the Swedes on the mainland had long excited the natural cupidity and ambitions of their
188

continental neighbours. Now, with a boy-king and an army believed to have passed its zenith, the Swedish Empire seemed to be a seasonable prey. All this might have come to nothing but for the revengeful machinations of a private individual. Patkul was a Livonian magnate who had been exiled and expropriated for insufficient cause by Charles XI. He it was who wove together with tireless industry and dynamic force all the rulers and Governments who coveted the Swedish inheritance. A league of Russia, Saxony, and Denmark had been formed in 1699 for the partition of Sweden; and very little had prevented Prussia from joining it.

The forces already seemed overwhelming. The three confederates expected to rob a child. Never was undeception greater: for there leapt from the Swedish throne this boy-king, deemed an easy quarry, who now burst upon Northern Europe as the most furious warrior of modern history. War at all times, in any direction, at any odds, was his insatiable demand. For eighteen years, until a bullet slew him in an hour of victory, he rushed with the frenzy of genius and of mania at the throat of every antagonist. Dauntless and implacable, with cold calculation and for a long spell a charmed life, Charles XII defended and wore out his country against all comers. With the help of William III and the Anglo-Dutch fleet he had already dictated peace to Denmark in 1701, and, swiftly appearing before Narva, had put Peter the Great to flight and destroyed the Russian army. Possessed by these successes, he had turned next upon Augustus, Elector of Saxony, who was also the elected King of Poland. In this double-faced monarch Charles discerned the hub of the conspiracy against the grandeur of Sweden. There was no glory, he said, in winning victories over Muscovites: it was too easy. The deposition of Augustus from the throne of Poland became for several years his ruling purpose. Although the Swedish forces he had left in the Baltic States were eventually overwhelmed by hardship and the Russian masses, Charles XII in 1702, 1703, and 1704 conquered the greater part of Poland, defeated the Russians,

Poles, and Saxons in the battles of Klissow (July 19, 1702) and Pultusk (April 21, 1703), stormed Cracow, captured Warsaw, and set up with some pretence of electoral legality a Polish king of his own.

This ferocious Northern War, conducted by both sides with the dullest savagery of barbarous ages, caused continuous anxiety to the founders of the Grand Alliance. At Versailles the hope of exploiting its complications, and if possible of enlisting the martial ardours of the Swedish King, was perseveringly pursued. The Court at Vienna might cherish possibilities of a combination with Russia for the advantage of the Empire; but the Sea Powers would have none of this. From the beginning they sought only to end or wall in a conflict which they could not but regard as a monstrous irrelevancy. "The northern crater was to burn itself out, shut off in every direction."[1] It was in this purpose that William III in 1701 had carried a Swedish army in his fleets to curb Denmark. As the great war with France developed Marlborough and Heinsius vigilantly discouraged every tendency of the Germanic states to turn their eyes to the north or to the east. The Empire in its increasing weakness was ready to obey this grave and imperious guidance. Prussia had appetites and movements in both directions which at times were nicely balanced; and the tortuous, equivocal course of Frederick I, with his invaluable Prussian troops, was an unrelenting worry. The chastisement of Denmark was held up to all the Germanic states accessible from the sea as a proof of what might happen to allies who looked in the wrong direction. How could they tell that England and Holland, with their wealth and their command of the Baltic waters, would not offer compulsive inducements to the Swedish fire-eater, and land his army at any point upon the exposed sea-coast? Such were the bearings and posture of the Northern War in the period at which our story has arrived.

But the years 1702 and 1703 also saw new countries and new

[1] Von Noorden, ii, 38.

forces drawn into the War of the Spanish Succession. The reverberations of the main quarrel roused a giddy excitement in all minds, and everywhere rulers and races with ambitions to satisfy or grievances to assert hastened to choose their sides and draw their swords. We have seen the same thing happen in our own time. Indeed, the parallel is curiously exact. Each of the chief combatants reached out for small allies, or sought to raise or foment revolts in the domains of the enemy. Bavaria and Savoy were thrown by their sovereigns or by their circumstances into the general war on opposite sides in the early eighteenth, just as Roumania and Bulgaria were caught up in the twentieth century. Moreover, the consequences, both to these small Powers arriving belated in the arena and to the principals in the quarrel, were very much alike in the two periods. The newcomers were set upon with fury by the champions they had affronted. The German treatment of Roumania in 1917 is but a repetition of the punishment inflicted by the allies upon Bavaria in 1704. The vicissitudes of Savoy may be set against those of modern Bulgaria. In both cases the decisive struggle was transferred for a while to new theatres and more distant battlefields.

In this chapter we have to tell how the cause of the Two Crowns was helped by the treason of Bavaria and the Hungarian revolt; how Anglo-Dutch policy endeavoured to succour the rebellion against Louis in the Cevennes; and how Savoy and Portugal were gained to the allies. We shall also show the often decisive relations which these subsidiary disturbances bore to the main event.

THE TREASON OF BAVARIA

While the fortresses on the Meuse were falling one by one to Marlborough's arms in 1702, a new spring of events began to flow in Bavaria which was ultimately to be decisive upon Marlborough's career and upon the future of Europe. Max Emmanuel, the Elector of Bavaria, was a politician without scruple and with a thirst for adventure. In 1701, before the fighting became general, he was in close intrigue with France,

and a treaty was signed whereby he received a monthly subsidy of a hundred thousand thalers[1] in order to build up a
Bavarian army, which finally amounted to twenty-one thousand
men. Thus in 1702 he was in a position of remarkable
strength among the states of the Empire. In March he went
a step farther and opened by a roundabout channel his designs
to Louis XIV. His lengthy letter, preserved in the Austrian
archives, sets forth as black a scheme of greed and deceit as has
ever been committed to paper. He wished, he said, to join
the party of the Two Crowns, and was willing to make war
not only upon the house of Austria, but upon the neighbouring German princes. For this he must have the guarantee of
France that whatever lands he conquered, "to which he had
no right," should be assigned to him in the final peace, and
that no such peace would be made by the Two Crowns which
did not provide for this. The continuance of the military
subsidy was also imperative. King Louis had not been wholly
satisfied with his previous attitude, and had allowed the instal-
ments to fall into arrear in order to make him define his
intentions.

The Elector proceeded to explain how he might be most
serviceable. If he entered openly into the campaign provision
would be made by the Grand Alliance to meet his attack; but
if he remained quiet and powerful until all the troops on both
sides were engaged, and then chose the best moment for throwing his weight by surprise into the scale, he would produce the
greatest effect in his power. For this purpose he proposed to
lull the Emperor into a false state of security by bargaining
with him for the use of the new Bavarian Army, and then
suddenly, when he had gained his full confidence and no precautions had been taken against him, he would strike what he
devoutly prayed might be a deadly blow. His first act would
be to seize by treachery in full peace the free city and fortress
of Ulm, on the Danube. As the only other first-class fortress
between Ulm and Passau was his own city of Ingolstadt a great
waterway, he pointed out, would be opened into the vitals of the

[1] The thaler—or dollar, as it is now called—exchanged with the pound sterling
around 4.86¾.

Empire and the Austrian Hereditary Lands, and even Vienna itself would soon be exposed. If, however, he took this plunge he must be assured that French forces up to 40 battalions and 60 squadrons would be sent him from the Rhine according to his needs. He felt, he concluded, he would never have such a chance again in all his life, and mentioned that he could hardly sleep for thinking about it.

All this seemed very good to the Great King. Every promise that Max Emmanuel desired was given, and the punctual flow of the military subsidies was resumed. The Elector thereupon, with many expressions of love and loyalty, began to negotiate with the Emperor for the hire of his troops. He offered to declare war upon France for a subsidy larger than that he had hitherto received from Louis, and to send an important part of his army to fight in Italy, provided that he himself were given the command of all the Imperial troops there. The Emperor and his Court were attracted by the proposal. They commended it to the Maritime Powers, and asked for their assent and their money. There was no difficulty about the money; nor in Holland was any objection taken against Max Emmanuel holding the Italian command. But when Wratislaw earnestly pressed complete acceptance upon England he met with an obstinate resistance on the question of command. Prince Eugene's brilliant campaign of 1701 and his recent hard-fought action at Luzzara had already made him famous and popular in London. Marlborough had conceived an instinctive admiration and liking for him. These views were shared by the Queen and Godolphin, and also by Nottingham, the Secretary of State. The idea of superseding Prince Eugene, then the greatest captain of the age, in the full tide of his success, by an unproven royalty, was deemed both foolish and ungrateful. The Secretary of State confronted Wratislaw with a letter in the Queen's own hand in which she declared she could not be a party to the displacement of Prince Eugene. Nottingham inquired why the Elector should not serve under Prince Eugene. No objection could be taken by England to that, nor to the provision of the money. But Wratislaw observed

193

that the precedence of an Electoral Prince over a Marshal of the Empire was so decisive that it could not even be questioned. The divergence between Dutch and English policy had now to be discussed between the Governments.

Meanwhile it was already September. All the armies were fully engaged in every theatre. The Imperial forces in Germany were involved in the siege of Landau, which seemed to be in extremities. The moment for which Max Emmanuel had plotted had come. On September 9, 1702, forty or fifty Bavarian officers, disguised as peasants bringing vegetables to the market-gate of Ulm, suddenly overpowered the sentries, and after a short struggle in which their leader was killed admitted the Bavarian troops, who were close behind them, into the defenceless city. The mayor and corporation surrendered to treacherous violence, having only time to send a messenger for help. The Elector had awaited the result of his master-stroke at a neighbouring castle, and as soon as the courier with the news clattered into the courtyard informed his councillors and officers that Ulm was his, and that he was at war with the Emperor. The officers applauded; the Ministers were dumbfounded; and subsequently the nobility and clergy of the whole of Bavaria testified their grief and alarm at what they regarded as almost an act of sacrilege against the Holy Roman Empire. But the deed was done, and Max Emmanuel stood at the head of an intact, well-equipped, and comparatively powerful army.

The news of the defection of Bavaria carried consternation both to London and to The Hague. The discomfiture of Wratislaw, who almost the day before had been pressing the claims of the Elector to oust Prince Eugene in Italy, can be imagined. Heinsius also felt that his judgment had been at fault. In both countries the injury to the Empire and to the cause of the Alliance was understood. But what was there to do? A fortunate coincidence, however, mitigated the first effects of this malign event. Max Emmanuel had miscalculated the resisting powers of Landau. Had he struck a fortnight earlier, or had Landau resisted a fortnight longer, it is probable that the Imperial army would have been forced to

194

abandon the siege. But when the Elector seized Ulm on the 9th Landau had already 'beaten the chamade' on the 8th.

What followed in Bavaria may be shortly related. The Elector sent a message to Marshal Catinat on the Rhine proposing a junction of their forces at Hüningen. But the Imperial Minister in Switzerland, having heard of the treason, armed his servants and caught the messenger and several other couriers with papers exposing not only Max Emmanuel's immediate plan but his further designs. Neither the Elector nor Catinat received their messages, and each deemed himself for some time betrayed by the other. No junction was effected between the French and Bavarian forces, and the Elector to gain time sought to protect himself from military chastisement by endeavouring to resume relations with Vienna. Meanwhile in October Prince Louis, the Margrave of Baden, marched up the Rhine from Landau and engaged Villars, who had replaced Catinat, in a serious action at Friedlingen. Each side had about sixteen thousand men. Both fell back in disorder and even panic; and both claimed the victory. Villars sent a despatch to Versailles so glowing that he received his marshal's baton forthwith. But when it was seen that he had been glad to recross the Rhine, and that no junction of his troops with the Elector seemed likely, it was felt at the French Court that his promotion was precipitate and their *Te Deums* premature. The year therefore closed with the Elector still separated from the French, and apparently seeking to make his peace with the Emperor. The Dutch, stung by having been deceived, were scornful of these negotiations. But Marlborough and Godolphin seemed impressed with the importance of dealing with Bavaria by force or treaty. Neither was possible in 1702. The grave change which had been produced in the strategic position did not impose itself as yet upon either side in an acute form.

THE HUNGARIAN REVOLT

During the centuries when the Turks preyed upon Central Europe Hungary and Transylvania became a borderland torn by repeated invasions, and frayed with ceaseless strife. The Magyar nobility and squires preserved a feudal character, and in their desperate need welcomed every form of German aid, even at the price of Imperial control. But when the victories of Prince Eugene and the Peace of Carlowitz at the end of the seventeenth century removed, as it seemed finally, the Ottoman pressure, a new view was taken of their respective rights and duties by the two races which had hitherto been content to fight side by side. The House of Austria conceived itself entitled to treat Hungary as rescued or conquered territory, and to assert Imperial sovereignty in its most uncompromising form. The elective monarchy of Hungary became hereditary in the person of the Emperor. A vigorous policy was launched against dyarchy and dualism in all their manifestations. A bureaucracy of German-born and German-speaking officials overspread the land. The old Hungarian Estates were to be reduced to impotence. A contribution of one-third of the expenses of the Austrian Army was permanently imposed upon Hungary without consultation with its representatives, and without the traditional immunity from taxation which the Magyar nobility and minor military chieftains had enjoyed during the troublous ages. Vienna would become the sole and undisputed centre of the Empire, and Hungary an Austrian administrative province governed and taxed in strict uniformity with the other Hereditary Lands.

It is easy to see why the struggle between these Imperial claims and the national pride and interest of the Magyars was fierce and unending. Almost every impulse which has ever roused revolt was now at work in its sharpest form. The nobles had hitherto dreaded the peasantry and the brigand chiefs whom generations of warfare had produced. All came together, and the full strength of the Hungarian nation ranged itself against the Empire at a time when that already decrepit body was engaged in a grievous war with the first of military powers. Franz Rakoczy, sprung from a famous Transylvanian family, had fled with a price on his head to Poland from Imperial vengeance. He now became the accepted leader of the rebellion. Strengthened by French money and the support of Louis XIV, he returned to Budapest, and in 1703 was at the head no longer of small bands of partisans, but of armies which sometimes assembled twenty thousand strong, behind which the ancient Constitution of Hungary stood, and administrations both national and local were soon taking shape and reality.

It is needless here to describe the cruel guerrilla or even war which followed; still less the tortuous negotiations by which it was continually accompanied. Suffice it that during the whole period with which we are concerned the Imperial Court alternated between indecisive combat and insincere caresses, and changed from severity to concessions according to the fortunes of the general war; while Rakoczy for his part revealed a strong personal ambition to become the hereditary ruler at least of Transylvania, and used the impulses of Hungarian freedom largely for that purpose. But the reactions upon the Grand Alliance play a well-marked part in our tale. The Sea Powers, on whom the weight and even more the cost of the war fell so heavily, were by this time thoroughly dissatisfied with the exertions of the Empire against France. Primarily, they observed, the quarrel lay between the Emperor and Louis XIV. None of the allies stood to gain from victory prizes comparable to those which would fall to the house of Hapsburg. Yet this sovereign seemed helpless in his own cause. Instead of throwing his weight into the main struggle against the common enemy, he preferred, it seemed, to persecute his subjects whom misgovernment had driven into revolt. The Court at Vienna clamoured ceaselessly for subsidies and for troops. But the Maritime Powers complained that if these were sent it would only by so much relax the Empire's efforts against France, and enable the strength of the Imperial forces to be thrown against the Hungarian insurgents.

Moreover, there was in both England and Holland a lively sympathy for these same insurgents. In Parliament the Whigs descanted upon freedom and the rights of peoples, while Tories dwelt upon the shortcomings of Continental allies. In the Dutch Republic the idea of establishing similar federal institutions in Hungary naturally found support. Neither the

English treatment of Ireland nor that which the States-General were soon afterwards to mete out to Belgium disturbed the complacency of their leaders' judgments about Hungary. The sympathies of the Maritime Powers for the Hungarian rebels strained the structure of the Grand Alliance. The Imperial Court resented the interference of England and Holland in the affairs of the Hapsburg monarchy, and not less the subversive doctrines which these republican or Parliamentary countries fostered. On the other hand, in the desperate straits to which the Empire was already reduced the money and arms of the Sea Powers were indispensable. Continuous friction resulted. No one charged with the duty of pressing for the mediation of the Maritime Powers between the Emperor and his rebellious subjects could have avoided giving offence at Vienna. The English Ambassador, George Stepney, was Whig-minded. This added an extra sting to his negotiations on behalf of the Hungarians. By the end of 1703 he was a most unpopular figure at the Imperial Court. A strong personal antipathy had grown between him and Wratislaw. Only increasing common danger kept ill-assorted allies together, and preserved Stepney in the discharge of his thankless though congenial duties.

The Rising in the Cevennes

The Huguenot peasantry of the Cevennes, long harried by the persecutions of Louis XIV, had broken into open revolt in 1702. Here was a furious war of religion as an enclave of the main struggle for power. Mysticism, murder, and retributory massacre spread through all that hard mountainous region between the Rhone and the Garonne. A warfare as pitiless as that of La Vendée a century later, and similar to it in many features, began to gnaw internally the strength of France. The Camisards, so called from the white shirts which were their only and easily doffed uniform, performed prodigies of daring and fanaticism against the regular troops of the Great King. Their struggles and torments deeply stirred the Protestant passions of the Sea Powers.

198

To give these martyr-peasants succour in their revolt against Popery and slavery was a dear desire spreading far beyond the lobbies of Parliaments or the tents of commanding generals.

But how to reach them in the depths of France? The Anglo-Dutch fleets were already able to make summer cruises in the Mediterranean, and in 1703 efforts were made to establish contact with the rebellion in the Cevennes. Two English ships under Sir Cloudesley Shovell, with money, arms, and agents, hung off the French southern ports. But so far every endeavour to pierce the land barrier had failed. Sympathy for the Camisards and the evident advantage of sustaining their resistance increased the desire of the allies to regain the Duke of Savoy.

THE RECONCILIATION WITH SAVOY

In the conflict between the Bourbons and the Hapsburgs, between France and the Empire, the Duchy of Savoy-Piedmont was cursed or blessed by the highest form of strategic importance. This small state, with its compact and loyal army, was the guardian of the Alpine passes. It rested with its rulers, the Dukes of Savoy, to decide upon occasion whether Austrian armies should invade the southern provinces of France, or French armies should deploy on the slopes of Piedmont for an advance into Northern Italy. The politics of the house of Savoy during the whole period of the wars of William and of Marlborough against Louis XIV consisted in selling the passes and reselling them to the highest bidder who was likely to honour his bond. Victor Amadeus carried this dangerous marketing to a high perfection. It was the deliberate policy of his house and Government to change sides from time to time for the sake of safety or profit. The defection of Savoy from King William's confederacy had been the prelude to the Peace of Ryswick. Victor Amadeus made marriages of high consequence with the family of Louis XIV. His elder daughter had married the Duke of Burgundy: the younger Princess of Savoy married the

Duke of Anjou. Thus in 1701 Victor Amadeus was father-in-law both of the heir to the French throne and of Philip V, the accepted sovereign of the Empire of Spain. He was, in fact, precariously astride not only of the passes of the Alps, but of the party of the Two Crowns.

Nevertheless his situation was uncomfortable. William, implacable over his desertion, had brushed him out of all consideration for the English throne, to which he had a contingent claim. The French marshals, although bound to respect a prince so well connected, were rough and contemptuous of the little state France had seduced. Even at the renewal of the general war the Duke and his advisers were filled with resentment against the patronizing arrogance of France. The brilliant campaign of Eugene in Venetia and Lombardy in 1701, the unexpected solidarity of England and Holland after the death of King William, the vigour, howsoever hampered, of Marlborough's operations in Flanders in 1702, caused the Duke of Savoy and his councillors to discuss among themselves whether it would not pay them to change sides again. The Roman Empire was Holy. The Sea Powers were not only militant but rich. Large subsidies were being paid to German princes far less cardinally set upon the map. Events which we have described made, as they occurred, a very deep impression upon the Court at Turin. Profound and perilous confabulations were held during the whole of 1702.

The first conclusion which Victor Amadeus reached was that he could raise his price against the Two Crowns considerably. The marriage-ties which his children had contracted seemed to be no brake upon the politics of Savoy-Piedmont. Accordingly he began to press both Paris and Madrid for morsels of the Spanish Empire; his appetites were directed towards securing the assistance of France in his succession to Mantuan Montferrat, and the assent of Madrid to his acquisition of Milan. These crude desires and all the possibilities arising from their disappointment became well known to both French and allied diplomacy during that year. But, whether from distrust

VICTOR AMADEUS II OF SAVOY

From a print in the British Museum

or disdain, or from inherent difficulty, Victor Amadeus' demands were ignored in the capitals of the Two Crowns. We need not complicate our story by intricate details, but by the end of 1702 it was realized in the secret circles of Europe that Savoy had asked her friends for more and had been refused—and even spurned. Victor Amadeus was soon deep in intrigues with the allies. Stepney at Vienna worked with the Imperial diplomats to bring him over. The transaction was dangerous, because a strong French army under Vendôme was actually in the Duchy, intermingled with the Piedmontese troops, and in control of many key-points. Vendôme, great-grandson of Henri IV, Marshal of France, and a fine soldier to boot, but with unpleasant personal habits, rode rough-shod over the occupied territory. The Piedmontese became hostile to the French troops; the negotiations of the Court of Turin with Vienna, with The Hague, and with St James's continued, and the French were soon suspicious of what was afoot.

Throughout the spring and summer of 1703 the relations between Savoy-Piedmont and France became increasingly strained. In July Vendôme convinced himself that Victor Amadeus was obtaining military information for the allies through his vivacious daughter, the Duchess of Burgundy. He sought authority from Versailles to disarm the Piedmontese Army and garrison the more important fortresses whenever he should judge it necessary. Plenary powers were given him.

This delicate situation was brought to a head by an astonishing breakdown in English diplomacy which was held to reflect seriously upon Nottingham as Secretary of State. In the secret councils at Turin there were two parties, pro-Austrian and pro-French. Victor Amadeus had, of course, rigidly excluded the Comte de la Tour, the advocate of France, from his underground negotiations with the enemy. But in August 1703 Richard Hill, the former tutor of Rochester's eldest son, whom Nottingham had publicly appointed Envoy Extraordinary to the Duke of Savoy—a job in itself and a hardy procedure towards one who was still an enemy prince—

and Aglionby, the English agent in Switzerland, addressed themselves to la Tour as if he were in their secrets and on their side. Consternation swept Vienna and Turin when this indiscretion became known. Nottingham and his colleague Hedges learned too late from Stepney the true state of affairs. "You will see," wrote Stepney to Hill on October 10, after the disclosure, "that the little Count de la Tour is not the man you took him for; and it were to be wished . . . this Court might have been consulted how far such application had been seasonable. . . ."

The consequences were serious. On September 29 Vendôme arrested a number of Piedmontese generals, disarmed such of the Duke's troops as were in his immediate power, and demanded the surrender of fortresses. "Never, perhaps," wrote Stepney to Hill, "was any affair transacted from the beginning to the end with so much negligence and indiscretion as this had been." However, the violence of Vendôme produced an unforeseeable reaction. Up till this stage Victor Amadeus was still balancing. He had not yet made his treaty with the allies. His exorbitance and procrastination had driven the Imperial agent at his Court almost to despair. Victor Amadeus was a proud and courageous turncoat. While weaving his webs of intrigue in the interests of his small country he never forgot that he was a soldier with a sword at his side. Indeed, he was capable of fighting with the utmost personal valour in the forefront of a battle which his policy required him to lose. He was smitten by Vendôme's high-handed action into an indignation in which an uneasy conscience played its part. Thereupon he threw himself into the arms of the allies. He turned to them for help "like a man whose house is burning over his head." The allies did not try to exploit his weakness. If he had still been in possession of an undiminished force and at the height of success, he could have secured no better treaty than was ultimately made. On November 8 the alliance between Savoy and the Empire was concluded. The Duke was promised an Imperial army of twenty thousand men; the upkeep of his own army was to be arranged with the Sea Powers. His ambitions about

Mantua and Milan would be gratified in allied victory, and he could look to further conquests in the south of France should the war flow prosperously into those regions. There were no illusions about these transactions in Vienna. Stepney wrote on November 7, "it is certain our new ally has no manner of bowels or other principles and cares for nothing on God's earth but his own dear self." This severe judgment paid too little consideration to the trials and needs of a small country between the hammer and the anvil of rival empires engaged in ruthless quarrel.

The wrath of the great combatants was forthwith focused upon the petty traitor states. The same hatred which the allies and the Empire felt for the Elector of Bavaria was now concentrated by France upon the Duke of Savoy. The desire to make examples of these recreants lent new possibilities to strategy. Moreover, each side felt bound to do its best for its own new adherent. Louis XIV conceived his honour closely engaged in sustaining Max Emmanuel and in wreaking vengeance upon Victor Amadeus. These sentiments stirred the allies with the same degree of bitterness in the reverse form, and cast their shadows forward upon the year 1704.

The treason of Bavaria had torn the entrails out of the Empire. The desertion of Savoy threatened to inflict an almost equal injury upon France. Just when, in the summer of 1703, the party of the Two Crowns believed they were masters of all Italy, the apparition of Savoy-Piedmont in the ranks of their enemies created a new, costly, dangerous front, second in importance only to Flanders itself. Nor need the evil stop at the frontiers of Savoy. If the Camisards' revolt continued, and if a serious invasion of France, sustained by the Empire and the efforts of the Sea Powers, could be launched from Savoy, a tremendous penetration of France might result.

The swift and exemplary chastisement of Victor Amadeus became an important aim of France. Hotfoot upon the news of the Savoy treaty, Marshal de Tessé overran the dukedom with a numerous army, and a converging campaign against

Piedmont under Vendôme and his brother the Grand Prior was prepared for 1704. From all sides—across Savoy, from Lombardy, and from the Milanese—the avenging armies would move towards Turin. It was confidently believed in Paris that the coming year would bring his reward to the Elector of Bavaria and his ruin to the Duke of Savoy. But, as we shall see, destiny chose other channels.

The Portuguese Alliance

Hitherto in the War of the Spanish Succession no attempt had been made by the allies to challenge the French usurper on the soil of Spain. This was impossible without a base in the peninsula. All through 1702 the English Cabinet sought to wean Portugal from its warm friendship with France. Powerful factors were upon their side. Portugal had suffered cruelly as a neutral from the blockade of the Sea Powers, which intercepted lawful trade upon the high seas, and choked the still more lucrative smuggling trade in English manufactures at its source. Pedro II had need to be a cautious king. His pompous Court, always threatened by palace revolutions and seething with the cabals of favourites and the disputes of noble would-be place-holders, rested upon a horde of provincial and colonial officials, alike lazy and corrupt, beneath all of which heaved and muttered the extremely nasty Lisbon mob. Here was no sure foundation for a throne or an audacious policy. The King sought ample guarantees. He saw with comfort the French ships cowering in Toulon before the English fleets. He observed the riotous command of the oceans which the allies exercised. He dreaded the effect upon the royal finances and the national temper of a quarrel with England. Accordingly he agreed in May 1703 to break with the Two Crowns, and throw in the luck of Portugal with the cause of the Sea Powers.

His conditions were exacting. The allies must advance through Portugal to the invasion of Spain, thus shielding his country from the wrath of France. He would provide 28,000 Portuguese soldiers, of which 13,000 would be at their expense.

They must add 12,000 English and Dutch troops. All must be under his royal command. Beyond all, the allies must directly challenge the sovereignty of Philip V by the personal presence in the invading army of the rival claimant, the Archduke Charles; and parts of Estremadura and Galicia, including the fortress of Badajoz, were to be taken from Spain to reward the new ally. These last requirements were the hardest of all to meet. The Emperor Leopold shrank from the departure of his beloved younger son to be cast upon a distant shore in a dubious adventure sustained by the arms of heretics. But far more grievous were the consequences upon the general war. The treaties of the Grand Alliance were based essentially upon the idea of partition. They had never presumed to claim for the Imperial candidate the whole of Spain. The addition of the clause in the treaty with Portugal that there should be no peace without Philip V surrendering Spain involved an immense enlargement of the war-aims of the Alliance and an almost indefinite prolongation of the struggle.

For this the English Cabinet and Nottingham, the Tory Secretary of State, were directly responsible. The Hapsburgs could not, of course, object to so full a recognition of their claims. Although at Vienna there were fierce disputes over the respective rights of Joseph, King of the Romans, and the Archduke Charles, the Emperor Leopold himself did his part by renouncing all rights to the Spanish throne. The Dutch were profoundly disturbed. Their opposition long prevented the incorporation of the additional clause of the Portuguese treaty in the general engagements of the Grand Alliance. Heinsius said to Stanhope that the article "that no peace shall be made till the House of Austria be in possession of the whole monarchy of Spain" was "of hard digestion."[1] The Dutch misgivings were to be only too well justified by the event. However, the will of London prevailed. England and Holland had the ships, the men, and the money, and England pulled all the strings. Accordingly the die was cast. Henceforth the war would be lighted up throughout the peninsula,

[1] Stanhope to Hedges, September 11, 1703; S.P., 84/226, f. 30.

and the French Philip V and the Austrian Charles III must themselves wrestle for the land and crown of Spain. Henceforth the allies, besides humbling Louis XIV, had to conquer the Spanish people.

The English Cabinet had made for themselves a very rosy picture of the Spanish-Portuguese scene. To their fancy the Portuguese were still the ardent guerrilla fighters who had liberated their country from the Spanish yoke in the previous generation. They looked to see the fiery shepherds and wine-growers of the highlands and lowlands of Portugal leap forward on their behalf in their ancient valour. But these doughty folk did not respond to English expectations. They liked the commercial treaty, but they did not want the war which was its price. It was without the slightest national enthusiasm that the Portuguese allowed themselves to be drawn into the European struggle. Queen Anne's Government overrated the martial efforts of the Portuguese: they misjudged the temper of the Spaniards. They had looked for hot struggles on the Rhine, the Meuse, and the Po, but they could not believe that this French intruder so recently thrust by his grandfather into the sovereignty of Spain could have taken any root in that soil. They expected that a patriotic Portuguese Army, sustained by a strong nucleus of the best troops in Europe, would march swiftly forward from Lisbon to Madrid, and that the Spaniards would welcome King Charles III as their deliverer and rightful prince. Indeed, the overbearing behaviour and methods of the French Ambassador, Grammont, and the French generals, who treated Spain, like Savoy, as if it were a conquered province of France, had already aroused a keen resentment among the Castilian nobility.

But against these flowed the current of Spanish hatred against the revolted vassal state which had wrested its independence from the motherland. The Spanish people recognized the event as a Portuguese invasion. Nor were their prejudices removed by the tales which reached them of the exploits of the English soldiery during the attack upon Cadiz. The pillage of churches, the rape of nuns, and later

206

the capture of the treasure at Vigo and the insulting of the Spanish coasts, roused the nation. To them the French King stood for the unity of a world-wide empire, and the defence of the national soil against freebooters. He was the man in possession. The allies and their candidate were invaders who in cold blood had proclaimed the partition of the Spanish dominions, and were now marching to the subjugation of Spain itself. Thus, while the Portuguese were lukewarm, the Spaniards, infuriated, rallied to Philip V, and he became their national champion in an hour when their old glories and immediate safety seemed at stake. When these passions were armed by the sharp sword of the Duke of Berwick, now a Marshal of France, the Spanish theatre became the scene of a series of clamant disasters to the allied cause which not even the thunders of Marlborough's victories elsewhere could drown.

We shall not anticipate the course of the Spanish campaigns. Their episodes each year must be judged in relation to the general war, but we must discern how Marlborough stood towards this immense widening of the conflict. It is certain that he did not resist it. He watched the Spanish theatre with the keenest interest. He yielded with hardly a grumble the troops which the London Cabinet sent for the expedition to Portugal. Although these troops were withdrawn somewhat unceremoniously from his command by Nottingham as Secretary of State, and he was thereby exposed to the violent protests of the Dutch, he took great trouble to pick good regiments, and aided—within limits—the enterprise as if it were his own. He concurred in the choice of the commanders, and was content to be weakened in the main sphere of operations. There is no doubt that individually he never looked upon the Spanish war as anything more than a diversion of French energies. His own eyes were constantly fixed upon the control of the Mediterranean and upon the Italian front. To have a good fortified harbour and naval base upon the coast of Spain, to pen the French fleet in Toulon, to take Toulon, to carry the war into France from the south, to sustain Eugene and the Imperial troops from the sea—

these, apart from his own task of coping with the strongest French army, were his aims. For the rest, the war in Spain, if kept within a certain scale, would tend to the dispersion of the French forces perhaps as much as those of the allies; and it was, finally, a concession to the Tory Party's views upon the art of war. Such a concession may have been inevitable: we cannot measure the forces at work within the English Cabinet and Parliament. That there was a great urge towards the Spanish theatre is evident. Indeed, we shall presently see Marlborough compelled to resist proposals to carry the bulk of the Queen's troops from Flanders to the peninsula. We shall see him forced to acquiesce for years in a lamentable drain of troops and money from his own forces to regions where nothing decisive could be gained. It did not prevent him from conducting his own operations successfully, but nevertheless it weakened his right arm.

He never explained his thoughts except in his letters at the moment, and, so far as we know, never indulged in retrospect of any kind. But there is a story about him at the end of his life which seems to reveal his inmost mind. In 1716 there was an alarm of French invasion. The Cabinet sent two Ministers to Blenheim to ask the advice of the Captain-General who had already undergone his first stroke, was partly paralysed, and spoke only with the greatest difficulty. The Ministers carried back from their interview only one recorded remark: "Keep the army together: don't divide it."

CHAPTER X

"THE GREAT DESIGN"

(1703, Summer)

MARLBOROUGH arrived at The Hague on March 17 and began forthwith to draw his forces into the field. This year he could concentrate the "grand army" eighty miles south of Nimwegen, around Maestricht. He reviewed his troops and garrisons, beginning with the English at Breda, and inspected all the fortresses of the Meuse from Venloo up to Maestricht. While he marshalled the troops and set all things moving with the utmost activity, he argued with the Dutch about the plan of campaign. The evident intentions of Louis XIV to make his main effort against the Empire, and to stand on the defensive against the Anglo-Dutch armies, could be countered either by sending large reinforcements to the Moselle or the Upper Rhine, or by decisive action in Flanders. The Prussian King had offered an extra corps of eighteen thousand men for service in the northern theatre, provided that it served as an independent command. Marlborough would have welcomed this, but the States-General, fearing political designs, rejected the powerful aid. There remained the resource of a battle gained among the fortresses, the consequences of which would instantly make Flanders and Brabant the decisive theatre. But Marlborough knew already too well that the Dutch Government and command would never commit themselves to this in cold blood. They might be drawn into a great decision of arms by the force of events, but they would not agree to it beforehand. He did not press them, therefore, to allow him to seek the enemy in the field under the best conditions. Within the limits and in the theatre to which he was restricted there were, however, opportunities of producing dominating results. For this purpose he had set his heart on the capture of Ostend and Antwerp. Ostend would give him a new direct communication with England: Antwerp was not only the northern keystone of the French lines, but, more important still, controlled the whole waterway system of the Scheldt, the Lys, and the canals, which with the Meuse formed the principal lines of advance through the fortress zone. These two great trading centres, if won, would open up Belgium to the commerce of the allies. The fall of the city and seaport of Antwerp would offset the successes which the French must certainly gather elsewhere, and it seemed almost certain that they would fight a battle in its defence. Moreover, the Tory Party would approve a campaign in which the Navy would play an important part, directed against the coast ports and with promising commercial reactions. It was not only good strategy, but good politics.

The States-General, like Louis XIV, were not averse from sieges. Sieges seemed the safest way of making war; but they looked in the opposite direction. The fortress of Bonn, mid-way between Cologne and Coblenz, was now the sole barrier to the navigation of the Rhine for three hundred miles from its mouth to Philippsburg. The capture of Bonn would seem to succour the Empire, with which it opened a sure communication. This enterprise had been prepared during the winter, and the Dutch had undertaken to have all in readiness before the end of March.

Marlborough deferred to the Dutch opinion on the understanding that the siege of Bonn should be begun early, pressed with extreme vigour, and disposed of in the early stages of the campaign. Ostend and Antwerp could follow later, if no time were lost. Leaving Overkirk between Maestricht and Liége to guard the line of the Meuse, he marched in the middle of April to the Rhine, forming with the Prussian, Hessian, and Hanoverian troops an army of 40 battalions and 60 squadrons for the siege of Bonn. So backward were the preparations that Cohorn, the expert on whom the Dutch were relying, at the last moment advised that the siege of Bonn should be put off till the autumn. But Marlborough would have none of this. His letters had best tell their own tale.

Marlborough to Godolphin

MAESTRICHT
April 16, 1703

* I find by Lady Marl. that you were gone to Newmarket, where I hope you will have good luck. Since my last I have been at Liége, where I saw the E[arl] of Ailesbury, but there was so much company that I had not time to speak to him, so that he has sent his steward to me here to let me see that his family would be undone if he had not leave to come for [back to] England. I told him the Queen's affairs would suffer if she should give him leave at this time. His steward is going to England, and will wait upon you, with the reasons that make him hope that he may obtain leave for the next term only, in which time he says he may settle all the affairs of his family, with his son. I can't tell whether this thing be only a pretence, and if real whether it may be reasonable for the Queen to do it as matters now are; but I promised the steward that I would let you know what his request was. I am assured here that my Lord Ailesbury has played the fool and changed his Religion.

Marlborough to Godolphin

COLOGNE
April 20, 1703

* Since my arrival here yesterday I have had a good deal of spleen, for instead of finding everything ready there is none of the boats with the ammunition and cannon yet come, so that Monsr Cohorn had proposed to me to let the siege alone till the end of the year. You know in my opinion I was never fond of this siege; but it has now made so much noise that I think it would be scandalous to avoid the making it now, so that I have given the orders for the investing of it next Wednesday, in the hopes that most things will be come by that time.

I have this day seen a very great procession, and the thought how pleased poor Lord Churchill would have been with such a sight has added very much to my uneasiness. Since it has pleased God to take him, I do wish from my soul I would think less of him. The news is so ill from Germany that I am afraid we shall make a very scurvy end of this campaign, especially if we should be so unhappy as to meet with great difficulty in this siege.

It is significant that, while Marlborough opens his heart about his dead son to Godolphin, he makes no reference to his feelings in telling his wife about the same procession. Evidently he was unwilling to revive Sarah's grief. There were very few things which he overlooked in his care for her.

John to Sarah

COLOGNE
April 20, 1703

* I came to this place last Night, and find I must stay here longer than I intended; for we want so many things here, that I shall not be able to invest the place before Tuesday. This day is a very great holiday in this place. I have seen a procession, in which there was several thousands of clergymen. I have got a very good house for my quarters. I wish I could have you with me, and you could go back without trouble; for I believe 'twill be a month before the siege is done. I own to you, that upon several accounts, I have at this time the spleen. For I see plainly that I can never be happy till I am with you, and do not trouble myself with any business: For I think every ill news has so great an effect upon my temper, that, if I continue serving, I shall be very miserable. *Tho' I must own at the same time, I have all the obligations imaginable to the Dutch; for they let me command, and do more than if I was their own General.* . . .

Marlborough to Godolphin

COLOGNE
April 24

Our news from Germany continues to be very ill, which gives us very melancholy thoughts on this side. The town of Bonn should have been attacked before now, but that we have been disappointed in everything. However, all the troops will be there to-morrow. I go from hence at the same time, and shall press the siege all that in me lies, for I shall be very uneasy till I am with the great army, hoping we may have time to do what is at my heart. After which we shall be the better able to defend ourselves against the French, when they shall think fit to be strong.[1]

Marlborough to Godolphin

CAMP BEFORE BONN
April 27, 1703

* . . . As we have no cannon yet come, we are very quiet, and the French are civil, for they have not fired above five or six cannon

1 Coxe, i, 241.

as yet. We shall begin to-morrow to make our bridges over the Rhine, for the fort on the other side is what Monsr Cohorn intends to attack first. The name of Cohorn frightens all the ladies of Bonn, which has given me an occasion of obliging them; for I have refused no one a pass to go to Cologne, amongst which are all the Nuns of a Monastery. . . .

John to Sarah

CAMP BEFORE BONN
May 1, 1703

If you had not positively desired that I would always burn your letters, I should have been very glad to have kept your dear letter of the 9th, it was so very kind, and particularly so upon the subject of our living quietly together, till which happy time comes I am sure I cannot be contented; and then I do flatter myself I should live with as much satisfaction as I am capable of. I wish I could recall twenty years past, I do assure you, for no other reason but that I might in probability have longer time, and be the better able to convince you how truly sensible I am at this time of your kindness, which is the only real comfort of my life [part effaced], and whilst you are kind, besides the many blessings it brings me, I cannot but hope we shall yet have a son, which are my daily prayers.[1]

Marlborough to Godolphin

CAMP BEFORE BONN
May 4, 1703

* Notwithstanding we have not all our boats with the Artillery, I have prevailed with Monsr Cohorn to open the trenches last night, which we have done with very little loss. We hope that all may be here by the time the Batteries will be ready, which will be by Tuesday next. In 12 days after our cannon fires we hope to be masters of this place, after which I shall lose no time in going to the Army on the Meuse. . . .

The siege of Bonn while the armies were still assembling was a serious undertaking. The obvious counterstroke for the French was Liége. Overkirk with the partially formed main army guarded against this danger, but was himself largely outnumbered meanwhile. Bonn was resolutely defended, and the garrison even sallied out upon their assailants.

1 Coxe, i, 227–228.

But Marlborough, commanding in person on the spot, used all his power. The Dutch and Germans who composed his army were stout troops, and the artillery was overwhelming. Never before had been seen such a concentration of cannon and munitions as shattered the defences and, indeed, the town of Bonn. Ninety large mortars, many of them six and eight inches in bore, with as much as thirty rounds a day each, five hundred smaller mortars, and over five hundred guns bombarded the doomed fortress. Its outlying works were broken and stormed in fierce fighting, and when the ramparts of the citadel were no more than one great breach the governor averted the final assault by an appeal for terms.

Meanwhile the two French Marshals, Villeroy and Boufflers, had, as expected, been instructed by the King to recapture Liége as a relief, or at the worst an offset, to the siege of Bonn. They too had made large preparations before the campaign opened, and fifteen thousand workmen and three thousand pioneers, together with the necessary stores, were already gathered behind the main French army around Saint-Trond. They had hoped, indeed, to begin the military year by this attack upon Liége. But Marlborough had provided for its solid defence. They now saw in Overkirk's army which lay between Maestricht and Liége an even more tempting prize. Villeroy had in his hand forty thousand men. Overkirk for some time had but fifteen thousand. Probably because of the stringency of supplies, Marlborough had left the English in their cantonments till April 30. He realized the French menace in sufficient time, and ten thousand English, well drilled and in the finest fettle, reached Overkirk on May 9, just before they were needed. On the same day Villeroy marched upon him, and his vanguard attacked Tongres, an entrenched post held by a Dutch and a Scottish battalion in Dutch pay. This handful of allied troops resisted for twenty-four hours the onslaught of the French army. They were not only brave, but lucky. Though forced to surrender at discretion, they fell into the hands of Berwick, by whom they were kindly treated. He hastened to assure the Scots that they were his countrymen and that "no man shall do you

MARSHAL VILLEROY
From an engraving after the painting by Hyacinthe Rigaud
British Museum

wrong." The delay gave time for Overkirk to arm and entrench a strong position under the walls of Maestricht and for Marlborough on the 12th to send a further reinforcement. On the 14th the whole French army drew up in order of battle: but after inspecting the defences and bethinking themselves of their general strategic instructions from Versailles the two Marshals decided not to try conclusions, and withdrew, somewhat abashed, towards their own lines.

Marlborough had measured carefully, and, as was proved, justly, all the factors; but we should not underrate his anxieties sixty miles away at Bonn. The fortress was at its last gasp, but meanwhile a disaster at Maestricht would be ruinous. The crisis at Maestricht arose on the 13th. It was not till the 15th that Bonn surrendered. He certainly passed an unpleasant forty-eight hours. This was the kind of situation he had to gauge many times over in his campaigns, and it is astonishing how almost invariably his summing-up of facts, times, and risks was right.

His reflections upon politics at home were set forth in a striking letter written to Sarah while the siege cannon thundered.

CAMP BEFORE BONN
May 13, 1703

* My head did ache so extremely the last post that I was hardly able to write, but I thank God it is now very well. I am very sorry to see by all your letters that the factions continue so extremely angry. As for myself I do assure you, I shall meddle with neither party, having no private ends of my own, but whilst I am in the world endeavour to serve her Majesty the best I can. I know by this method whichever party is uppermost will be angry with me, so that at last the Queen will be obliged by them to let me retire. If she be satisfied with the sincerity of my intentions for her service, I shall then be most happy, for I do flatter myself that I shall behave myself so here that this part of the world will be convinced that I think of nothing but what may be most for the Queen's service, and the good of the Common Cause. If you approve of what I now say, which I promise you I can never be brought to alter from, I should then beg you would endeavour to bring yourself to the same temper; for, my dearest soul, when we come to live together my happiness will depend upon our having but one thought in order to which we must renounce all parties and content ourselves in praying for the Queen's long life, and that France may never have it in their power to impose laws upon England. You will be apt to think by this letter I have the spleen. I do assure you that I am far from it, but it proceeds from the unreasonable partiality I see in both Parties.

John to Sarah

Camp before Bonn
May 16

* . . . I have been so often disturbed this night with messages out of town, they having begun to capitulate, that I am very uneasy, the post being ready to go. I am afraid we shall not agree on the capitulation; for they ask much more than we are willing to give; but our affairs go so ill upon the Meuse that we shall lose Liége if this business be not quickly ended. I will keep this open till the last minute to give you a further account.

[Later.] The Governors of the Town have at last agreed to what I have offered. And in one hour I shall be in possession of one of the gates. They are to march out on Friday, but I shall not stay to see them, being resolved to be with the army on the Meuse on Friday from whence you shall be sure to hear from him who loves you with all his soul. My humble duty to the Queen.

He adds, with a characteristic touch of that vile parsimony in small matters which has made him the butt of history:

I hope she will excuse my not putting her to the expense of an express to bring the news of Bonn being taken.

This piece of shabbiness has hitherto escaped attention: but we feel bound to bring it to light. The man must be judged as a whole. Here is a general in the full activity of war, in close contact with the enemy, with difficult allies around him and grave situations to face, who can stoop to save a paltry twenty pounds of public money in the announcing of his own success. It is probable that in Marlborough's armies this kind of thing went on all the time;

216

and it is only now and then that it can be exposed. This ill-assorted combination of the daring commander ready to put all to the push and a cheese-paring Treasury clerk is one of the burdens his defenders have to carry.

Family affairs played a large part in Marlborough's letters from the front, and we must here mention the marriages of his younger children, in which he took so great an interest. His third daughter, Elizabeth, had married early in 1703 the Earl of Bridgewater. His youngest daughter, Mary, had now reached her sixteenth year. She is described by the Archdeacon in the flowery terms usually applied in those days to young ladies of quality. She was, we learn, "exquisitely beautiful, lovely in temper and no less amiable in mind than elegant in person." She was a star to the brave in the Army. Peterborough wished her to marry his son, Lord Mordaunt, whom we shall admire later. Lord Tullibardine also pressed his claims. The reader will remember the gallant Earl of Huntingdon, who while still recovering from his wounds at Kaiserswerth bribed the soldiers to carry him forward at the head of the assault upon Venloo.[1] His letter to the Duke asking for Mary's hand is a fine specimen of eighteenth-century courtship and a worthy tribute coming from so heroic an officer:

> * In a point on which all the future happiness of my life depends, I thought my concern would be so great, that I should not be able to express myself to your grace by word of mouth. That consideration obliges me to put this paper My Lord into your hands and your thoughts on the perusal of it must determine whether I shall be happy or miserable. My hand trembles at what I am to write, lest my boldness offend those for whom I have the greatest veneration and respect.
>
> I saw yesterday at Court my lady Mary Churchill. I had often heard of her charms but never before thought so many perfections could have enriched one person. From the moment I saw her, I felt what my respect forbids me to mention, and what I cannot describe.

1 See p. 147 n.

I have since taken the resolution to acquaint your Grace with it, to throw myself at your feet and to beg I may have leave to adore her and endeavour to do what man can do to merit such a treasure.

Fortune shone on none of these extremely eligible young men. Marlborough was determined not to unite his family with that of Peterborough. He wrote from Vorselaer (July 8, 1703):

> *What you write me concerning 102 [Peterborough]'s son, I think you have done very well in disengaging yourself from that proposal for I have heard that he is what they call a Raskell, which never can make a good husband.

About Huntingdon we have only a laconic sentence in one of the Duke's letters, written very late in the campaign of 1704: "Lord Huntingdon is now with me; he is grown very like his father and mother, which is the worst thing I can say about him."

The choice of John and Sarah inclined from the beginning to Viscount Monthermer, son of the Earl of Montagu, and apparently Mary's views were not discordant. The Duke, however, thought his would-be son-in-law far too young even in those days of early matches to be engaged. In his letter to Sarah from the siege of Bonn he set forth his objections.

May 16

> *You desire to know what I would have you answer to 139 [the Earl of Montagu]. You know my mind in that matter, but whatever you do in it, I shall like it; but I am very confident whenever you shall see the young man and Miss Mary together, you will think she is too much a woman for him. However you cannot do better than to advise with the Lord Treasurer what is best to be done, for the proposal is very good if the young man were some years older.

And again:

John to Sarah

HANNEF
June 25, 1703

> *I am very glad you are parted so well with 139 for a great many things happen in a year's time, which may make this match more or less reasonable. I can give you no other reason

Lady Mary Church
ill 4th Daughter to
John Duke of Marl
borough Wife to
John Duke of Mont.
agu.

THE DUCHESS OF MONTAGU

By permission of the Duke of Marlborough

than what I have already against it. However, I find something within me against the match; for should Miss Mary not esteem the young man, it is neither title nor estate that can make her happy; but of this whenever I have the happiness of being with you, we shall have time to talk of it. She being the only child we have to provide for, I should hope with the blessing of God, we ought not to despair of making her happy.

The marriage did not take place until March 1705, and in the following month a dukedom was conferred upon the Earl of Montagu. As in her sister's case, Queen Anne bestowed ten thousand pounds upon the bride.

But John had a personal hope which filled his inner mind. Both he and Sarah longed for another son.

John to Sarah

Friday, June 3

What troubles me in all this time is your telling me that you do not look well. Pray let me have, in every one of your letters, an account how you do. If it should prove such a sickness as that, I might pity you, but not be sorry for it; it might yet make me have ambition. But if your sickness should really be for want of health, it would render me the unhappiest man living.[1]

I have just received your letters of the 6th. What you say to me of yourself gave me so much joy, that if any company had been by, when I read your letter, they must have observed a great alteration in me.[2]

John to Sarah

THYS
June 7

I have had yours of the 18th, by which I find you were uneasy at my having the headache. It was your earnest desire obliged me to let you know when I have those little inconveniences of the headache, which are but too natural to me; but if you will not promise me to look upon my sicknesses as you used to do, by knowing I am sick one day, and well another, I must not be

[1] Coxe, i, 228.   [2] Ibid.

219

punctual in acquainting you when I am uneasy; for I would be just to you, and not make you uneasy. I think you are very happy in having dear lady Mary with you. I should esteem myself so, if she could be sometimes for an hour with me; for the greatest ease I now have, is sometimes sitting for an hour in my chair alone, and thinking of the happiness I may yet have, of living quietly with you, which is the greatest I propose to myself in this world.[1]

Marlborough returned to the Meuse not only with relief at the ending of a crisis, but full of ardour to begin the campaign as he had always wished. With the fall of Bonn and the retreat of the Marshals wide prospects opened, and he unfolded to his generals and to the Dutch Government what he called "the Great Design." The phrase is his own; it recurs in his letters. Such a phrase is unusual in his matter-of-fact style. One of the barriers between history and Marlborough is his self-restraint. We have none of the splendid invocations with which Napoleon led his armies and excited the French nation. There is an endless flow of hard sense. At the worst he is "uneasy," or will "pass his time ill." At the best he will make the enemy "uneasy," or "do some service for the Queen," if only they will "venture." And even these careful under-statements were confided only to a select audience in a secrecy which, so far as he knew, would never be broken, and was never broken in his lifetime. But now and here we have "the Great Design."

Marlborough to Godolphin

MAESTRICHT
May 19

I shall to-morrow send an express to The Hague to see how far they have prepared for what I call the great design; so that we may not lose time in endeavouring to put it in execution. Before I left Bonn, measures were taken for the embarking 20 battalions of foot, if it be possible to get boats enough, and 21 squadrons of horse are to march the nearest way to Bergen-op-Zoom, where they are to join the 20 battalions that go by water. These troops are to take the most advantageous post

---

[1] Coxe, i, 228–229.

near Antwerp, after which there will be care taken to join more troops to them. If this design of Antwerp can be brought to perfection, I hope we shall make it very uneasy for them to protect Brussels and the rest of their great towns. I am speaking as if we were masters of Antwerp, *but as yet the two marshals threaten.*[1]

Since this was one of his most cherished and most complicated schemes, and since it miscarried, it is worth some attention. The field armies were almost exactly equal in units, but the allied units were the stronger. The Sea Powers had a superiority of perhaps 73,000 to 67,000 men. But these numbers are uncertain because behind each of the armies were the garrisons. The French, for instance, had no fewer than 63 battalions spread in their fortresses, and the allies a much smaller number. It depended upon the tactics employed to what extent these garrison reserves could be used. The Dutch were eager to undertake another siege, and Marlborough as usual wished to fight a battle. Although this looked more hazardous, it offered really a larger safety. A siege lasted for weeks and a battle only for a few hours. The margin of allied superiority was scarcely sufficient to undertake a siege, because the moment they had divided their armies for that purpose the French could draw freely from all their garrisons. On the other hand, if the initiative were retained and a number of French fortresses simultaneously threatened by an aggressive field army it would be the French who would have to disperse, and Marlborough could strike at their remaining army. Thus a siege was in fact to risk both the initiative and the superiority.

Forced by the Dutch to adopt the least favourable measure, Marlborough had devised a plan which cast siege warfare in an offensive form. To this end he used the waterways at the delta of the Scheldt to move troops and stores quickly and secretly to the northern front while still keeping his main army in the south. The transportation of 20 battalions from Bonn, on the Rhine, to the neighbourhood of Bergen-op-Zoom, near the coast, was favoured by the current of the rivers,

1 Coxe, i, 245.

which carried the troop-barges forward night and day far quicker than men on the march; while the necessary cavalry rode swiftly across country. Thus the first phase of the operation was the unexpectedly rapid concentration in the north, while all the time the main armies faced each other at the other end of the theatre. All this was easily accomplished.

The second phase was to force the dispersion of the French troops in the north. For this Cohorn, assisted by the fleet, was to attack and lay siege to Ostend. Ostend is sixty miles from Antwerp. Bedmar, the Spanish-French commander in Antwerp, would thus be compelled either to divide his forces out of all supporting distance or to lose the highly valued seaport. Marlborough foresaw that nothing less than the fear of losing Ostend would tear him asunder.

The third phase depended upon the timing and upon the strict obedience of the secondary commanders. On zero day Marlborough would move first towards the French main army to pin it and then north-west towards Antwerp. Two days later Cohorn would attack Ostend, and Spaar west of Antwerp. This should produce the division of Bedmar's forces, while Marlborough held the two Marshals so closely that no help could be sent him. On the sixth day Opdam would advance against Antwerp from the north-east. Spaar would attack from the west, and Marlborough would be close at hand near Lierre with the main body. If Bedmar did not divide his forces Ostend would fall, an important prize would be gained, and further combinations would become possible. If, on the other hand, Bedmar defended Ostend, Opdam and Spaar would have a good superiority against him at Antwerp, and no help could come to him from the main army facing Marlborough. The French could choose between losing Ostend or Antwerp or both, or as an alternative weakening their main army, which Marlborough could then attack.

But Marlborough would have required the authority of Napoleon to compel this accurate execution of his intricate plan. Actually the Dutch commanders were not at all interested in Ostend. They were not attracted by opening

222

any new line of communication from the sea to the English forces. They preferred English drafts and stores to pass through Holland. Cohorn used his influence at The Hague to substitute for the siege of Ostend a pillaging excursion into the Pays de Waes (the region between Antwerp and Ostend), from which his office entitled him to receive 10 per cent. of any contributions exacted. Now, this diversion was

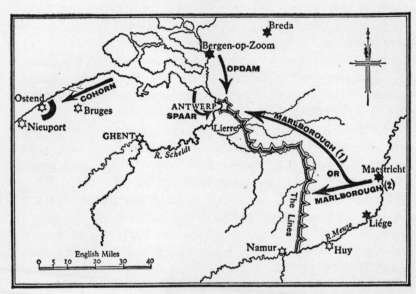

"THE GREAT DESIGN"

not sufficiently remote from Antwerp to make Bedmar divide his forces beyond the power of swift recovery; and consequently Marlborough's combination would not become operative.

While the forces were taking their new positions in the north, and while Cohorn was busy at The Hague, Marlborough sought to draw Marshal Villeroy southward farther away from Antwerp, hoping that by manœuvres he could place himself nearer Antwerp than the French main army. For this purpose he pretended with many elaborate refinements a siege of Huy. But the French had the advantage of their lines, behind which they could move in safety and

223

along which they had stores of food and forage. Moreover, as the map will show, these lines, following the course of the Demer, bulged out convexly. Thus Marlborough must traverse the arc while Villeroy could follow the chord. Marlborough therefore required a considerable start to win a 'race to Antwerp.'

By the end of May Villeroy was lured down towards Huy,

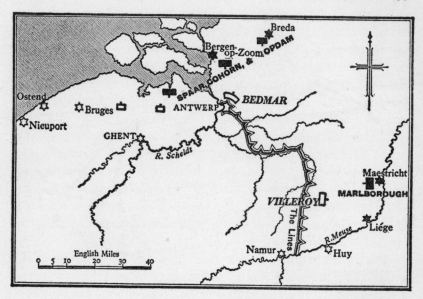

THE JUNE SITUATION

and almost as far from Antwerp as was Marlborough, and the Dutch army which was to begin the operations was gathered to the north of Antwerp and along the seaboard. But already at his camp at Thys Marlborough received the disconcerting news that Cohorn had obtained permission to substitute for the siege of Ostend the raid into the Pays de Waes. The Duke saw at once that this change of plan would spoil his combination: and that his elaborate attempt to make siege and manœuvre warfare serve the purpose of battle, or bring about a battle which neither French nor Dutch could avoid, would not succeed. From Thys he wrote to Godolphin on May 31:

224

I am afraid the diversion M. Cohorn is gone to make in Flanders, will not oblige them to make any great detachment; for his design is not on Ostend, as I desired . . . It is no wonder that Cohorn is for forcing the lines; for as he is governor of West Flanders, he has the tenths of all the contributions.[1]

Both the main armies lay very close to one another, and the French had the remarkable spectacle of Marlborough remaining, with a slightly superior force, for eighteen days of the campaigning season motionless, inert, seemingly unwilling to fight or unable to manœuvre. The Marshals waited likewise in perplexity. We now know the reason. All this time Marlborough was beseeching Heinsius and the States-General either to allow him to deliver a battle or to make Cohorn attack Ostend.

"I am now by my temper so inclined to quietness," he wrote to Godolphin (June 25), "that you will believe me when *I assure you, that no ambition of my own inclines me to wish a battle, but with the blessing of God, I think it would be of far greater advantage to the common cause, than the taking of twenty towns, so that as far as I can influence, I shall be far from avoiding it.*"[2]

Almost the whole of June thus passed in a tense immobility, the two principal armies facing each other at a few miles distance, or sidling this way or that in constant readiness for battle. But now the Dutch began to carry out as a disconnected operation and in the wrong way the northern part of Marlborough's design. On June 26 the attack from the seaboard began. For some days their movements had puzzled Bedmar. He felt himself about to be assailed, but at which point on his lightly guarded sixty-mile front from Antwerp to Ostend he could not tell. On the 27th Cohorn and Spaar fell from opposite directions upon the north-western salient of his lines and pierced them, Cohorn with scarcely any loss, Spaar after hard fighting. The Pays de Waes thus lay open to Dutch incursion, pillage, and contribution. The unwisdom of the Dutch action now became plain. The mere raiding of the countryside and the levying of a contribution, though

[1] Coxe, i, 246.　　　　[2] *Ibid.,* 250.

pleasing to Cohorn and his troops and vexatious to the enemy, failed to make Bedmar change his general conceptions. He remained rightly concentrated in Antwerp. Cohorn's action was only a flourish, and a feint which did not deceive.

There was a second more disastrous error. Opdam, who was to attack Antwerp from the direction of Bergen-op-Zoom, should never have moved until the Cohorn-Spaar operations had had time to draw some reinforcements from Bedmar, nor above all until Marlborough and the main army had come near enough to support him. Nevertheless, the next day, June 28, Opdam, with 13 battalions and 26 squadrons, advanced in this faulty combination to Eckeren, four miles from Antwerp. Here he was in great danger. The three Dutch forces were widely separated from one another, and the French and Spaniards were concentrated in superior strength in the city close to Opdam. His subordinates, Slangenberg at their head, pointed out to him that he might be attacked by the enemy with fifty battalions, or at least three times his numbers. They prevailed on him to send his baggage to the rear. But for the rest he stood his ground, seemingly unconscious of his peril.

No positive information of their offensive had been sent by any of the Dutch generals to Marlborough, still sixty miles away at Thys. But evidently he had news of their movement; for on the 27th he suddenly broke his camp before daybreak and marched in the direction of Antwerp. Villeroy within a few hours was keeping pace with him within his lines along the road Landen-Diest. There could be no doubt that Villeroy could reach Antwerp before Marlborough. But if Opdam took care of himself the allied armies could still concentrate before Antwerp for battle with somewhat superior forces. However, on the 29th Villeroy learned of the Dutch incursion into the Pays de Waes, and also of the arrival of Opdam at Eckeren. He perceived at once that Opdam could be destroyed. On the night of the 29th he sent Marshal Boufflers, with 30 squadrons of cavalry and three thousand Grenadiers, helping themselves forward by holding on to the horsemen's stirrup-leathers, to join Bedmar, with orders

226

to pass through the city of Antwerp and fall upon this exposed Dutch force. Villeroy, weakened by sending this detachment, marched the next day in anxiety lest Marlborough should attack him. But Marlborough did not know what he had done, and in any case was forbidden to seek a battle without specific authority from The Hague. During the 30th both armies were marching on parallel lines towards Antwerp through ceaseless rain and terrible mud. The French had every advantage of the short-cut and the stores of forage behind their lines. Marlborough, without knowing all the

facts, was already deeply alarmed about Opdam. On the 29th he had sent him a most urgent warning of his danger and advised his immediate retirement towards Bergen-op-Zoom. But before this message could reach Opdam the blow had fallen.

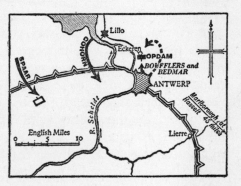

ECKEREN

Early on the morning of July 1 Boufflers, reinforcing Bedmar with his cavalry and Grenadiers, who had marched nearly forty miles in twenty-four hours, debouched from Antwerp in four columns, and fell upon Opdam. Boufflers had nearly forty thousand men against ten thousand. Luckily for the allies, this large force did not immediately strike its quarry. Berwick says they had "to beat about the country for several hours as hunters would seek a boar." It was not till the evening that the surprise became effective. Opdam found himself enveloped by swiftly approaching superior forces. His line of retreat lay along a causeway to Lillo; but the French cavalry and dragoons, sweeping round his left, cut across the causeway, and had they promptly dug themselves in upon it would have caught everybody. Fierce fighting began. The French troops, strained to the utmost by their march, were met by the stubborn Dutch foot, and

227

several brigades were not only repulsed, but fled in panic back into Antwerp. The ground was divided by dykes and watercourses, and a soldiers' battle began.

Opdam had a humiliating personal experience. With a few officers and horsemen he got separated from his troops, and, believing all was lost, galloped off to Breda. From here he sent two letters, one to Marlborough and one to the States-General, reporting that his army was destroyed. The messenger to Marlborough was captured by the French. The other letter reached The Hague after nightfall. The Council of State met together at Heinsius' house in consternation. Their action was worthy of their greatest national qualities. They at once sent Deputies to organize a front before Bergen-op-Zoom. At the same time they resolved to fill the gap in their forces which the destruction of Opdam's corps seemed to cause by hiring further contingents from Germany. Trusted emissaries took the roads to Münster and Berlin forthwith upon this quest. But meanwhile the Deputies who were on their way to the army met other tidings.

When darkness had fallen on July 1 the fighting was at its height. It continued in much confusion throughout the night. Opdam had disappeared, but on the bloodstained dyke stood Jacob Hop, Treasurer of the Republic. Strengthened by his authority and determination, General Slangenberg took command. Under his orders the Dutch, tough and desperate, beat off the superior numbers of the assailants, stormed and overwhelmed the French cavalry who lay across their line of retreat along the causeway, and when morning dawned were marching in stubborn array towards safety and Lillo. The hand-to-hand fighting in the afternoon and night had been so violent and disordered, and the Dutch at bay had shown such discipline and fury, that Antwerp was full of fugitives, and the French thought at first they had lost not only their prey, but the battle. It was not until daybreak that they realized they at least possessed the field. They hastened to proclaim their victory, set themselves in imposing array, and advanced with drum and trumpet.

They had indeed, if they had known it, finally ruptured "The Great Design." But Slangenberg, with the bulk of the Dutch troops, was beyond their reach.

This was the joyful news which met the Deputies as they hurried towards Bergen-op-Zoom, and they returned at once to report to the States-General that, although Opdam had run away and reported his army lost, Slangenberg had not despaired of the Republic and had cut his way out with heavy losses but in good order. Actually each side had lost about two thousand men killed and wounded, and the French had captured six cannon, nine hundred prisoners, and the Countess of Tilly, who was visiting her husband in male attire. (Berwick says "disguised as an Amazon.") The French boastings of victory and of their trophies did not mar the thankfulness of the Dutch at so narrow an escape.

We must now remind the reader of General Slangenberg. We met him last ten years ago at Walcourt when he and Marlborough from the two opposite flanks had fallen upon Marshal d'Humières's imprudently exposed army. Slangenberg's career had not been cheered by success. He had fought his way through William's wars, but his rancorous temper and vicious tongue had marred his fortunes, and he was still only a subordinate. Now in the hour of disaster he had emerged, a stern, embittered man, as the saviour of his country's honour. He was acclaimed with the wildest enthusiasm by both the oligarchy and the mob. His dispatches from the battlefield were modest, but upon this wave of national applause and in his just sense of his own deserts, the hatreds and jealousies which had long festered in his breast burst forth from him in a passion. All the reputation he had gained in that grim night he used to assail not only the conduct but the loyalty of the English Commander-in-Chief. He declared that Marlborough out of spite had left Opdam exposed and unsupported; that when Opdam's jeopardy was apparent he had neither sent him reinforcements (which was physically impossible) nor attacked Villeroy's army (which he was forbidden to do). Opdam, though his personal position was weak, seemed also inclined to associate himself with Slangenberg's charges. We can imagine the unpleasant character of these reproaches from such a man at such a time. But Marlborough's authority in Holland was deeply founded. His friendship with Heinsius, his hold upon the confidence of the Dutch, his position as the Queen of England's Captain-General, were immediately found to be unshakable. There was a storm of criticism. The Dutch pamphlets during this summer are full of bitter references to the "foreign Commander-in-Chief" and his "unheard-of" maxims of war.

But all this abuse recoiled as a wave from the rock. It was Slangenberg who suffered. In Lediard's words, "he lost by his tongue what he had gained by his sword." The incident is interesting to us as a measure of the strength which Marlborough had acquired. That strength could not procure him an effectual command of the confederate army, but it was entirely unaffected by this sensational attack. There is no trace of his offering any explanation or excuse. His letters during the race to Antwerp narrate the event in his usual unmoved, matter-of-fact style, and from them we may now read in his own words, written day by day, the story of this fierce minor drama of the war.

John to Sarah

Sunday, July 1

I have been in so perpetual a hurry, having marched five days together, and sometimes not coming into the camp till eleven or twelve at night, that I have not been able to answer so particularly your two last letters, as I shall always be desirous of doing. We have been obliged for many reasons to rest this day. However, it gives me very little rest, being obliged to have the general officers with me for regulating the next three days' march, so that I am obliged to take this time of writing, although I have several officers in my room talking about me; but as I love you above my life, so my greatest pleasure is writing to you, or hearing from you.[1]

Marlborough to Godolphin

July 2, 1703

. . . I am afraid the lucre of having a little contribution from the Pais de Waes, has spoiled the whole design. . . .

[1] Coxe, i, 253.

230

If M. Opdam be not upon his guard, he may be beat before we can help him, which will always be the consequence when troops are divided, so as that the enemy can post themselves between them. But we have given him such timely notice, that if he has not taken a safe camp, he will be very much to blame. . . .

Since I sealed my letter, we have a report come from Breda, that Opdam is beaten. I pray God it be not so, for *he is very capable of having it happen to him.*[1]

Marlborough to Godolphin

THIELEN
July 5, 1703

* As I was sealing my last letter to you, we were alarmed from Breda that Monsr Opdam was beaten. The news coming from himself we did not doubt it. His letter that he wrote to me was taken by a French party, so that I do not doubt but they will print it. He wrote the same account to the States that the whole army was lost, which put them under great apprehension. They met at twelve o'clock that night, and sent immediately three of their body to Berg-op-Zoom, to take care of that Frontier, and sent us a copy of what they had done. But they were not long under these apprehensions, having received a true account of the action from *Mons. Hop who had the honour of seeing more of it than the General that should have commanded.* He [Opdam] is gone back from Breda to the army. It is certain the troops did all as well as men could do, and certainly had the advantage over the French. However they will pretend, and make the World believe they had the best of it, and prove it by Opdam's letters. The enclosed is the copy of my letter to the Pensioner yesterday by which you will see my thoughts as to what I think we ought to do for the good of the Common Cause. The consideration of that makes me give my opinion so freely. I am very sensible that were I more cautious I should be less liable of being found fault with, but as long as I think I am in the right I shall venture for the good of the whole.

The French Army, and all their cannon fired three rounds yesterday in the evening. I suppose it was for the success the Elector of Bavaria has in the Tyrol; for he meets with no opposition. This will give the Emperor great trouble, as to the Communication with his troops in Italy. If the Dutch will

1 Coxe, i, 254, 255.

not venture some thing at this time, I am afraid all Germany will have but too much reason to be angry with us.

. . . It is not to be imagin'd what our poor Foot has suffered in their last marches by the excessive rains we have had. My service pray to all with you.

In his letter to Heinsius he said:

THIELEN
July 3

. . . If you have a mind to have Antwerp, and a speedy end of the war, you must venture something for it. I have not consulted the generals, so that you must consider this as my single opinion; but if this should be approved by others, and be thought fit to be put in execution, you must then act as the French do, by drawing out of your garrisons all the battalions that are possible; *for those that can make the greatest fire will carry this matter.* And I think all officers will agree with me, that if they opiniatre the defence of the lines between Antwerp and Lierre, and we should force them, they having a river behind them, it will be next to impossible for them to get off. On the other side, if they should take the resolution not to defend the lines, then the siege may be made with all the ease imaginable. Upon the whole matter, I take the good or bad success of this campaign depends upon the resolution that shall now be taken.

. . . I am confident if you miss this occasion, you will repent it when it is too late.[1]

This melancholy miscarriage reveals Marlborough's qualities as a general as well as any of his victories. His letters show his sure-footed comprehension and measurement of all the factors and forces at work. He foresaw the uselessness of Cohorn's raid. He knew at a distance, with almost uncanny prescience and far better than Opdam on the spot, the danger in which that strange military personage stood. He received the news of the downfall of his own plans without discouragement, and instantly formed others to restore the position. All the time while bearing the brunt of responsibility, and vexed by every kind of senseless obstruction, his vigilant, tireless mind has plenty of room for family affairs and for

1 Coxe, i, 258–259.

love-letters to Sarah. Afflicted by the most trying provocations, hampered and blamed, the sport of jealous and foolish rivals, the first army of France on his hands, battle possible any day at a few hours' notice, he only shows the more plainly his massive superiority alike over events and men, and over friend and foe.

CHAPTER XI

"VICTORIOUS WITHOUT SLAUGHTER"

(1703, Autumn)

THERE was such good Parliamentary support in England for a campaign designed to capture Ostend and Antwerp that Marlborough, despite Slangenberg's virulence and the perturbation in Holland, was able to press hard for the second attempt. Marlborough's letter to Heinsius of July 3 had put the question of a main trial of strength in its most direct form. A council of war of all the Dutch commanders was ordered by the States-General to meet at Bergen-op-Zoom. Marlborough did not at first attend; and at this moment the feeling among the Dutch generals was hot against him. His proposal to force and attack the lines between Antwerp and Lierre was rejected. He refused to accept the first rejection. He repaired in person to the council. Again and again he reiterated his request. At last he actually wrung an assent, in form at least, from this unfavourable tribunal. It was at length resolved to "come to an engagement." The decision of the experts at Bergen-op-Zoom was thereupon remitted to the statesmen at The Hague.

Marlborough did not delude himself. He was gloomily certain that Villeroy would retire behind his fortifications as soon as the whole allied army advanced upon him, and that the Dutch would refuse to attack him there. The event warranted these misgivings. Before daylight on July 23 Slangenberg marched from Lillo to join Marlborough, and the whole army of the Sea Powers advanced upon the French camp. "I take it for granted," wrote Marlborough to Godolphin the night before, "that as soon as they know of our march they will retire behind their lines . . . I think it is one thousand to one they do not stay, for they can be behind their lines in one hour's march."

As soon as the heads of the allied columns were discerned

234

Villeroy burned his camp and stores and swiftly retired within the fortifications of Antwerp and the Lines. Further councils of war ensued. After hours of fruitless discussion Marlborough could only end the conclave by asking all the members to express their views in writing. "I see enough, I think, to be sure the Lines will not be attacked and that we shall return to the Meuse. I intend to go out to-morrow morning with a body of horse in hope to get near enough to view the lines."

The reconnaissance confirmed the Dutch generals in their opinion. What they saw of the strength of the works produced the worst impression upon them. Marlborough was still earnest for a general assault, and we do not know how he proposed to deliver it. But all the others resisted obdurately. Whether he or they were right was not proved. It would certainly have been a frontal attack upon a fortified position defended by an army four-fifths as strong as his own. It was then agreed to abandon the attempt upon Antwerp, and nothing remained but to return to the Meuse and lay siege to the minor fortress of Huy as a consolation.

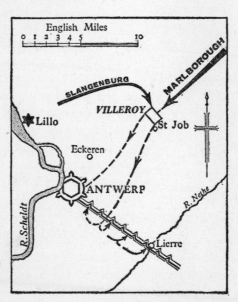

VILLEROY'S WITHDRAWAL

To Godolphin, who voiced the English disappointment at the relinquishing of the Antwerp plan, Marlborough wrote:

HOUTHALEN
August 6, 1703

I am but too much of your mind, that the going back to the Meuse is, as the French expression is, a pis aller. But as Cohorn has managed his business for these last six weeks, we had nothing

235

else to do. I know that Huy will make very little noise in the world. However, if we will [must] make the war in this country, it is very convenient for us to have that place. Our superiority is not so great, but that the French may reasonably expect to make us uneasy, when we shall be obliged to divide our forces, as we must do when we make the siege. If they give occasion, I hope we shall venture, by which God may give us more success *in three or four hours' time,* than we dare promise ourselves.[1]

On August 2 the allies, leaving Cohorn, who had quarrelled with Slangenberg, sulking on the seaboard, marched back southward. Villeroy kept pace with them inside his lines. On the 14th they arrived at Turinne. A corps under the Prince of Anhalt invested and began the siege of Huy, while Marlborough moved to Val Notre-Dame to cover the operation. The town and fortress of Huy lies on the Meuse amid picturesque wooded hills and steep bluffs rising from the river midway between Liége and Namur. It was still a point of strategic importance in the opening phase of the Great War. The investment was completed on August 15.

Amid these vexations Marlborough was keenly occupied with his family.

John to Sarah

THIELEN
August 4

* Upon your saying something to me in one of your letters of the company 53 [Lady Harriet] keeps, I wrote to her myself, not taking any notice of [mentioning] what you had said, that she could never find any lasting happiness in this world, but from the kindness of 27 [Mr Godolphin[2]], so that she ought to omit nothing that might oblige him. You must not ask her for this letter; but I should be glad to know if it has had any effect, for I love her, and think her very good, so that I should hope if she commits indiscretions, it is for want of thinking. I know you are so good and kind to them all, that I need not desire you to persist in letting her see her ruin, if she should govern herself any other way than you would have her. I know she loves and esteems you so that you may with kindness do much with her.

1 Coxe, i, 264.   2 Her husband, Francis Godolphin, afterwards the second Earl.

Many things may happen that the world may think will vex me, but nothing can go very near my heart but what concerns your dear self, and our children, and the Queen's welfare.[1]

By this time a dearer hope than "the great design" had died, and Sarah's health seemed seriously affected. She mourned both for her son, and that she could never bear another. We do not know what she wrote to her husband; but he made a great reply.

John to Sarah

OP-HEEREN
August 13

I have received yours of the 23rd, which has given me, as you may easily believe, a good deal of trouble. I beg you will be so kind and just to me, as to believe the truth of my heart, that my greatest concern is for that of your own dear health. It was a great pleasure to me when I thought that we should be blessed with more children; but as all my happiness centres in living quietly with you, I do conjure you, by all the kindness I have for you, which is as much as ever man had for woman, that you will take the best advice you can for your health, and then follow exactly what shall be prescribed for you, and I do hope you will be so good as to let me have an exact account of it, and what the physicians' opinions are. If I were with you I would endeavour to persuade you to think as little as is possible of worldly business, and to be very regular in your diet, which I should hope would set you right in a very little time, for you have naturally a very good constitution.

You and I have great reason to bless God for all we have, so that we must not repine at his taking our poor child from us, but bless and praise him for what his goodness leaves us; and I do beseech Him, with all my heart and soul, that he would comfort and strengthen both you and me, not only to bear this, but any other correction that He shall think fit to lay on us. The use I think we should make of this His correction is, that our chiefest time should be spent in reconciling ourselves to him, and having in our minds always that we may not have long to live in this world. I do not mean by this that we should live retired from the world; for I am persuaded that, by living in the world, one may do much more good than by being out

1 Extract,

of it, but at the same time to live so as that one should cheerfully die when it shall be his pleasure to call for us. I am very sensible of my own frailties; but if I can be ever so happy as to be always with you, and that you comfort and assist me in these my thoughts, I am then persuaded I should be as happy and contented as it is possible to be in this world; for I know we shall both agree, next to our duty to God, to do what we ought for the Queen's service.[1]

John to Sarah

VAL NOTRE-DAME
Aug. 16

I am so very uneasy since I received yours of the 23rd of the last month, that I shall have no rest till I hear again from you, for your health is much dearer to me than my own. It is impossible for me to express what I feel, having seen by my Lord Treasurer of the same post, that he thought you very far from being well. For God's sake let me know exactly how you are; and if you think my being with you can do you any good, you shall quickly see you are much dearer to me than fame, or whatever the world can say; for, should you do otherwise than well, I were the unhappiest man living. We invested Huy yesterday, and I am afraid it will be a fortnight before we shall be masters of the castle. I pray God your next may put me more at ease than I am at this present.[2]

Marlborough to Godolphin

VAL NOTRE-DAME
August 16th, 1703

* Since my last I have had none of yours, and the wind being in the east I am afraid I shall not have any for some time, which makes me very uneasy, for your last has given me great unquietness as to my Lady Marl. ['s] health. For God's sake let me have a particular account; and if she does not go to the Bath with the Queen, I hope her Majesty and yourself will prevail with her, to enter into such a course of physic as she shall be advised to, or that the Queen will take her to the Bath with her: for I am very sure to leave her alone will not be good for her health. I am sure too [if it would] do her any good, with the Queen's leave, I would immediately come over, notwithstanding that I am very sensible how the world would censure me; but I hope she will be governed by the Queen and you, so as that I may

1 Coxe, i, 229–231.   2 *Ibid.*, i, 229.

make an end of this campaign with some quiet of mind, which
I can't do if I do not hear that she is in a good way; for I have
no ambition or other thought left, but of serving the Queen to
the utmost of my power, and ending my days quietly with Lady
Marl.

I came to this place yesterday. The bridge below the town
of Huy was made in the afternoon, and that above the town will
be finished I hope this night, so that we are now landing the
artillery. But the hills all about Huy are so very steep that I
am afraid we shall not set the cannon to the batteries till this
day senight.

While the Dutch were effectually paralysing Marlborough
in the Low Countries, and frittering away the months in
which they had a local superiority, the course of the general
war turned sharply and sourly against the allies. The grand
conception which the treason of the Elector of Bavaria and
the progress of the Hungarian revolt had enabled Louis XIV
to form was being brilliantly executed. In Italy Vendôme
held the flower of the Imperial troops, twenty thousand
veterans under Starhemberg, fully occupied. For the whole
course of the summer the Austrians were confined in their
entrenched camps by overwhelming opposition. Meanwhile
the main resources of France were concentrated in Alsace,
and acted from Strasburg. The combination of Tallard and
Villars completely dominated this theatre. While Tallard
pinned the Margrave to the defence of the Lines of Stollhofen, Villars plunged deep into Germany to join the Elector
of Bavaria. On March 11 he had captured his bridgehead,
the fortress of Kehl, opposite Strasburg. A choice was open
to him. He could join with Tallard in driving the Margrave
from his lines, and then take the easy valleys round the north
of the Black Forest; or he could attempt to traverse the lonely
passes to the south. He chose the mountain road. His vanguard had left Offenburg on April 27, and he followed with
the main army on April 30. In his memoirs he describes how
the slightest organized opposition would have prevented his
march. But the Margrave could not believe that Villars
intended to lead thirty thousand men through the heart of

the Black Forest. Villars was therefore opposed only by the local German militia, and on May 8 he dined with the Elector at Riedlingen, on the Danube. The long-sought-for junction had at last been effected. A Franco-Bavarian army far stronger than any force of which the Empire could dispose stood in the centre of Germany with power to move in any direction.

The French plan unfolded step by step. In June Vendôme, leaving Starhemberg blockaded in his camps, began to move upon the Brenner towards the Tyrol. At the same time the revolt in Hungary assumed a new importance. It had begun as a rising of Roman Catholic peasants against Protestant landlords. Under the influence of French gold and the pressure of French diplomacy it had now become a national Hungarian rebellion against the Emperor. The Protestant landlords armed their Catholic tenantry against a common foe. There then began those disastrous forays in which at times before the end of 1703 the rebels plundered and burned almost to the gates of Vienna. Under these triple thrusts the entire structure of the Empire threatened to dissolve. The exertions of 1702 had ruined its finances; the disasters of 1703 broke its military power. Of what use was it to think of campaigns on the Rhine, of conquests in Italy, or of the Spanish inheritance, when the Austrian Hereditary Lands were the prey of the rebel and the spoiler; and when the venerable capital of Central Europe, Vienna itself, might in a few months witness the triumphal entry of Max Emmanuel, or endure the ravages of the outlaw Rakoczy? Here was this great power of the Empire, which was pledged to place ninety thousand men in the field against France, now completely absorbed by its own perils and internal stresses, able only to cry aloud for help from those allies which it had so woefully failed. Yet the downfall of the Empire meant the loss of the war.

The dyke-mind of the Dutch was possessed by the desire for a strong fortress barrier defended by the largest possible army. Huy commended itself to them as a preliminary to the capture of Limburg and, in a future campaign, the regaining of Namur. These seemed to their statesmen and their generals objectives at once practical and satisfying. But Marlborough felt the war in every theatre. He suffered with the Margrave on the Rhine or on the Danube, with Eugene now trying to quell or appease the Hungarian rebels, with Stahremberg marooned in Italy. He held the nominal command of the largest and finest armies on either side in any quarter. A battle won by these armies even in the fortified zones of the Netherlands would "in three or four hours" change all the values, and the impingement of all the forces throughout Europe. How shameful to sit idle in superior strength at such a time! How horrible to contemplate the penalty which 1704 would exact for the sloth of 1703!

MARLBOROUGH'S PROPOSAL

The Dutch Field Deputies and all the generals gathered round him at Val Notre-Dame, the headquarters from which he covered the siege of Huy. A vehement council of war was held on August 24. Once again he proposed a plan of battle. He demanded a general attack upon the lines, which in this part of the country between the river Mehaigne and the minor fortress of Léau he considered "contemptible." The nature of the country on this sector would allow the whole allied army to be employed. In a battle upon a six-mile front the advantage would rest with the larger army and the heavier fire. The French Marshals would not be able to meet such an assault upon an equal front. Either they would retire, or a trial of strength under favourable conditions would ensue. In Flanders the defeat—perhaps destruction—of the French army and the rupture of their vaunted lines would open fine prospects. In Europe it would stem and turn the tide.

Again the discussions were interminable. This time all the generals except the Dutch—even the commanders of their own mercenaries—agreed with Marlborough. But the Dutch were solid, and the deadlock was complete. Both sides drew up their reasons in writing for submission to The Hague. Marlborough's paper, which was signed by the generals of the English, of the Danes, of the Lünebergers, and of the Hessians, thirteen persons in all, declared:

> If we do not attack the enemy in this place, with the finest troops that can be seen, and such superiority as we cannot expect to have next year, it will be evident, not only to our Allies (to their great discouragement), but the Enemy may with reason boast that these lines, which they will make stronger every day, are an invincible barrier against the troops of the Allies. . . . The Enemy being superior in Italy, and in the Empire, and being out-numbered no where but here, the Eyes of all the Allies are fixed upon us, and they will have cause justly to blame our conduct, if we do not do all that is possible to relieve them, by obliging the Enemy to call back such succours into these parts, which is not to be done but by pushing boldly.[1]

Against this the Dutch generals contended that the choice lay between attacking the lines or besieging Limburg. "Without doubt the first would be the more glorious attempt, but . . ."; they then proceeded to elaborate the difficulties of the ground to be attacked, and all the many dangers and obstacles that would be encountered, even if the first assault were successful. For this purpose they enlarged upon the strength of the various positions in rear of the lines. There was one position to which they drew particular attention. "For instance, that of Ramillies, where, their right being extended to the Mehaigne, near Taviers, and their left towards Ramillies, and Autréglise, they will have a narrow aperture of but 1200 paces to defend."[2]

Marlborough was not convinced that this dreaded position

1 *Dispatches*, i, 165, 166.   2 Lediard, i, 263.

of Ramillies was incapable of being attacked with success. On the contrary, he believed that it, like others, could be mastered by the manœuvres and resolute fighting of a good and powerful army. He must have meditated a great deal upon this already well-known position at Ramillies, and he saw no reason to be afraid of it. It is noteworthy that the French engineers who had sited the lines in 1701 noticed its serious defect. It was concave, and the defenders would not be able to move troops from one flank to the other as quickly as the assailants. The engineers therefore excluded it from their line of defence. Nearly three years were, however, to pass before Marlborough was able to prove with only equal forces that their judgment and his own were right.

The Dutch generals concluded by urging the siege of Limburg, but added, "Whatever resolution shall be taken, we whose names are underwritten will not fail to contribute all we can to facilitate the execution of it."

On August 25 Huy capitulated. Marlborough in his congratulatory report to the States-General on the success, "though small," sent them the opposed conclusions of the council of war, and his own appeal and warning:

. . . The Allies rightly expect that we on our side should do something striking [*éclatant*]; the situation of their affairs even demanding prompt relief by a powerful diversion which would oblige the enemy to retire from the Empire. I can assure your High Mightinesses that this is very much expected in England and also without doubt in Holland, which would gain the greatest advantage. I can even say that in our case it is very necessary, for there are signs that people would be in a bad humour at home this winter with such a superiority if the campaign went by without something considerable. For the rest I cannot forbear from observing to your High Mightinesses it would seem that according to the arguments of the other generals we are obliged to act on the defensive; and those who agree with them must admit the increase of the enemy's strength next year will be such that we cannot hope for the same superiority; so that it will no longer be possible to think of making war on the Two Crowns in this country. . . . Success would be very glorious . . . and could still lead us very far

243

before the end of the campaign, provided that the matter is taken up without losing a moment.

He concluded:

> So far as I am concerned, I feel that your High Mightinesses are sure that I shall always be ready to expose myself everywhere for the welfare of the Common Cause.[1]

Fruitless counsel—vain appeal. The States threw it back to their Field Deputies; their Field Deputies threw it back to their generals. The attack upon the lines was forbidden. The siege of Limburg was prescribed.

Even the most hostile Continental historians are struck by Marlborough's resiliency. Every action that he thought vital to the success of the war was denied him. His opinion as Captain-General and deputy Captain-General of the two armies was brushed aside, as though he were a suitor with a doubtful case before some small tribunal. He preserved an imperturbable demeanour. The usually censorious Klopp writes:

> We see the extraordinary pertinacity of this man who does not relax his efforts at any misfortune, at any lack of foreign insight or goodwill, but with the same tirelessness renounces one favourite plan in order straightway to adopt another. The correspondence of Marlborough with the principal Dutch Field Deputies, Geldermalsen and Hop, never reveals any irritability on his side, but, on the contrary, continual deference, whether real or assumed, to their opinion. At this time he laid before Geldermalsen a proposal to reform the discipline of the Dutch army which implied his complete confidence in the Deputy.[2]

Count Goes, the Ambassador, has left us a contemporary comment:

> It is to be regretted that all important affairs are handled here with such confusion. And yet it cannot be otherwise under the present constitution of the Republic. Greater confusion still is to be expected unless Divine Providence grants what there is no sign of at present, that a true head take over the conduct of

---

1 *Dispatches*, i, 167.　　　　2 Klopp, x, 377.

military affairs. For every burgomeister and every alderman here is determined to understand the profession, and register his vote how Europe must be regulated. The experts dare not speak out decisively against them.[1]

But, as we shall see from Marlborough's letters, his stress of soul and inward vexation were so great as to make him physically ill. To be thus continually thwarted and forbidden to carry out what his genius told him was right, and what his knowledge of the whole war declared vital to the Common Cause, roused passions in his breast, the more tormenting because borne with apparent composure. He burned with suppressed anger; he was wracked with headaches; a profound loathing for the conditions of his task possessed him. He spoke no word of complaint or menace before subordinates, but he resolved to be quit of such stifling responsibilities. This should be his last campaign. He would serve no more under intolerable conditions. He bore all the responsibility before Europe and before his professional opponents, and yet was constantly prevented from doing justice to his task.

Marlborough to Heinsius
September 10, 1703

* I do call God to witness that after I had seen the Lines upon Wednesday and Thursday I was confirmed in my opinion that we should have forced them with the loss of very few men. We should have taken their lines by storm with very little loss. But the discord in our camp will encourage the enemy, who knows everything that goes on among us. But even if I were given millions I would not again serve in the field with such obstacles and forced to depend upon the unanimous consent of the generals. I would rather die than put up with anything like it again. No plan remains secret, and with such procedure as this there cannot be any discipline in the camp.

The States can send to me in the camp as many Deputies as they like, and I will always satisfy their judgment, but if the States are upon the whole of the opinion that my services in the field are generally of any use, *I will for the future command the troops that are in the pay of England,* and the States can supplement

1 Goes' dispatch, September 21 ; Klopp, *ibid.*

them by as many battalions as they think advantageous to their own interest.[1]

Not so far away across the narrow seas the peaches were ripening in his garden at Holywell. The trees he had planted were growing up, and the trout stirred in the fish-ponds. He had affluence now, the highest rank, and a name already famous. The formidable enemy was the least of his troubles. All his strength was consumed by his friends, allies, and subordinates. On every side—in the field, at The Hague, in Parliament—opponents, rivals, detractors, plied their arts with bristling diligence. Was it strange that home, peace, rest, his children, Sarah, presented themselves in irresistible contrast? But then, the Queen—the Common Cause—the unbroken might of France! A deep longing to retire possessed him. He would not act in haste. At least he would wait until he had calmed his spirit and recovered his health. But he must have relief: he must break away from futile, interminable disputations with jealous or obstinate subordinates. He would go somewhere where he would not see their faces for a while. If all they would do was to besiege Limburg, at any rate he would have this excursion for himself. On September 6 he announced that he proposed to conduct the siege of Limburg in person. He handed over the command of the covering army to Overkirk, and hastened to a scene of local action where "I shall have none about me but such as seek to do my bidding." This remedy for his mental distress proved for the time being effective. Directing the siege, planting the batteries, mingling with the troops, tramping the trenches, in the fresh air and under fire, he regained in a fortnight his poise and good humour. His blood was cooled, his head-aches departed; and yet ever and again when he thought of how he had been baulked, of wasted opportunities, of a campaign marred, and of a world war which had definitely turned against the allies, his wish to leave the field and the service rose up again within him. But his letters can best tell the tale.

[1] Von Noorden, i, 352.

SARAH, DUCHESS OF MARLBOROUGH
Michael Dahl
National Portrait Gallery

"VICTORIOUS WITHOUT SLAUGHTER"

John to Sarah

VAL NOTRE-DAME
August 23, 1703

* I am very sorry to find by yours of the 3rd that you were not then perfectly recovered. We have so many here that think they have a right of being consulted before anything is positively resolved, that I am not able to tell you what will be the next step after this business is over; but I can let you know that my own opinion is that nothing is to compare to that of forcing the lines, that if I can be able to influence any, it shall [be] for that attempt; for the lines on this side are really contemptible, so that I can't but think when they shall see us in earnest they will not dare defend them. . . .

You may be sure that I shall do what I can to be early in England this year; but I am afraid it will be impossible for me to be there before the end of October, for the Dutch officers have so many disputes amongst themselves, that should I leave the Army before they receive their orders for their winter quarters, I am sure some misfortune would happen to them; but I shall endeavour to make this campaign shorter than the last. . . .

Marlborough to Godolphin

VAL NOTRE-DAME
August 30, 1703

* You will see by the answer to my letter I wrote to the States that they are unwilling to decide against their own Generals. . . . I thought we should certainly have attacked the lines, but the Dutch Generals having again this day insisted upon the not attacking of the lines, but for the making of the siege of Limburg, the Deputies have again this night sent another express to The Hague; so that I believe this matter at last will end with the Siege of Limburg, after which I shall be thinking of coming to The Hague; and then I may be in England against the time you desire; *for I shall not be very fond of staying with an Army that is to do no more but eat forage.*

If I leave the Army some time before they go to garrison, it would be for the honour of the English that the right wing should be commanded by an Englishman, and that can't be, there being several Lt. Generals amongst the foreigners that are older than our Lt. Generals; so that I would beg the favour of the Queen, that I might have a commission sent me for my

247

brother, he being the eldest Lt. G., to be General of the Foot. I desire nobody might know of the commission, for if I did not leave the Army before they went to garrison, I would not make use of the commission.

My Lady Marlborough has given me so many assurances that she will take care of her health that I am much more at ease than I was; for tho I am pressing people here with the hazard of my life to do what is good for themselves, yet I assure you, I have no other thoughts of happiness but after all is over, to be grateful to the Queen, and to deserve the continuance of your friendship, and end my days quietly with my Lady Marl.; so that should she do other ways than well, I were the unhappiest man alive.

The first paragraph of the following letter has an ugly significance which a later chapter will explain.

Marlborough to Godolphin

St Trond
Sept. 6, 1703

* When I wrote to you by the last post I was so tired, and my eyes so sore that I hardly knew what I wrote. *I shall be sure to quarter the English so as that they may be embarked in 24 hours,* and if you approve of it, I am very certain when I shall be at The Hague I can settle the matter so, as that if there should be occasion, the Queen might have what number of troops she pleases; for as I am fully persuaded if Holland were ruined, England could not be happy, so if England should be invaded, Holland could not subsist; that if France, *or Scotland* should disturb England, I am confident all honest people here would be very ready to help her Majesty with all their forces.

I dare not say to you what I think of some of those gentlemen that have hindered us from forcing the lines; but I am very confident before this campaign is ended they will be ashamed of it, for they begin already to say that if they had had more cannon they would not have been against it.

I am going to the siege of Limburg so that I believe I shall be a fortnight from this army, in which time I hope to recover my health, for the unreasonable opposition I have met with for the attack of the lines has heated my blood so that I am almost maddened with the headache.[1]

1 Extract.

Marlborough to Godolphin

ALDERBEESTEN
Oct. 11, 1703

* I find by my Lady Marl. of the 20th, this will find you at Newmarket, where I hope you will have had good luck, and perfect health. Since I see by your last the convoy [of battle-ships] can't be in Holland till the middle of the next month, I shall continue longer in the Army than I intended; for I do not care to be above four or five days at The Hague.

We have as yet no news of the King of Spain's arrival at Düsseldorf, so that I am not certain whether I shall wait upon him there or in Holland; but I shall order it so that it shall not keep me one day longer on this side, I being very desirous of being with you; for I really am so weary of all the business of this world, that I have no pleasure but in the expectation I have of being with you and Lady Marl. . . .

What I am going to say does not proceed from my being at the head of the Army, for I hope this is my last year of serving; but I beg of you for the good of England to consider what measures ought to be taken; for, if it be true that an offensive war must not be made in this country, I have but too much reason to apprehend that the consequence of that would be that the Dutch would not think themselves safe. I think they have been much to blame in not venturing something this summer; but that must not let me forget that when they are ruined, we are undone. You can judge of this better than anybody, so that I could not forbear letting you have my thoughts, not knowing but you might think something proper for me to do before I leave this country. . . .

The negotiations with Portugal, in describing which for convenience we have somewhat pressed upon chronology, had reached their conclusion in July; and the Emperor's second son, the Archduke Charles, already proclaimed King of Spain by the Grand Alliance, was now to set out to conquer his kingdom. For this purpose he counted upon an Anglo-Dutch corps of veterans, and upon Portugal as an ally and as his base.

'King Charles III' of Spain arrived at Düsseldorf on October 16. It was arranged that Marlborough should meet

249

him there. Many compliments of interest to aristocratic Europe were interchanged. Marlborough made a remark the significance of which will soon appear. "I have just had the honour of putting Your Majesty in possession of Limburg." The young King replied, "I hope to be yet more indebted to your valour for the reduction of other places to my obedience." After an animated conversation he took from his side a sword richly set with diamonds, and presented it to Marlborough with the words, "I am not ashamed to own that I am a poor Prince, having no other inheritance than my cloak and my sword. My sword may be serviceable to Your Grace, and I hope you will not esteem it the less because I have worn it a day. I hoped to present it to you at the head of that gallant army with which you have performed such great actions." Marlborough kissed the hilt and replied, "This sword acquires an additional value in my eyes, because Your Majesty has condescended to wear it; for it will always remind me of your just right to the Spanish crown, and of my obligation to hazard my life and all that is dear to me, in making you the greatest prince in Christendom."[1]

But neither these amenities nor the action and exercise of the siege of Limburg affected Marlborough's resolve to quit the command.

The capture of Limburg ended the campaign. As the fastness of Guelders, protected by its morasses, had also been starved out during the summer, Spanish Guelderland and the whole of the Bishopric of Liége had been restored to the allies. The capture of Limburg and Guelders raised issues which shook the structure of the Grand Alliance to its foundations, and were of the same nature as those which finally dissolved it. Guelders had been taken by the Prussian general Count Lottum. Louis XIV had already offered Spanish Guelderland to the new Prussian monarchy as a bid for an alliance. Frederick I had with many backward glances spurned the temptation. He not unnaturally claimed as good payment from the allies for his loyalty as he would have

[1] Coxe, i, 291.

received from France for his desertion. But the Dutch wanted Guelders for themselves. It was to be part of their barrier. The States-General demanded that the stronghold should be placed in their charge, and their Commissioner thrust himself forward with warrant and proclamation. But the Prussians said that the fortress captured by Prussian blood must be garrisoned by Prussian troops. They did not care whether it was counted as part of the inheritance of the house of Hapsburg, or whether it fell within the disputed sphere of the Dutch compensation claims. There they were, and there they stayed.

Limburg raised in an even more acute form the rival claims of Holland and the Empire. Here the Empire had the law and the Dutch the force. The Empire was failing in all its obligations to the Alliance. Barely a fifth of the troops it had engaged to march against France were in the field. The Emperor had already craved and received succour. Marlborough had prevailed upon the States-General to send their General Goor and twelve battalions to aid the Margrave between the Rhine and the Danube. While, however, the Hapsburg Empire revealed month by month its awful collapse as a fighting unit, its rulers abated no jot of their titular and sacred rights. Limburg was a part of the Spanish Netherlands—no mere Guelderland or Bishopric, but undoubted Belgium. By all the causes for which the war was being fought it belonged to the Spanish monarchy. But the Dutch, who maintained in their solid persevering manner over 100,000 troops in operation against the enemy, meant to have for themselves Limburg and all the Belgian fortresses Marlborough might take as part of the Dyke, and also for their commercial profit. And here force was on their side. This direct collision between the Empire and the Republic, both indispensable allies, confronted Marlborough with a crucial task. Perhaps one of his reasons, apart from temperamental self-indulgence, for taking the siege into his own hands was the need for him to be in physical control at this diplomatic storm-centre. The representatives of the Empire, strong in their indefeasible right, proceeded to assume the government of Limburg; and the Dutch, with brawn and bayonets, and that kind of rough justice which asserts itself among allies in war whatever the parchments say, pushed the Imperial Commissioner from their path with complete indifference to all the consequences.

Here Marlborough acted the statesman as decisively as he ever acted in the field. He met the pretensions of the Dutch, the appeals of his invaluable friend Heinsius, and the physical obtrusiveness of the Dutch agent, with uncompromising resistance. No one knew better than he the strength of the Dutch and the weakness of the Empire. But if the Grand Alliance was to continue, this seizing of territory as booty wherever the armies marched, without regard to treaties and hereditary rights, must be stopped. He stopped it. The municipal administration of Limburg was transferred to the Imperial Ambassador. It is true that the Dutch, in default of Imperial troops, garrisoned the place, and collected the revenues, but the title-deeds were preserved intact for a future peace conference. The Limburg dispute was the first stage in the famous Dutch Barrier question which, in spite of all the victories yet to be gained, was slowly to rend the alliance. These discordances were an unfortunate preliminary to the fresh demands which Marlborough must make upon the States-General for further sacrifices and risks to save the Empire.

The Dutch alliance was indeed creaking. Parliament had only consented to provide an additional ten thousand men at the beginning of 1703 on the condition that the Dutch abandoned their habit of trading with the enemy. The States-General had agreed to this, but had not kept their word. Pressed as they were for money to carry on the war, they could not in practice deny themselves the earnings of the lucrative French carrying trade; and all their wealthy citizens who lived by this brought, as may well be imagined, every kind of pressure to bear upon the assembly. But the House of Commons was indignant at this process of nourishing France with the one hand while fighting her with the other.

The Dutch had a counter-grievance. Nottingham, as Secretary of State, had sent Marlborough peremptory orders to embark four battalions for the expedition to Portugal. Marlborough had obeyed the lawful command of Crown and Parliament. He had even, in spite of his vexation, taken pains to make sure that the battalions selected for this special service should be of the best quality and up to strength. But he saw and explained with apprehension the effect which the arbitrary withdrawal of English troops from the Netherlands would produce upon the Dutch. The quotas had been fixed by treaty. "I cannot but say," Marlborough wrote to Godolphin, "that the Dutch argue very justly. If the Queen can without their consent take these men, she may by the same reason recall the rest; and by the same reasoning they are at liberty to reduce as many as they please of their army."[1] He begged Godolphin to prevent Hedges and Nottingham treating the Dutch Ambassador roughly when he waited on them in strong protest.

Meanwhile the year 1703 drew to a grievous conclusion for the allies. The two Marshals had successfully discharged their minor part in the Low Countries. They had maintained themselves against superior armies with only the loss of three lesser fortresses out of more than thirty which they held. Elsewhere France had triumphed. The French were dominant in Alsace and upon the Upper Rhine. Their bridgehead from Strasburg to Kehl opened the road to Bavaria. Villars had traversed the Black Forest and joined the Elector. Vendôme, advancing upon the Brenner, had isolated Starhemberg in Italy. The genius of Prince Eugene was absorbed in the distracted war councils of Vienna or in attempting to placate or crush the Hungarian insurgents. The Empire, unyielding in its legal rights, unbending in its ceremonial, was at the last gasp.

On the other hand were consolations of various kinds. Villars was soon at odds with the Elector. The audacious Marshal wished to march upon Vienna with the combined

1 The Hague, October 30, 1703; Coxe, i, 292.

Franco-Bavarian army, which at the end of June amounted to nearly seventy thousand men. But Max Emmanuel took a different view of policy and strategy. He coveted new

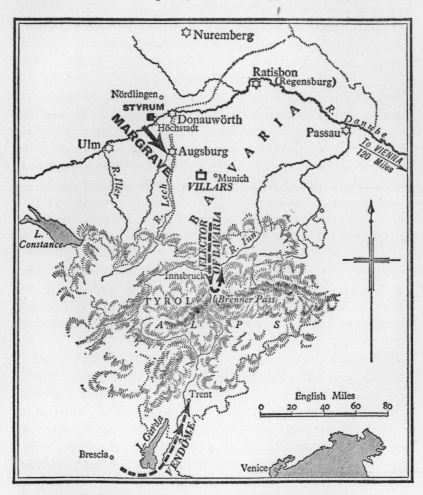

THE CAMPAIGN IN BAVARIA AND THE TYROL

territory. He marched into the Tyrol from the north, while Vendôme assailed it from the south. Leaving Villars to guard Bavaria from the Margrave and his generals, he established himself at Innsbruck. Simultaneously Vendôme advanced from Brescia towards the Brenner. The French had reason to expect aid from their sympathizers among the discontented Tyrolese nobility. But these hopes were dashed by the violent patriotic reaction among all classes in the Tyrol against the double invasion and the exactions which the Elector was already levying upon the northern districts. The Tyrolese when roused were among the finest troops in Europe. Their Landsknechte had formed the heart of the armies which had fought the French under Maximilian and Charles V, and won Italy for the Hapsburgs in the sixteenth century. The old traditions were still alive, and the musters were carried through with almost the speed of the great days. A peasant rising in the valley of the Upper Inn spread in a week through the whole of the Tyrol. The lesser noblemen and peasants served side by side with the high aristocracy. Together they swiftly hustled the Elector out of their country. Vendôme at the same time was brought to a standstill at Trent before he could even enter the Brenner, and his army played no part in the general war from the beginning of July to the middle of September. Max Emmanuel's attempt upon the Tyrol thus ended in failure—rapid, complete, and ignominious. The episode was disastrous to French prestige throughout Italy. It was watched by no more attentive eye than that of Victor Amadeus.

Meanwhile elsewhere the position grew steadily worse. At the end of July the Margrave, leaving General Thüngen to guard the Lines of Stollhofen against Tallard, joined his other lieutenant, Count Styrum, who confronted Villars on the Danube. Crossing this river in August, he entered Bavaria and laid siege to the free city of Augsburg. His position threatened the Elector's retreat from the Tyrol and at the same time exposed Bavaria to ravage. The Elector, drawn by these needs in front, and impelled by the vigorous Tyrolese at the rear, hastened home. His arrival with his well-trained Bavarians transformed the scene. He was able, on the one hand, to besiege Ratisbon, and, marching with his main body, joined Villars opposite Count Styrum on the Danube. Styrum lay across the French communications with a force of eighteen thousand men. He

255

posted himself before the town of Höchstadt, of which we shall hear more in another year. Villars and the Elector, crossing the Danube by the bridgehead fortress of Donauwörth, marched upon him with combined forces. On September 20 Count Styrum, taken between two fires, was

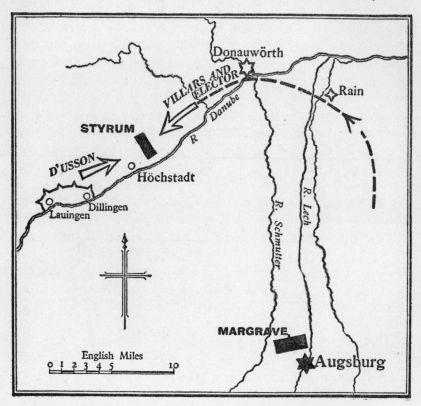

THE FIRST BATTLE OF HÖCHSTADT

defeated in a severe action at Höchstadt and retreated in disorder upon Nördlingen. The Margrave was now himself in turn cut off at Augsburg, but he managed to escape across the Danube and retired into the Black Forest north of Lake Constance. Thus it was the Elector who took the free city of Augsburg; and Ratisbon, the seat of the Imperial Diet, also fell into his hands. The result, therefore, of these complicated marchings and counter-marchings was grievously adverse to the Empire. Moreover, Tallard had also been active. In spite of his strong superiority, he had not dared to attack the Lines of Stollhofen, but he had taken the fortress of Old Brisach in September, and in October invested Landau.

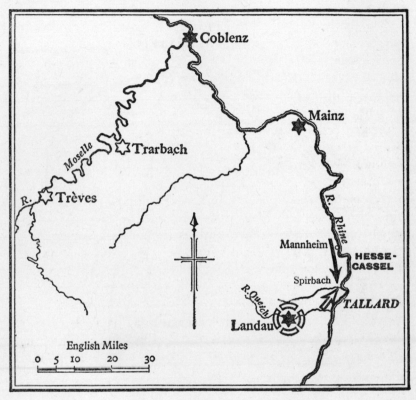

SPIRBACH

In spite of these successes the quarrel between Villars and the Elector grew to a height. The Marshal felt that his grand design against Vienna had been sacrificed for minor and disjointed operations, one of which had been a grotesque failure. His breach with Max Emmanuel became irreparable. Louis XIV had no doubt where his interest lay. He discarded his Marshal in favour of his ally. He deemed the Elector the ablest German prince of the age, with the best army. He

257

regarded the Bavarian alliance as the keystone of his policy in Germany. He foresaw decisive results by this agency and channel in the coming year. He recalled Villars to Versailles, and sent him to cope with the rising in the Cevennes. Marshal Marsin succeeded Villars in the command of the French army in Bavaria.

Marlborough had put the bulk of his army into winter quarters, and was forced himself by the political situation and the insistent appeals of Godolphin to return to England. He had resolved and had obtained the Dutch consent to make a lodgment on the Moselle. The Prince of Hesse-Cassel, with 22 battalions and 30 squadrons, was sent from Coblenz with orders to retake Trèves and Trarbach and settle himself in winter quarters there. He was now diverted to the relief of Landau. But this enterprise gravely miscarried, and in the middle of November Tallard, who had received heavy reinforcements, fell upon Hesse-Cassel at Spirbach and routed him with slaughter. This action decided the fate of Landau, which surrendered to the French at the end of November.

The Dutch were well satisfied with the campaign of 1703. They struck a medal with Queen Anne on the obverse, and on the reverse Marlborough on horseback being presented with three keys in a basin by a nymph adorned with a mural crown. The inscription was truthful. "Victorious without slaughter, by the taking of Bonn, Huy, and Limburg."

We can imagine with what measured words and gestures and inward scorn and sorrow Marlborough received these local tributes. He never ceased to think of the war as a whole. To him the wide scene of strife and struggle, which spread through so many lands and involved the fortunes of almost all the nations, was but one. He saw himself only an actor in a single theatre without power, yet the presiding mind of the entire confederacy. These three fortresses were all that could be gained in the Netherlands during a year of definite superiority. Meanwhile what had happened in Germany? What ruin impended upon the Empire? And what chance, if the Empire fell, for the allied cause? While the sturdy, obstinate, short-sighted Dutch clapped their hands and struck their medals, Marlborough and Louis XIV were agreed in their measure of 1703. Versailles knew the year had been disastrous for the allies. France had run risks in the Low Countries in order to lay broad and deep the foundations of future conquests in Germany and Austria. In the Northern sphere they had not even lost Antwerp. Of what avail would Bonn, Huy, and Limburg be compared with the fall of Vienna and the destruction of the Hapsburg monarchy, for which all was now prepared? What would be the fate of the Dutch? What would be the value of the petty successes of an English adventurer, not even a prince, a mere Queen's favourite, the son of a country squire, when the large armies, which would force a separate peace upon the Empire in 1704, turned their victorious bayonets upon the Netherlands? Let him strut in his new dukedom; let his Queen be flattered with ill-founded praise; let them have their medals! The year was approaching when the long, profound designs and strategy of the Great King would bear their golden fruit—absolute victory of the French armies in the East. Then might the Republic and England beg for such terms as the magnanimity of Europe's master would accord.

Our General saw all this as clearly as his foes. It was with the deepest feelings of grief and fear for the public cause and a distaste for the part he had to play that he took leave of his Dutch admirers. He saw that this fleeting hour of "victory without slaughter" was probably the prelude to slaughter without victory. The attitude of the States-General and the Dutch oligarchy towards him was that of loving masters to an indispensable servant, without whom they would suffer disaster, but whom they nevertheless were determined to control. "No battles" was still their rule; and how well it had answered! The illustrious Duke, the dauntless commander, the link of the Alliance, so skilful, so reasonable, so reassuring, was the man of all others they needed. If only they could keep his fighting propensities within bounds! And had they not succeeded during two whole years? Had they not re-

conquered wide territories and important fortresses? Was
not the hostile cannonade driven now far to the southward?
Was not the Republic relieved from all danger of invasion?
Not even could they hear the sound of guns. And might

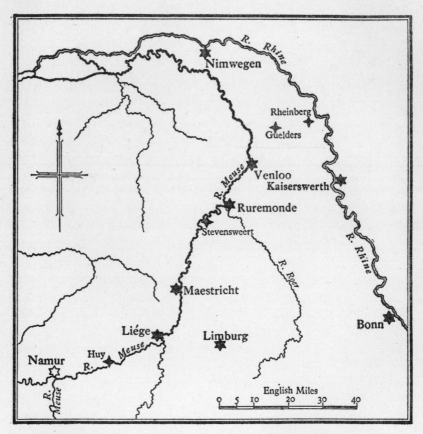

FORTRESSES OF THE MEUSE AND RHINE, END OF 1703

not all have been cast away "in three or four hours" if they
had let him fight a battle—he who had never fought a battle
in his life? They were equally grateful to him for what he
had done, and for what they had compelled him not to do.

But he had tempted them so often, pressed them so hard,
coaxed them so much, and his reasonings on the general war
were so grave, that in their hearts were serious misgivings.

Marlborough was plain with Heinsius and his colleagues. They were deeply conscious of the unspoken reproach which his sombre reception of their compliments conveyed. Perhaps he had been right after all. It would be awful if the Empire fell. How wonderful if the lines had been forced and the army of the two Marshals had been broken up in the field! Was this Ramillies position really so strong as their generals had declared? Thus the Dutch searched their hearts as they conducted their Deputy Captain-General to the quay.

CHAPTER XII

THE QUEEN'S COMMANDS

(1703, Winter)

SINCE the days of Job no man's patience has been more tried than Marlborough's in 1703. The year had begun with the death of his only son. It was to end in a melancholy breach with his beloved wife. We have seen how his campaign had been spoilt by the Dutch, and the endless vexations which the "many-headed Republic" inflicted on its own servants. He returned to England heartily sick and weary of his command, and determined, whatever might happen, never to exercise it again under similar conditions. But the situation awaiting him at home was not less baffling and distasteful.

The violence of the High Tory attacks upon the conduct of the war put the Whig Party in an awkward plight. Although the Whigs were angry because they had no larger share of the offices, they had hitherto most loyally voted the supplies and sustained the policy of a great land war; but they expected results. Without victories and solid gains they saw themselves stultified and pilloried in the party fight. They were the war party. The Tories said it was *their* war. "Now there is being reaped in the Continental war," sneered the High Church Press, "the poisonous crops of a pernicious sowing. But none save the Whigs with their eagerness for a loan [a reference to the Whig connexions with City finance] and their ambitious King of Dutch descent have sowed the seeds." As the year closed under its succession of heavy blows—defeats in the field at Höchstadt and Spirbach, the loss of the famous fortified cities, Augsburg, Ratisbon, and above all Landau—as the French grip closed on the Upper Rhine and the Moselle, as the Empire broke down everywhere, as the Dutch would venture nothing, and Marlborough came home with little to show, the Whigs felt that as a party they must reconsider their position.

There was much to be said for their leaders making a triple arrangement with Marlborough-Godolphin and the Dutch. Such a combination might plough its way through the less highly wrought substances; but would Marlborough agree? Would or could the Dutch play the part assigned? The Lords of the Junto[1]—eminent, wealthy, powerful, uplifted above the crowd, masters of their party, the famous Ministers of King William's reign, nursing the wounds and insults they had received from the new régime; convinced that they had the secret of British greatness and British freedom in their keeping—coldly and massively reached a definite decision. There must be an end to the friendly relations they had preserved with Marlborough and Godolphin. The Whig Party—its strength in the Commons, its majority in the Lords, its landed magnates, its City financiers, its chapel going folk of every class, the entire Dissenting interest, all their orators, pamphleteers, and newspapers—must turn their fire in a new direction. The whole Cabinet must be subjected to an unsparing Parliamentary and public onslaught. Even those Ministers who were most conciliatory in party matters, and were at the same time most resolute for the war, must be assailed equally with their more partisan and less patriotic colleagues. Marlborough must be accused of military incompetence. Marlborough and Godolphin must be charged jointly with the malevolent wasting of the subsidies and with a deliberate frustration of the projects of the war amounting to malignant treachery against the State. Language of this kind, it was felt, would outstrip all Tory abuse of Marlborough and Godolphin, and save the Whig Party from the reproach of having drawn the nation into a disastrous war. The war was right: the policy was good: King William was a true prophet; but his majestic designs were being cast away by corrupt, incapable, and malicious Ministers who fattened upon the cruel misfortunes of the times and feared lest even victory might put an end to their evil reign. This seemed the most promising line; and the

---

[1] Wharton, Somers, Halifax (formerly Charles Montagu, the ingenious Chancellor of the Exchequer), Orford (Admiral Russell), and Sunderland.

whole Whig Party worked themselves up on it. Both parties therefore delivered their full blast of competitive calumny against Marlborough and Godolphin.

Accordingly Marlborough was assailed by the Whigs in speech and pamphlet as a supporter of the Occasional Conformity Bill, as a suspected Jacobite, and as a bigoted defender of the Prerogative of the Crown. They accused him—of all men—of acting defensively in Flanders, while wasting national strength upon useless naval expeditions. The Tory attack took exactly the opposite form on nearly all points. The Whigs were angry because he had not allowed them a larger share of the offices: the Tories because he would not let them drive out what Whigs there were. But both parties agreed in abusing him for prolonging the war for his own benefit. The schism in the Cabinet had been growing more bitter all through the year, and now was notorious. Nottingham, the High Tory Secretary of State, backed by Jersey and Seymour, and Hedges harshly asserted their party view and party interest within the Government, and made no scruple of working with Rochester, and the mass of their party outside, against Godolphin and Marlborough. Not only did they oppose their policy, but they revealed their secrets, and sought to cast the blame for every misfortune and difficulty upon them. Opposed by conviction and party tenet to England's large share in the Continental war, they laboured to make it unpopular, and recked little if it were unsuccessful.

Many methods lay to their hands: of these, the first was to become strong critics of the Dutch. Every shortcoming of the Republic in its obligations as an ally—its tardiness in supplying ships or money; its underhand trading with the enemy; nay, its interference with Marlborough's military plans—was used to prove the unwisdom of being so deeply involved with so perverse and selfish a State. They did not care what ill-will was bred between the two countries. The sooner the Dutch were left to defend their own frontiers for themselves, the sooner could England resume her natural traditional Tory policy of seeking colonies, trade, and loose

264

alliances by naval force and expeditions. Marlborough's ambition to lead armies in Europe, they suggested, clouded his judgment. No doubt, they hinted, it was most agreeable to him to receive his large salary from the Dutch, his perquisites and allowances from other allies, in addition to his pay as Captain-General; but why should England be dragged on to the mainland to waste her life and treasure and the splendid opportunities which offered overseas, to gratify the selfish desires of an individual? When Ministers set on foot such propaganda their followers could hardly be blamed for spreading it.

During the whole of the summer Godolphin had been worried out of his life by incessant attempts to isolate him from his own party and supplant him in the Queen's favour. He repeatedly appealed to Marlborough to allow him to resign. Marlborough, burning inwardly against the Dutch Deputies and generals, who thwarted him on every occasion, brought his plans to nought, and sullenly forbade the battle which would have cleared the air and established his authority, had, nevertheless, to bear all this in silence, lest his enemies at home should use his complaints to mar the alliance. There is no doubt that the two "Great Ministers," with the weight of the war and the Grand Alliance on their hands, were now strained to breaking-point.

When they turned their gaze from the fierce feuds and intrigues of English and Dutch politics to the general war, it was only to encounter an even darker scene. For the new campaign Louis XIV was placing in the field eight separate armies, each commanded by a Marshal of France. Villeroy in Flanders, Tallard on the Rhine, Marsin with the Elector on the Danube, Vendôme in Piedmont, his brother, the Grand Prior, in Lombardy, La Feuillade in Savoy, Villars in the Cevennes, and the Duke of Berwick in Spain, were all preparing for a decisive effort in the coming year. Nor could there be much doubt where the fatal blow would fall. The Empire was the prey, and Vienna the prize. The contingents from different German states paid by the Sea Powers were still available for the defence of Southern Germany;

but a further advance of the French and Bavarians would recall them all, in accordance with their subsidy treaties, for the local defence of their own home lands. The defeat of the Empire spelt the ruin of the confederacy and the final triumph of France. Meanwhile, as we have seen, the States-General had little thought beyond gathering the largest numbers of Dutch, auxiliary, and English troops for the defence (without battles) of the approaches to their own frontiers; and the English Parliament was moving powerfully towards leaving them to do this by themselves.

Marlborough realized with sombre conviction that the general defeat of the allies was approaching. The components of the confederacy would make separately what terms they could with the conqueror: a supreme Catholicizing monarchy of Gallican stamp would be erected upon the continent by French bayonets; and Protestant England, little England with its six million people, with its trade and newly planted Empire, would be left alone to face the wrath and appetite of this enormous rival.

Since no coherent plan for common action could be devised; since even his sword-arm in the field was fettered; since his every movement was baulked by clinging hands and censured by shrill voices; since responsibility with odium, but without power, was all that was offered, and even that dreary situation grudged—why should not the Captain-General and the Lord Treasurer yield these awful burdens to those who coveted them so ravenously? Why not retire from "these uneasy and troublesome broils"?[1] Why struggle further for the privilege of being involved in a vast catastrophe? Their would-be successors pressed avidly forward. Why not let them have their wish? He and Godolphin had done their best. Their consciences were clear. Each had his consolation: fruit-trees grew at Holywell, and horses ran at Newmarket. They could utter their warnings, and they could depart each to his abode. There is no doubt that both were sorely tempted. Public men under unfair stresses have often used such threats as a

1 Marlborough to Harley, October 11; Bath Papers, H.M.C., i, 56.

manœuvre for reviving their authority. There is every reason to believe that in this case both were sincere, and viewed in deep despondency their thankless and, as it seemed, hopeless duties. The word 'galley' became a favourite in their correspondence. * "We live the life of *galley slaves*," wrote Godolphin to Harley.[1] "It is much better *to row in the galleys* than have to do with such as are very selfish and misled by everybody who speaks to them," wrote Marlborough to Hedges in July.[2] It was not that Marlborough feared the task: the task was not confided. It was not that he felt unequal to it. Indeed, part of his trials consisted in seeing so clearly what ought to be done, and was prevented. Give him a reasonably free hand to direct the war-policy even only of the two countries of which he was Captain-General, even only for a year, and he felt sure he could transform the scene. But to be at once burdened, paralysed, and abused was more than could be endured.

But now Queen Anne struck her blow for the victory and the greatness of her country. She had reigned barely two years, but far behind her, it seemed, lay the "sunshine day," that brief space after the weight of Caliban had been lifted from her shoulders and before the weight of his cares was fastened there instead. She felt the distress and rising temper of those about her, the servants she knew best and trusted most. She resolved to draw them together around her in a new endeavour. Putting aside for the time being all her feelings about Whigs and Tories and her honest, inevitable differences with her bosom friend, she wrote Sarah a letter, magnificent and momentous, which ranks her with Queen Elizabeth and the greatest sovereigns of the English line.

WINDSOR
Saturday

The thoughts that both my dear Mrs Freeman and Mr Freeman seem to have of retiring gives me no small uneasiness, and therefore I must say something on that subject. It is no wonder

1 Portland MSS. (undated).   2 Coxe, i, 273.

at all that people in your posts should be weary of the world, who are so continually troubled with all the hurry and impertinencies of it; but give me leave to say you should a little consider your faithful friends and poor country, which must be ruined if ever you should put your melancholy thoughts in execution. As for your poor unfortunate faithful Morley, she could not bear it; for if ever you should forsake me, I would have nothing more to do with the world, but make another abdication; for what is a crown when the support of it is gone. I never will forsake your dear self, Mr Freeman, nor Mr Montgomery, but always be your constant faithful servant; and we four must never part, till death mows us down with his impartial hand.[1]

It was the Cockpit against the world.

Sarah was evidently the channel by which the exasperation of the General and the miseries of the Treasurer were brought home to the Queen. The Queen abandoned none of her convictions, but by writing such a letter she made it plain to her servants that she made common cause with them, and would do all that was necessary to help them, even though much was contrary to her personal views. She must have been very weary of her interminable discussions with Sarah upon the relative demerits of the Tories and Whigs. Her placid, unalterable Tory prejudice bore unmoved for months and years the vivacious, shrewd, persuasive, or often rasping assaults of one who was still her dearest friend. But now, when the glory of England was at stake, she subordinated her party politics and her side of the argument with Sarah to the

---

1 This letter bears only the day of the week, and has usually been assigned to early June (*cf.* Coxe, i, 273–4). But the postscript, hitherto unpublished, makes it plain that it was written in the autumn, and, we think, late in October, just before Marlborough returned home:

Sunday

∗ "I am very sorry dear Lady Sunderland has got so great a cold, and extreme glad you persuaded her not to come hither *for ye sharpness of ye air now* yt she is not well and ye change of beds would have made her worse. She need have no scruples about her going to Althrope before she comes hither, and I hope she will not think I can be so unreasonable as to take it ill. I am very sorry dear Mrs Freeman thinks it necessary to make any excuse to her poor unfortunate faithful Morley for ye length of your letter, and ye concern you were in for dear Lady Sunderland. I'm sure nobody can have a more tender feeling for you in everything than I have, particularly on these occasions. I pray God bless you, and preserve you from all manner of misfortunes." (Blenheim MSS.)

supreme need. Her magnanimity and her sense of proportion expressed the genius of the English race in adversity.

Sarah's letters throughout the year give no sign of her appreciating the nobility of the Queen's gesture. Imbued with her conviction that only in the Whigs and in modernism could a sure basis for war and politics be found, she pursued her advocacy. We cannot trace even a dint to mark the impact of this great appeal. But Marlborough was moved in every fibre of his being. Under the captaincy of his mind and the smooth surface of his manners his soul flamed within him. He would endure all things and dare all things: he would not despair: he would not lose patience: he would find a way to make the Queen victorious, or perish in the attempt.

It was November 10 before he got home, and his first few days were occupied at Windsor in the ceremonies preceding the expedition of the Archduke Charles, now proclaimed King of Spain, to invade through Portugal the kingdom which he claimed. Compliments, jewels, and valedictions having passed, the Archduke embarked at Portsmouth on board the *Royal Catharine,* with a fleet of battleships and transports, on his unpromising adventure; and Marlborough turned to face the political situation.

With regard to the command of the armies the Whigs had a definite plan. Marlborough must be removed. The country could run such risks no longer. Moreover, his resolve never to take the field again under the Dutch restrictions of the 1703 campaign was widely known. Through King William's old friend Portland the Whig leaders discussed with the Grand Pensionary whether the supreme command might not be transferred to the Elector of Hanover, the lawful heir to the English throne. Thus the Prince who was to preserve the Protestant succession and restore the Whig supremacy would be at the head of the armies, leading the English troops, and ready, should the Queen's health fail, to claim his Parliamentary rights with all the advantages of armed force. It was hoped that Marlborough would consent to advise the proposed new

Commander-in-Chief. This scheme was duly brought before him. Through Sarah and Sunderland, wife and son-in-law, he had contact with the Junto and must have received early and accurate accounts of their designs. To the astonishment of every one in the secret Whig circles, Marlborough agreed at once to the plan. He declared himself ready as commander of the English Army to serve under the command of the Elector, and to use his best endeavours. "Marlborough himself," wrote Portland to Heinsius, "seems to be *very strongly* drawn to this plan, and will be relieved and contented to be under the Elector's orders."

There is scarcely any doubt that Marlborough meant what he said. Not only was he sickened of his treatment by the Dutch and wearied by the clatter of eloquent malice directed upon him in England, but also he saw a way of procuring a better direction of the war as chief of the staff under a royal head than as titular commander. He lent himself fully and frankly to the scheme. That it failed was no fault of his; and here again we see the unfathomable mystery which Marlborough's character presents. Did he know all the time that the Dutch would never agree to the transference of the command to so considerable a prince of the German Empire who himself provided a substantial mercenary contingent? Was he always sure that this Whig proposal would be choked in the inundations of Dutch obstinacy? There is no telling. We think that he had reached a point in human endurance when he did not care what happened to his own career; that at this moment ambition was utterly quenched. He would serve the Queen wherever it would help most.

The Dutch executive were staggered at this development. They had conceived themselves throughout the year in imminent danger of a widespread domestic revolt against their authority and the continuance of the war. They knew their generals hated Marlborough. All their experts said his notions of war were unprofessional and unsound. But the more the men who knew him thought about losing him the less they liked it. And how would they enjoy this German prince at the head of their armies? So they took no decision. Once again their natural obstructiveness stood them in good stead. They let the weeks slip by, and the campaign of 1704 drew near in its appalling panoply.

The winter afforded a tense example of English party and Parliamentary struggles in the midst of European storm. For all the Captain-General's suave demeanour, Nottingham and his Tory colleagues knew what he thought of them. They resolved to marshal all the Tory forces and launch an offensive which would break up the Government. Well did they know, and Marlborough recognize, the weapon in their hand. On November 23 they caused, or connived at, the announcement in the *Gazette* of the impending introduction of another Occasional Conformity Bill. Godolphin and Marlborough learned of this intention only when they read it in the official Government publication, and two days later Mr Bromley, a private Member, but leader of the Churchmen in the House of Commons, presented the Bill under what every one might suppose to be Ministerial countenance. It was immediately carried by a large majority of Tories, supported by Non-Jurors and Jacobite Members.

In that dark hour of the war this measure drove, and was meant to drive, a wedge which would split the Cabinet, sunder the parties, and embroil the two Houses. It was also calculated to estrange Marlborough and Godolphin from their party and Parliamentary majority, and at the same time to excite the High Church sentiments of the Queen and make mischief between her and Sarah's open-mouthed Whiggery. The Tory Ministers resolved to force an issue at all points, and, believing themselves capable of gaining the control of the State and of the war, with open insolence to their colleagues encouraged their followers and partisans. The Whigs, the Nonconformists, and the money-power of the City were roused by fear to fury. The challenge was plain to all: a trial of strength was opened. It must be remembered that, though Marlborough was recognized at this time as a skilful commander who could outmanœuvre the French and take fortresses and recover territory in a manner unknown under King William, he had never been allowed to fight a battle, and had no historic achievement to set against the sneer that he was only "a general of favour." There was no surpassing prestige to subdue faction. As for the safety and interest of the State, the Tories, with a complete scheme of war and policy in which they were thoroughly drilled, conceived themselves well able to judge of that.

But they could not know what had passed between the Queen and her trusted friends; nor how she had determined to suppress her personal feelings in what she deemed a national interest. The second Occasional Conformity Bill found her in a very different mood from the first. Then she had been an enthusiast for the measure. Now she thought it unseasonable, although no doubt right in itself. The royal speech, drafted by Marlborough and Godolphin, but cordially assented to by the Queen, had expressed at the opening of the session her earnest desire "of seeing all my subjects in perfect peace and union among themselves," and urged concentration upon the war peril. She was not blind to the factious calculations which inspired the aggressive measure, and was alarmed by the passions which it roused among her subjects and in her most intimate circle. She was torn between her deepest religious and political convictions and her trusted friends to whom she had pledged herself. In a letter to Sarah she reveals the stresses through which she passed. This time she would not compel her husband to vote against his own heart. She wrote:

> To ease your mind I must tell you that Mr Bromley will be disappointed; for the prince does not intend to go to the House when the bill of occasional conformity is brought in. But at the same time that I think him very much in the right not to vote in it, I shall not have the worse opinion of any of the lords that are for it; for though I should have been very glad it had not been brought into the house of commons, because I would not have had any pretence given for quarrelling, I cannot help thinking, now 'tis as good as passed there, it will be better for the service to have it pass the house of lords too. I must own to you that I never cared to mention anything on this subject to you, because I knew you would not be

QUEEN ANNE
Edmond Lilly
By permission of the Duke of Marlborough

of my mind; but since you have given me this occasion, I cannot forbear saying that I see nothing like persecution in this bill. You may think it is a notion lord Nottingham has put into my head, but upon my word it is my own thought.[1]

It is impossible to have a clearer revelation of her mind, of the relations of the two friends, and of the severity of the crisis.

Marlborough and Godolphin repeated their tactics of the year before, but with much more effrontery. They left no stone unturned to procure the rejection of the Bill. They threw all their influence—and it was weighty and far-reaching —against it. But at the same time they voted for it, and when it was rejected they signed the protest of twenty-three Tory peers against its rejection. Thus malice was met by guile, and faction baffled by deceit. And this was no more than was right and necessary for the public safety and the peace of the realm.

We may imagine the condition of the Cabinet on the morrow of the Bill's defeat. The Ministers faced each other across the council-table with mutual scorn. Both sides understood every move in the game. The rage and disappointment of the Tory Party were extreme. They accused Marlborough and Godolphin of having tricked them by double-dealing and hypocrisy, and forgot who had compassed the destruction of colleagues and the downfall of much else besides. They even extended their reproaches to the Queen in rhymes and pamphlets. They classed her with King William. They raised the cry "The Church in danger." This at least would wring her heart. But here they overreached themselves. Anne, who loved the Church so dearly, was indignant that it could be thought in danger under her rule. She reacted strongly in the opposite direction. She was filled with resentment against the Tories, and prepared herself thenceforward for the political changes which were obviously imperative to the cohesion of the Government.

Marlborough's breach with Nottingham had begun in the spring of the year.[2] He had written to Godolphin on April 6:

1 *Conduct*, p. 166.
2 The following letters are in Coxe, i, 270–280.

If Lord Nottingham continues being so impertinent as to join with Sir Edward Seymour and others to obstruct business, I think it were much better to be plain with him, than to suffer him to go on in that way; for by that he will be much abler to do mischief than if he were out; and I am very much mistaken if he will care to part with his place.

Again, on June 11:

I am very sensible by a letter I have received from Lord Nottingham that there will be an ill use made this winter of the Dutch ships coming so late. As much as I hear of the behaviour of Lord Nottingham, if there were anybody proper to be put in his place, he could do less hurt to the business of the queen if he were out than where he now is.

And on June 14:

. . . There is nothing more certain than what you say, that either of the parties would be tyrants if they were let alone; and I am afraid it is as true that it will be very hard for the queen to prevent it. I think nothing should be omitted to do justice, and then God's will be done. What you say of lord Nottingham concerning the park is very scandalous, but very natural to that person. I wish with all my heart the queen were rid of him, so that she had a good man in his place, which I am afraid is pretty difficult.

And to Sarah, from the same camp at Hanef:

. . . Some of them might, in my opinion, be removed, as 15 [Lord Jersey] and 42 [Lord Nottingham]; but who is there fit for their places? I do protest before God I know of none. I am of your mind that if the queen spoke to lord Rochester in the manner you mention in your letter, I believe it would make him very cautious; not that I think it would make him honest, but he would be afraid. The conversation that was between lord Rochester and the Speaker [Harley] is no doubt the language that he entertains the whole party with; and if they can once be strong enough to declare which way the war shall be managed, they may ruin England and Holland at their pleasure, and I am afraid may do it in such a manner as may not at first be unpopular; so that the people may be undone before they can see it. I can't say a word for the excusing the Dutch for the backwardness of their sea preparations this year;

but if that, or anything else, should produce a coldness between England and Holland, France would then gain their point, which I hope in God I shall never live to see; for our poor country would then be the miserablest part of all Christendom; for we should not only lose our liberty, but our religion also must be forced, and those gentlemen that would be helping to this would then be as miserable as others; for the French, when they are the masters, make no distinctions.

He was equally indignant with Nottingham's associates. "We are bound," he wrote to Sarah on June 14, "not to wish for anybody's death, but if 14 [Sir Edward Seymour] should die, I am convinced it would be no great loss to the queen nor the nation." Of Hedges he wrote to Godolphin on July 22:

. . . If you should oblige him in this and in almost everything he asks (if his temper be what I am told it is), the queen must expect that he will, underhand, endeavour to obstruct everything, which I am very sorry for, but I am afraid it is true.

On the other hand, he repulsed with the nearest approach to severity that occurs in any of his letters to Sarah her suggestion of making overtures to the Whigs, and especially to his son-in-law Sunderland:

ALDERBEESTEN
Oct. 11, 1703

I see by this last letter that you have mistaken my meaning in some of my letters; for though I may have complained of some you call your friends, yet it never entered into my thoughts that they should be spoke to in order to have a better thought of me; for I know they would be as unreasonable as the others in their expectations, if I should seek their friendship: for all parties are alike. And as I have taken my resolution of never doing any hardship to any man whatsoever, I shall by it have a quiet in my own mind; not valuing nor desiring to be a favourite to either of them. For, in the humour I am now in, and that I hope in God I shall ever be of, I think both parties unreasonable and unjust. I am very sensible of several errors I have committed: but I must not endeavour to mend them by running into greater: so that I shall make complaints to neither, but endeavour to recommend myself to the world by my sincere

275

intentions of governing all my actions by what I shall think
is for the interest of my queen and country. I hope in God
this will agree with what you desire, and then I can have no
uneasiness.

Harley, who as Speaker and in a sense the Government
Chief Whip lay so much in the centre of the House of
Commons, had explained the almost universal tide of opinion
flowing against the Continental war. Even Godolphin was
affected by it. Marlborough wrote, "If both parties agree
that the war must not be offensive in this country, I am very
much afraid the Dutch will not think themselves very safe
in our friendship." By this characteristic understatement he
meant that if the English troops were withdrawn from the
Continent the Dutch would make a separate peace with
France.

> However, I cannot but be much concerned; for if this country
> is ruined, we are undone, and then 10 [Sir Charles Hedges] and
> his friends may succeed, which otherwise is next to impossible.
> There are a thousand reasons for preserving our friendship with
> the Dutch; for as we save them, so they must preserve us from
> the arbitrary power of 19 [the Pretender] and 1 [Middleton]
> which must be entirely governed by 3 [Louis XIV].
>
> May God preserve me and my dearest love from seeing this
> come to pass; but if we should quarrel with 24 [the Dutch]
> I fear it might happen.

He sent a curt message to his son-in-law Sunderland, who
as a member of the Whig Junto had proffered the support
of the party in return for a full share in the Government.

> . . . Tell Lord Sunderland that I thank him for his letter, and
> that I hope I shall always continue in the humour I am now in,
> that is, to be governed by neither party, but to do what I think
> is best for England, by which I shall disoblige both parties.
> But as long as I have quiet in my own mind, I shall not care;
> for as I had rather be without employments than have them,
> I shall need none of their protection.

It had for some time been plain that the Government must
be reconstructed before the new campaign began. This

must have been the principal topic at the regular meetings which now took place at least twice a week between Marlborough, Godolphin, and Harley. The episode of the Occasional Conformity Bill only emphasized the need. Nottingham and the High Tories could not be allowed to continue their attack upon the Administration from some of the highest positions inside its structure. It seemed likely that the Queen would be distressed by parting from so eminent and experienced a statesman, whose personal character and morals she respected, whose outlook on politics and religion she largely shared. If the dismissal or resignation of Nottingham could be procured, the whole basis of the Government would have to be changed. Mr Speaker Harley was the only man who could fill the gap. He commanded the goodwill of a large number of the moderate members of both parties, and his influence upon the House of Commons was incomparable. It seemed feasible, if the Queen would consent, to break with the Tory Highflyers in the Council and in Parliament, and form a Government of the centre, which it would be easier for the Whigs to support. On this basis, once the supplies had been voted and Parliament had risen, the war might be carried on during the coming year. No steps could, however, be taken yet. Nottingham's position was too strong to be imprudently assailed, and Harley, who was thoroughly at home in the House of Commons, was by no means eager to enter a different and to him novel circle as Secretary of State. The characteristics of a new Administration were, however, defined in the minds of this triumvirate, whose consultation and concord formed what was virtually an inner Cabinet.

The relations between England and Scotland were moving, with most other great affairs, towards a climax. We have seen how Marlborough had found it necessary to quarter all the English troops for the winter "so that they might be embarked in twenty-four hours," and how he had arranged before leaving The Hague that "if there should be occasion the Queen might have what number of troops she pleases." These precautions were directed against a French invasion of

Scotland, or a hostile declaration by Scotland, or a revolt, or a combination of these calamities. The general election in Scotland in the summer of 1703 had resulted in the success of the Opposition parties. The temper of this free Parliament, the first since the accession of William III, manifested itself in three Acts. The first was an Act which forbade any future sovereign to declare war without the consent of the Scottish Parliament. This meant that if Queen Anne should die, Scotland could withdraw from the war. The second Act, for securing the Protestant religion, affirmed the Presbyterian establishment, and denied even toleration to Episcopalians. To both these measures Anne had been forced to give a reluctant assent. But the third, the Act of Security, proclaimed the probable approaching severance of the Crowns. Its most significant clause provided

> that when Queen Anne died the Scots Parliament might choose her successor, who was to be of the Royal line and a Protestant, *but who should not be the same person as the English successor unless England had previously satisfied Scotland as to her conditions of government and of complete freedom and equality of trade.*

This wild session had ended in September, and before the Edinburgh Parliament met again the Queen's Government had lost every vestige of control over it. The position at the beginning of 1704 was that the Scots were planning to compel the Queen to sign the Act of Security and a Militia Act to create a Scottish army, by tacking them to the Money Acts required for the prosecution of the war. These courses had still some way to run, but it seemed probable that if they were persisted in the outcome would be a civil war in which Scotland would become the ally of France. This was a hideous prospect.

The last domestic problem was the recruitment. All voluntary methods had been exhausted, and the treaty strength of the forces in the field could only be maintained by some form of compulsion. This was already customary for the Navy. Parliament and the naval ports were used to the press-gang. Tories and Whigs alike were for the Navy. It was the defence of the island, and no menace to its constitutional rights. But compulsion for the Army touched all the most sensitive spots in the body politic. The want of logic which had marked John Hampden's resistance to the exaction of Ship Money from counties that did not border on the sea had deep roots in national life. The seizure of men to be soldiers against their will seemed to challenge English liberty in a manner quite different from the seizure of men to be sailors, which, of course, was only what had to be done in time of war. Still, the strength of the armies had to be maintained, and after endless wire-pullings and Parliamentary management the necessary authority was at length obtained by the split Cabinet from the faction-ridden Parliament. The solution adopted was simple. The able-bodied unemployed were caught wherever they could be found and, to use a familiar modern term, "deemed to be enlisted" in the Army. But many of those who had voted for the measure did not scruple to turn its unpopularity against the Government and against the war which they had promised to support.

The increasing gravity of events at home, and the imminent resumption of the war along all its fronts, weighed heavily upon every one who was not diverted by the excitement of party politics. Harley not only was the best judge of House of Commons opinion, but took great pains to inform himself of public feeling throughout the country. He had a number of agents of remarkable quality and discernment, who prowled to and fro in the land from Cornwall to Scotland sending him their reports. Daniel Defoe was one of these; Paterson was another. It is in one of Paterson's letters that we find the best epitome of the situation:

> The face of affairs both at home and abroad requires another kind of resolution and vigour than, perhaps, ever yet appeared in the councils. *Two or three choice men should show another sort of courage and resolution than you and they have done yet in this reign.*[1]

It was in this temper that Marlborough now revolved the strategic problems of 1704.

1 Portland Papers, *H.M.C.*, iv, 71.

CHAPTER XIII

THE GENESIS OF BLENHEIM

(1704, Spring)

IN a war involving nearly the whole world it was natural that each campaign should offer to both sides a wide choice of plans, for and against any one of which there was much to be said. Each plan had to be weighed not only on its own merits, but in relation to all the others in the general setting of the war. The wonderful results which followed Marlborough's march to the Danube have led historians and biographers to hail the idea as if it were in itself an inspiration of genius. In fact, however, it was only one of the more daring moves upon the board which must have been present in the minds of all the chief authorities carrying on the war, and the only questions open about it were: Was it the best, and could it be done? But these were the riddles of the Sphinx.

The Empire had been crying for help throughout the whole of 1703, and as its plight grew worse it cried the louder. Wratislaw was the principal mouthpiece of the appeal. In him the Emperor had an agent of tireless activity and the highest persuasiveness and tact. He knew the desperate straits to which the Empire was reduced; he had the whole picture of the war in his mind; he saw deep into the politics of London and The Hague, and he had the confidence of Marlborough and Heinsius. In his importunity he moved to and fro between all the Courts and headquarters of the confederates emphasizing the peril of the collapse of the Hapsburgs and its imminence, and begging for troops and money. He further urged that, to avert the defeat and break up of the alliance, the main effort of the allies in 1704 must be made outside the Netherlands. A successful offensive upon the Moselle by an Anglo-Dutch

280

army would have advantages. It would set free the Imperial forces under the Margrave of Baden to make head against the Elector of Bavaria. An offensive on the Upper Rhine would be better; for then the allied armies would be nearer together and able to help one another more. But most of all he pressed for the gathering together of all available troops to strike down the Elector and close the awful gap which exposed the heart of the Empire. All this was the natural, obvious point of view for the Emperor's representative to take. But Wratislaw rendered fine service to his master in pressing upon Marlborough the boldest course of all, in choosing the occasions of his advocacy, in preserving the best contacts, and in smoothing away difficulties and misunderstandings. If Eugene, now head of the War Council in Vienna, did not ask Marlborough to come to Bavaria with an army, it was not because he did not desire it above all things; but because he thought it was beyond hope. Wratislaw, in personal relation with Marlborough, and comprehending the pressures to which he was subjected, did not despair. Nor did he risk anything by asking for the best: it might be the surest way of getting at least the second best.

As early as February 1703 the Imperial Envoy had urged upon Marlborough the dispatch of an auxiliary corps to meet the Bavarian danger. Marlborough did not oppose this, but, being then absorbed in "the great design" against Antwerp and Ostend, and hoping for a decisive battle in Flanders or Brabant, he only induced the States-General to spare twelve Dutch battalions.

The command of this not inconsiderable detachment was entrusted to a Dutch officer who plays a part in our story. Lieutenant-General van Goor was a soldier of whom Marlborough had formed a very good opinion and with whom he had established intimate relations. Goor quarrelled with the Margrave. He condemned his conduct of the campaign of 1703. He had criticized his long, futile marches, and the military disasters which had resulted from them seemed to justify his complaints. Goor's criticisms

281

were shared by many of the higher allied officers in the Imperial Army. On the other hand, the Margrave protested to the Emperor against the indiscipline of his generals, and singled out the Dutch and Saxon officers for special censure. He mentioned that they considered their comfort to such a degree that "on the march they appeared in nightshirts."[1] However this may be—and it certainly requires some explanation—the tension between Goor and the Margrave was to reach a climax on November 12. The Margrave ordered Goor to supply from the Dutch contingent a garrison for some small place. Goor displayed the instructions of the States-General that the Dutch troops were not to be split up into small parties. When the Dutchman persisted in his refusal the Margrave, as Imperial commander, had his sword demanded of him, and placed him under arrest. It is not difficult to guess how the Dutch received this information. They suggested that the Margrave should send General Goor back to Holland, not forgetting *to send his twelve battalions with him.* Here were to be additional complications.

Meanwhile, in August, Wratislaw wrote again to Marlborough, making the suggestion that he should meet Eugene at The Hague in December and assert his authority over the Dutch. This imprudent procedure was deftly put aside by the Duke, who confined his reply to expressing his fear that Eugene would not be able to get to The Hague, and his hope that Wratislaw would be there himself.[2] When Marlborough, at the close of the campaign, went to meet the Archduke Charles at Düsseldorf, Wratislaw was on the spot. He laid his case before Marlborough, who listened with his usual attention, conversed agreeably, but said nothing. Proceeding to The Hague, the Envoy pleaded with the Pensionary. Heinsius, knowing too well what his countrymen would feel, turned the subject. For the moment the question dropped, and the Parliamentary

1 P. Röder von Diersburg, *Kriegs- und Staats-schriften des Markgrafen Ludwig Wilhelm von Baden* (two vols., 1850), i, 270 *et seq.*
2 Wratislaw to Marlborough, August 1, 1703; Marlborough to Wratislaw, August 20, 1703 (Blenheim MSS.).

conflicts which filled the season when the armies were in winter quarters absorbed all attention.

Marlborough was, of course, pondering how he would fight his campaign of 1704, if, indeed, he were called upon to do so. He had come home in November determined that he would not repeat his odious experiences of the late campaign in the Netherlands. Upon this his decision was final. If he were to command it must be upon the Moselle or the Upper Rhine, and the Dutch must give him proper control of the army. He had already attempted to make definite preparations for this end. His decision to quarter the corps of the Prince of Hesse-Cassel upon the Moselle for the winter, and for that purpose to capture Trarbach and Trèves, had been frustrated by that Prince's defeat at Spirbach when he was diverted to the relief of Landau. But Marlborough's design for the first stage of the campaign of 1704 is inherent in this movement.

Whether he was, at this time, weighing the chances of a campaign on the Danube can never be known. If he harboured such ideas, he would probably have concealed them from Wratislaw, for many conditions would have to be exacted from the Emperor before it would be worth while to entertain so adventurous a scheme. It was for Wratislaw to ask and for Marlborough to give. It was easy to ask and hard to give, and this was certainly not a time for him to commit himself, even if it were in his power. He conferred with Wratislaw at the end of January on the eve of a visit to The Hague to discuss the war plans for the year with the Dutch. Marlborough then said, "It is my intention to induce the States-General to decide upon a siege of Landau, or a diversion on the Moselle. I should be very glad to march there myself, but as it is difficult to move the Dutch to a defensive, which would at the same time be an offensive, I should be able to get at most only 45 battalions and some 60 squadrons for that purpose. Should I take Landau I would supply the Margrave of Baden with as many troops as possible, so as to enable him to overthrow the Elector of Bavaria."[1]

[1] Wratislaw's dispatch of January 29, 1704; Klopp, xi, 92.

He authorized Wratislaw to report this statement both to the Margrave and to Prince Eugene, as well as to the Emperor. He strictly enjoined that nothing should be said to the Dutch; he would deal with them himself.

There were three important points in this statement. He was resolved, first, to fight outside the Netherlands; secondly, to have an independent army (for the numbers he specified corresponded exactly to the troops in English pay); and, thirdly, he sought the overthrow of the Elector Max Emmanuel. Of these the second is the most remarkable. The Anglo-Dutch forces had been so long intermingled under King William and in the present war that the separation of those paid by the Queen from those paid by the States-General would be a startling departure from the ingrained habits of the two allies. Marlborough had been forced to this decision by the treatment we have described, which rendered military success impossible. He must have a separate army under his own orders, and he would perhaps go himself as far as Landau. More than that could not then, and cannot now, be said of his intentions up to this time.

The Duke started for The Hague in very severe weather on January 26. The winter had been so bitter and tempestuous that his yacht was the first vessel which "for six weeks had ventured to navigate the German Sea."[1] He landed at Rotterdam three days later. He found opinion and affairs equally unpromising. There was great anxiety about the peril to the Emperor and the Empire, combined with an obstinate helplessness to take any steps to avert it. Marshal Villeroy was said to be expected in Brussels before the end of February. Marlborough wrote to Godolphin:

> If he should come I hope he will not stay; for our magazines will not be ready till the beginning of April, before which time these people have made me promise to be back, so that my stay in England is likely not to be worth the crossing the seas twice. But my desire of being with you and Lady Marlborough is such that I would come, although I were to stay but a day.[2]

[1] Coxe, i, 304.   [2] February 8/19; ibid., 306.

The financial position of the Republic was precarious. No receipts at all had come from two out of the seven provinces. All the subsidies to the German auxiliaries, as well as that newly promised to Savoy, were in arrear. The bulk of the war expenditure for the year could only be met by borrowing under adverse conditions. A wave of pessimism and pacifism was sweeping across all classes. There was a deep-seated fear in the States-General of the consequences of sending any large detachments of troops away from the Netherlands. This fear did not arise only from nervousness about their frontiers. There was a domestic cause. The party schism which divided the provinces and towns of the Republic was at this time most menacing. The memory of the two de Witts being torn to pieces by a mob maddened by their country's danger was still recent and vivid in all minds. The dispatch of any large body of troops to Germany might be the signal for a panic and a popular uprising. The stability no less than the defence of the Republic seemed to the dominant party in the States-General to require at once the maintenance of the largest armies, and their retention at home. Against such dangerous timidity Heinsius seemed powerless.

We must suppose that by this time Marlborough had examined in very considerable detail the possibilities and methods of carrying the war to the Moselle, to the Upper Rhine, or to the Danube, and that the essential features of all these three plans were marshalled in his mind. The unfavourable atmosphere at The Hague enjoined upon him the utmost reserve. He made his opinion known that no lasting successes against France were to be gained in Brabant and Flanders, but he did not commit himself to any alternative, not even, at this stage, to an emphatic advocacy of the Moselle. He so comported himself as to leave it to the Dutch themselves to make the suggestion. He took, however, a second definite step towards a concentration upon the Moselle. He ordered the generals of the Hanoverian and Cellian troops in the joint pay of the Sea Powers, Bülow and Somerfeldt, who stood between the Elector of Bavaria and

Nuremberg, to move towards the Moselle. When Count Goes protested that Nuremberg would be exposed, Marlborough shrugged his shoulders and answered, "But the diversion on the Moselle has been wanted on behalf of the Emperor, and, as you tell me, it is still wanted. To run to extinguish the fire everywhere at once is impossible. Emperor and Empire must themselves make every effort in their power: otherwise, I can see no result."[1] It is impossible to fathom the working of his mind from his manipulation of the different factors. Whether he intended by this move to bring matters to a head, or whether his schemes as yet went no farther than the Moselle, cannot be stated. At any rate, this movement increased the alarm, and should spur the efforts, of the Empire and of the German princes, and it presented the idea of a campaign on the Moselle to the Dutch in the agreeable form of some of their troops actually coming nearer home.

Marlborough left The Hague for his brief return to England seriously concerned by all that he learned there. He wrote to Godolphin:

> I shall be sure to take the first wind that will carry me to sea, for I am very impatient to be with you, having finished everything as far as this country is capable, for nobody here has power to conclude anything; *but Providence makes the wheel go round*, and I hope the blessing of God will make us succeed much better than we can propose to ourselves.[2]

And to Sarah (February 20 or 21):

> For this campaign I see so very ill a prospect that I am extremely out of heart. But God's will be done; and I must be for this year very uneasy, for in all the other campaigns I had an opinion of being able to do something for the common cause; but in this I have no other hopes than that some lucky accident may enable me to do good.[3]

This was the style in which he always wrote before his greatest adventures. The same note of gloom, almost of despair, also preceded both Ramillies and Oudenarde. Oddly enough, we usually find him in a sanguine mood at the

[1] Dispatch of Count Goes, February 22.   [2] Coxe, i, 306.   [3] *Ibid.*

beginning of his least successful campaigns. The explanation was that after any great success he saw the next move, and it filled his mind; but at the same time the allied states, feeling all danger past, relaxed their exertions and let loyalty slip. When a new crisis arose, he had a freer hand to deal with a worsened situation.

"If this wind continues," he ended his letter, "I hope the king of Spain will make use of it, and that I shall have the happiness of being with you." The wind held, and he embarked on the 22nd with the first tide. But the yacht ran aground and was stranded by the ebb. He leapt into a small boat and reached the Brill, where he went on board a frigate, the *Dolphin*, and sailed for home. He must have made a fine passage, for he landed at Gravesend about eight the following night and reached London early the day after.

The German princes, headed by the Elector Palatine, now joined their appeals for the succour of Germany to those of the Emperor. Marlborough's orders to the Hanoverian and Cellian troops to descend the Rhine tortured the Empire. The Dutch, deaf to German solicitations, and angered by the Margrave's treatment of General Goor, had finally sent an imperative order to that officer to bring his troops back to Coblenz by April 15, and seemed inclined to suggest that his force was all that could be spared outside the Netherlands, and then only for the Moselle. Marlborough was supplicated by Wratislaw, aided by Count Lescheraine from the Elector Palatine, to permit the Hanoverians and Cellians to delay their withdrawal. At first, on February 29, he was obdurate. He had, he said, already given the orders for their march. In answer to Wratislaw's demand for reconsideration the most he would say was, "I do not reject it: time will show." A fortnight later he consented to suspend the order provided the Dutch would agree.

Meanwhile Wratislaw continued almost daily his entreaties to Marlborough to "come to the aid of the distressed German fatherland"; and more and more he urged that he should come in person. The astute Ambassador seems to have felt

287

that here he was pressing the Captain-General where he wanted to be pressed. He gave important assurances that if Marlborough would come, the Emperor would "meet all his wishes." The Margrave of Baden and the other Imperial commanders would defer to his judgment. The whole authority of the Imperial Crown would be cast against the Elector of Bavaria. His destruction would be the sole object of the campaign. On the other hand, he declared that if the Commander-in-Chief allowed the large English army to be used only to guard the Dutch frontier, while the Emperor, the faithful ally of England, was overwhelmed by superior force, the fortunes of the Empire would not fall alone, but would in their collapse bring down the whole. And if Marlborough, out of deference to the Dutch, confined within the narrow ambit of their supposititious patriotism, failed to rise to the occasion, on his head before Europe and the English Parliament would the blame fall. Thus Wratislaw wrestled with Marlborough during the whole of March, and thus Marlborough, continually obtaining conditions, consented to be wooed.

He had serious need to explore the ground thoroughly. The politics of the German princes made a strange embroidery of half-friendships and hungry ambitions. We have described the motives and conditions which had induced the so-called 'treason' of Max Emmanuel; but what was the position of Prince Louis of Baden, the commander-in-chief of the Emperor? He too was a sovereign prince. Bavaria was his near neighbour. He was united to its Elector by personal friendship. The triumph of the French armies which might well be expected would raise Max Emmanuel to the Imperial throne. How then would the Margrave of Baden stand if he had been his chief and most active opponent in the field? Such suspicions might prove unfounded; but the tendencies from which they arose could not be ignored. Before Marlborough could hazard the Queen's army in the depths of Germany, he must be as sure as possible that he would not be obstructed or even betrayed by the general with whom he was to act.

The attitude of Frederick I also deserved deep study. The new Prussian Kingdom was voracious. If Max Emmanuel could win Swabia and much else at the hands of victorious France, could not Prussia obtain Franconia with its fertile plains of Nuremberg from the same unfortunate event? Could not a side deal be made between the King of Prussia and the Elector of Bavaria, whereby if Swabia were added to Bavaria, Prussia should take Franconia? Was there not, then, an underlying common interest between the Prussian King and the recreant Elector? There were plenty of brave troops to be had from Prussia at a price in gold and territory. By the treaty in which the Emperor had recognized his new kingship Frederick I was bound to provide eight thousand men for the Grand Alliance. Now that Franconia was menaced by the advance of the Franco-Bavarian army towards Nördlingen and Nuremberg, the Prussian King offered nearly double this quota. As before the campaign of 1703 he had been willing to send eighteen thousand Prussians to join the Anglo-Dutch army on the Meuse or the Moselle *provided they constituted an independent command*, so now he offered fifteen thousand men to protect Franconia on the same condition. The Dutch—not, we may be sure, without weighty reasons—had declined his former offer. The Circle of Franconia now were similarly shy of grasping the strong rescuing claw; and the Emperor, who shared their misgivings, had replied with suitable gratitude that eight thousand men would be enough.[1] But further, Frederick I desired above all things the recognition of his kingship by the greatest of monarchs. At Ratisbon, where the Diet sat under the involuntary safeguard of Bavarian rebel bayonets, the diplomats whispered that the kingdom of Prussia might one of these mornings be recognized by Louis XIV.

These examples suffice to illustrate the dangerous web of German affairs. Marlborough was aware of these shifting, indeed sinister relations. As James II's confidential agent, as William III's plenipotentiary, he had for a quarter of a century peered intently beneath the surface of the

1 Lamberty, iii, 460.

European scene. His information about the various states and princes of Germany was as carefully collected and sifted as his military intelligence, of which, indeed, it was an integral part. He had to measure the potential movements of his allies with as much care as those of the enemy, or his own marches and the supply of his own troops. Whether these evil tendencies would become dominant in 1704 turned upon belief or disbelief in the victory of France. Fear and hatred of French ascendancy would not hold the Alliance together beyond the hour when hope of beating France departed. Then Germany and Europe must accommodate themselves to the new dispensation, and prudent princes must not be unprepared for that. The Grand Alliance quivered at this moment in every part of its vast fragile organization. Marlborough saw that without some enormous new upholding force it must come clattering down. Could he impart that force, or would he, if he tried, only be buried in the ruins? No wonder as he listened to Wratislaw's advocacy he weighed all things carefully in his massive scales.

When, on March 21/April 1, the news arrived of General Goor's definite order of withdrawal, Wratislaw protested violently. "The carrying out of this order," he said, "would set Marshal Tallard absolutely free to throw a new and large reinforcement into Bavaria. I beg you to protest, so that the States-General do not heedlessly gamble with the very existence of the Empire."[1]

At this point Marlborough revealed a different attitude. He promised to use all his influence with the States-General to cancel their order. "But," he said to Wratislaw, "I cannot accomplish anything except by word of mouth. I beg you to go over with me." Wratislaw declared he would never leave his side.

Thus when Marlborough returned to The Hague in the third week of April two most important points were established. The leading personages in Holland had made up their minds that some kind of campaign on the Moselle was inevitable, and that they would have to play their part. The second

1 Wratislaw's dispatch, April 1, 1704; Klopp, xi, 98.

COUNT WRATISLAW

By permission of 's Rijks Prentenkabinet, Amsterdam

was that, unknown to the Dutch, Marlborough had procured from the Imperial Court satisfactory conditions for a campaign on the Danube. The Dutch authorities had taken a big step forward without suspecting any ultimate desire, and the Empire spread a carpet of welcome at his feet. We cannot pronounce how far these advantages were the result of the designs of Marlborough or of the course of events. He must by now have studied in hard detail the elaborate mechanism of a march to the Danube and also of the campaign in Bavaria if he got there. This comprised, first, the military disengagement from the Dutch of whatever army he could gather; secondly, the safety of the Netherlands in his absence; thirdly, the movement of his army up the Rhine and through the German states; fourthly, the movements which the French would make when they saw what he was doing; fifthly, the supply and financing of his army and its re-equipment through Germany as might be necessary at every stage; sixthly, the opening of a new and natural line of communications into Germany once he had entered the Danube basin; and, seventhly, how to coerce or crush the Elector of Bavaria. None of these matters could be left vaguely to chance, and, as we shall see from the marvellous smoothness with which everything was executed, all must have been foreseen and prepared. He had, we know, only a very small group to explore and implement his plans, and all manner of arrangements that would now be made automatically by a general staff had to be devised and settled by him and his personal military secretariat. Even now he could come to no decision till he saw how he stood with the States-General. But there is little doubt that from now onward he meant to march to the Danube unless prevented by the enemy.

It was, of course, indispensable to have some authority from the Queen and the Cabinet before entering upon the discussion with the States-General upon which action would follow. Wratislaw therefore prepared a memorandum for presentation to Queen Anne on behalf of the Emperor, to which a formal and constitutional answer would be given by the Secretary of State in Queen Anne's name as partial protection from impeachment should the fortune of war go ill. Marlborough, Godolphin, and Wratislaw sat together upon this document while it was still in draft. This shows that it was brought forward by Wratislaw at their instigation, or at least with their collusion, and not, as Klopp supposes, to put pressure upon them. Wratislaw's dispatches give the gist of their discussion. All saw that the separation of the Queen's forces from the Dutch would gravely perturb the leaders of the Republic. They canvassed the timidity and despondency which might result. It was a question how far this might go—possibly even to the breaking up of the alliance and a separate peace. Wratislaw argued that Holland in its political confusion and deadlock would not be capable of deciding to quit the Alliance before the end of the summer at the worst: whereas the Empire, if not delivered, would fall to pieces long before. If the advance of the English army into the midst of Germany were successful, all would be well; if not, "there would not be much more to lose." This dour logic was accepted. Marlborough and Godolphin approved the memorandum, invited the Ambassador to present it to the Queen, and promised to bring it before the Cabinet.

It is impossible that such a tense conversation could have taken place between three men whose lives and fortunes were all involved and whose hearts beat as one in the general cause without all the cards being thrown on the table. Godolphin certainly knew henceforward what Marlborough meant to do. No one can ever know what Marlborough, or Sarah—so far as she was instructed—said to the Queen, and Anne certainly would not have greatly concerned herself with the strategic significance of the various theatres mentioned. But it may be taken as certain that she knew that her army was to be sent very far into Europe to save the Empire, and that she meant that it should go, and desired to bear the consequences, whatever they might be.

We have thus examined the genesis of the Blenheim campaign. It will be seen that Wratislaw, going beyond his instructions, pleaded for it; that Marlborough, at a moment which cannot be fixed, undertook it; that Godolphin shared the responsibility; and that the Queen, trusting in her devoted servants, issued the commands they desired of her. Archdeacon Coxe states that this decision was taken "through the agency of Prince Eugene, with whom he [Marlborough] had secretly arranged the whole plan of the campaign."[1] And in a footnote he refers to "letters from Eugene to Marlborough, in the Blenheim papers." We have found no such letters in the Blenheim Papers. There is, on the contrary, a lengthy message from Eugene to Marlborough of the middle of February, sent through Whitworth, the English envoy at Vienna, in which there is not a hint of Marlborough coming to Germany.[2] It seems certain from the account we have given that until at least the middle of April neither Eugene nor anyone in Vienna had dared to hope for the good tidings which Wratislaw was able to convey. Although the Ambassador was the author of no discovery or invention, although he ran no risk and incurred no major responsibility, his clear view and earnest assiduity in these memorable events entitle him to long renown.

While all these public troubles and stresses fell upon Marlborough, there was suddenly thrust upon him the torment of a personal trial. We have not hesitated about publishing the poignant letters which follow, and from which we can to some extent reconstruct the story. The complaint is always made that Marlborough has never been made known in his soul and human nature to history. We have his youthful escapades; we have his chequered middle life; but thereafter he appears only as a commander, as a functionary, or as the builder of a private fortune. The exposure of every detail of Napoleon's life, the searchlights which are cast upon the character of Frederick the Great, have not dimmed their grandeur to modern eyes. And after more than two hundred years have passed there is no reason to conceal intimate facts about a great man's life from public knowledge. Moreover, in our human state there is no separation between public

1 Coxe, i, 316.
2 Whitworth to Marlborough, February 13, 1704 (Blenheim MSS.).

deeds and personal psychology, and the story of the one would be incomplete without the other.

Sarah had been smitten to the core by the death of her son. It affected, said one observer, "not only her heart, but her brain." It had "near touched" her head, wrote another.[1] The hope to which she had clung of bearing another son had failed in the summer, and she underwent not only grief, but those profound changes which mark the sad climacteric in a woman's life. Some time at the end of the year she persuaded herself that John had been unfaithful to her, and was obsessed with the idea that he was intriguing with, or "sending to," some lady upon whose identity Time has cast a decorous veil. It would seem from the letters that Lord Sunderland had made mischief in family, as well as in political, affairs. He had said something to his mother-in-law which had thrown her into paroxysms of rage and distress. Husband and wife had been happy in a brief spell together at Holywell, and this trouble fell upon them when they came back to London to meet the insistent demands of public affairs.

John to Sarah

LONDON
[*April* 1704]

＊When I do swear to you as I do that I love you, it is not dissembling. As I know your temper, I am very sensible that what I say signifies nothing. However, I can't forbear repeating what I said yesterday, which is that I never sent to her in my life, and may my happiness in the other world as well as in this depend upon the truth of this. If there be aught that I could do to let you know my innocency I should be glad to do it, tho I am sensible you can never esteem me: so that long life is not what I wish for, but after my death you may have juster and kinder thoughts of me than is possible for you to have of me whilst I am living. You say that every hour since I came from St Albans has given you fresh assurances of my hating you, and that you know I have sent to this woman; these two things are barbarous, for I have not for these many years thought myself so happy by your kindness as for these last five or six days, and if you could at that same time think I hated you I am most

1 Lady Pye to Abigail Harley, April 14; Portland Papers, *H.M.C.*, iv, 59.

miserable. And for the last which you say you are sure of, may I and all that is dear to me be curs'd if ever I sent to her, or had anything to do with her, or ever endeavoured to have.

Marlborough to Godolphin

Friday morning

* You know the tender concern I have for Lady Marl.; so that I need not tell you how unhappy her unkindness makes me. I would have seen you this morning, but that I am not fit for any company. But if I can I will wait upon you on Sunday.

John to Sarah

Saturday

* After your kind way of living with me since we came last from St Albans, which made me think I should always be happy, I did little expect to have had anybody put you in so ill humour as to make me so miserable as I am at this time. [As] for your suspicion of me as to this woman, that will vanish, but it can never go out of my mind the opinion you must have of me, after my solemn protesting and swearing that it did not gain any belief with you. This thought has made me take no rest this night, and will for ever make me unhappy. I know not what to say more but do assure you in the presence of God this is the truth of my soul.

John to Sarah

* I do call God to witness, and as he may be merciful to me the last day, that when I came home this last time I loved you so tenderly that I proposed all the happiness imaginable in living quietly with you the remaining part of my life. I do to my great grief see that you have fixed in you so very ill an opinion of me that I must never more think of being happy.

If the thought of the children that we have had, or aught else that has ever been dear between us, can oblige you to be so good natur'd as not to leave my bed for the remaining time, I shall take it kindly to my dying day, and do most faithfully promise you that I will take the first occasion of leaving England, and assure you, that you may rest quiet that from that time you shall never more be troubled with my hated sight.

My heart is so full that if I do not vent this truth it will break, which is that I do from my soul curse that hour in which I gave

295

my poor dear child to a man that has made me of all mankind the most unhappiest.[1]

We can add nothing to these letters except to set them in their frame.

To complete the picture of Marlborough at this moment we must remind the reader of two papers. The first is the report of the Jacobite agent Hooke to the "pretended Prince of Wales" of April 22.

> Some days before leaving for Holland Lord Churchill had me sought out, and made me so many promises, and gave me such proof of the rightness of his intention to wish to pay the debt which he had recognized so long was due to your family, that I could have no doubt of his sincerity.
>
> He seemed astonished that the Duke of Berwick had been sent to Spain and engaged so far afield, and he asked me how you could have consented to such a thing. I told him that you had already written to me on the subject, and that the Duke's employment in so considerable a post would be certainly highly advantageous for our common interests. I perceived, however, that he thought that the Duke would have been more useful in the theatre where he was last year.
>
> He directed me besides in his absence to go and see Lord Godolphin and let him know anything which I should receive of importance to you and to your family.[2]

The foolish Jacobite scribes and many English historians might seek in this document an additional proof of Marlborough's treachery to the Protestant Succession. Here he was, intriguing again with the Court of Saint-Germains and professing allegiance to the Royal Exile. Anyone of average intelligence who reads Hooke's report in its context of events will realize that Marlborough saw the Jacobite agent only in order to deceive him and to pump him. He was making a supreme exertion and staking life, fortune, and honour in an attempt which was hostile in the last degree to the Pretender's interests; and as a part of the mystery and darkness with which he enveloped his military designs, as

---

1 This cannot refer to anyone but Sunderland.
2 Carte MSS., 209, f. 430. See also Vol. II, pp. 73-4.

a piece of information that could hardly be fitted into any scheme, he sent these agreeable, soothing messages through Hooke to Saint-Germains, and through Saint-Germains to Louis XIV. At the French headquarters the obvious effect of Hooke's report would be to reduce their anxiety about Marlborough's possible activities.[1] He took so much trouble about so many small stratagems that we cannot tell whether this particular manœuvre was actually important or not. But its purpose needs no further pointing. Even the dullest of the Jacobites or the most prejudiced of our historians can see that it was not against England or Queen Anne that Marlborough was using his arts. Incidentally he seems to have gained the valuable certainty that Berwick, whose qualities he admired and respected, would be safely out of the way in Spain. There is another aspect of Marlborough's communications with the Jacobites when he was at the head of anti-Jacobite armies—namely, espionage in the highest circles, to which we shall recur later in the story.

The second document is a letter from Marlborough which finally decided the new combination upon which Queen Anne's Government must be based pending the result of the campaign about to open. Marlborough's political information was as good as his military intelligence. It is the General who reveals to the Treasurer the intrigue which threatens the Government with mortal danger. On April 8 Marlborough sent the following letter to Godolphin as he was about to embark from the Harwich quay.

I could not leave this place without acquainting you with what has been told me respecting lord Nottingham. The Speaker will be able to let you know how much of it may be true. I am assured that he tells his party that the queen is desirous to do everything that would give them satisfaction, but that she is hindered by you and me; that he is so convinced we shall in a very short time put all the business into the hands of the Whigs, that if he cannot get such alterations made in the cabinet council as he thinks absolutely necessary for the safety of the church, he would then quit; that he would speak very plainly to you and

1 The document is in the French archives.

myself before I left England, and that his opinion was that in the next session, *they should tack to the land tax the bill of occasional conformity,* and that of accounts, which was the only way of making them pass the house of lords; for then you and I would be zealous for it, notwithstanding our inclinations. If all this should be true, as I really believe it is, he is in my opinion doing Her Majesty all the hurt that he is capable of.[1]

He sailed again for the wars on this same day. With him were Wratislaw, his brother General Churchill, Cadogan, Orkney, and many other officers, and, of course, Cardonnel. A fleet of transports carrying four infantry regiments and several thousand drafts convoyed by battleships and frigates accompanied him. He must have bade a grim farewell to England. Sarah was at the waterside. The breach between them was not closed. She had repulsed his passionate appeals. She handed to him as they parted a paper setting forth her position and containing several painful things. She knew that he was going upon a high and dangerous enterprise, that there was desperation in his mood, that he would be in the forefront of great battles, that she might never see him again. Yet he was her whole life.

His feelings about his own affairs and his country's fortune were sombre. The national and political situation was dangerous and hateful. On every side were jealousy and baseness. The Tory Party was still harrying the Dissenters. The Whigs and Tories hated each other worse than the foreign enemy. The Lords and Commons were at bitter variance. Scotland seemed to be moving, not to union with England, but to a separate peace with France and a neutrality which could only mean civil war. The Cabinet struggles were burning swiftly into crisis. The old arrangement had broken in pieces, the new had not yet been established. Even the throne of the Queen seemed to quiver. Beyond the cold, rough sea bristled all the obstinate, intricate confusions of Dutch politics, and the cracking structure of the Grand Alliance; and beyond them all—if only he could reach them—stood the foe.

1 Coxe, i, 310.

CHAPTER XIV

TREPANNING AN ARMY

(1704, April)

THE strategic results of Bavaria joining France and Spain in 1702 resemble curiously in many points those that followed the accession of Turkey to Germany and Austria in 1914. The enemy in his central position had gained a state which lay across the circuitous communications of the allies. The defection of Bavaria separated the large, loosely knit, ill-equipped, but none the less indispensable mass of the Empire from the rest of the confederacy, in the same way as the hostility of Turkey cut Russia off from the allies in the Great War. The isolation and forcing of the Empire into a separate peace in 1704 seemed as certainly fatal to the allied cause as the same events in Russia would have been in 1915. Exactly the same issues arose on both occasions among those responsible for the safety of Britain and her friends. Should relief be given to the cut-off member of the alliance by striving to pierce the fortified lines in Flanders or by swiftly striking down the new opponent locally, and restoring the exterior communications of all the states leagued against the Central Powers? On both occasions grave differences of opinion prevailed which aggravated the difficulties of decisive action. But there was also a great contrast. The allies of 1914 could, if they so resolved, strike down Turkey with ease and swiftness by a naval or amphibious operation. Their forbears in 1704 could only reach Bavaria by a long and hazardous march across Europe and amid its moving armies.

Marlborough and Wratislaw arrived in Holland on April 21. "With Marlborough's journey," wrote Hoffmann to the Emperor, "the conduct of foreign affairs will be transferred from London to The Hague."[1] Unfortunately

1 Hoffmann's dispatch of April 16.

at this juncture Heinsius was ailing. His burdens bowed him down. Already in the winter he had seemed to an English observer "not just the same Pensioner we had here six years ago."[1] Now he showed plain signs of mental and physical exhaustion. He shrank from decision. It is impossible to say whether he knew what Marlborough really purposed. Certainly he did what he could to help him as far as he could see. But a new chapter had opened in the affairs of the Alliance. The war-policy had been settled between England and the Empire. Only at the final stage were the wavering yet obstinate States-General to be consulted.

Marlborough in fact was now acting in sole responsibility. He found the Dutch in the worst of moods, resolved to keep all their forces in Flanders, except, as a great concession and for the sake of agreement, to allow fifteen thousand men to go to the Moselle. He warned the Deputies for Secret Affairs at the outset that Louis XIV would open the campaign by sending another French corps to reinforce the Elector in Bavaria. It would therefore be wrong to recall the troops paid by the Maritime Powers which were already on the spot. His first trial of strength was taken upon this, the easiest issue. The four provinces of Guelders, Groningen, Zeeland, and Utrecht argued none the less for the recall of the troops; but Marlborough, aided by the Pensionary, gained the support of the Deputies of Friesland and Overyssel, and, above all, of the Deputy for the predominant province of Holland. After many hours the decision was reached not to withdraw the troops from Germany for the present. This marked a first and definite success.[2]

The Duke then proceeded to argue for a strong campaign upon the Moselle. The fifteen thousand troops suggested were useless; they bore no proportion to any plan. A good army must be formed there which he would command. As

1 Hill to Nottingham, November 3, 1703; Blackley, *Diplomatic Correspondence of Richard Hill*, i, 277.
2 Goes's dispatch of April 29.

the anxious debate rambled on Marlborough disclosed day by day a little more of his intentions. It became clearer to his audience that he had made up his mind. Presently he mentioned that, if opportunity offered, he would join battle with the enemy without consulting the States-General or the Field-Deputies. A hum of disapproval swept the crowded council chamber. Not even the late Stadtholder-King, declared the Zeelanders, had possessed such plenary powers.[1] Zeeland even spoke of "secession."

There must be an end to all this. The hostile armies were now coming into action in every theatre. On May 2 he struck his decisive blow. Having put his views to the three Dutch Generals with whom he could work best, Overkirk, Dopff, and Goor,[2] he requested a meeting with the heads of the Government in the house of the Grand Pensionary. Here the Dutchmen saw a different Marlborough. Hitherto their valued Deputy Captain-General had always submitted to their final judgment. He had pleaded with them often, long, and persistently in 1702 and 1703; but they had always found that the final word rested with them. This day it was otherwise. Marlborough declared that he meant to march with the whole of the English and English-paid troops to Coblenz. He displayed upon the table the Order in Council he had obtained, in circumstances already described, from the Queen. When the Ministers sought to continue the argument he silenced them with hauteur, the more impressive because unwonted. He observed that, this being the definite order of the Queen, he could not permit himself to criticize or discuss it. He charged them so to inform the States-General.

That night he wrote to Godolphin:

THE HAGUE
May 1

By the advice of my friends that I advise with here, I have this afternoon declared to the deputies of the States my resolution of going to the Moselle, and that I would leave this place on Monday.

1 Goes's dispatch of May 2.
2 This officer had not been recalled from his command. He was merely summoned to the conference.

There having been some speeches in the States-General, particularly by some of the Zeelanders, that it was not safe to let their troops go so far from their frontier, my friends were of opinion that I ought not to consult the States any farther, than to declare my resolution of serving there. I shall not know till to-morrow how far they will be satisfied with this. . . . Since I have no thought in this matter but what is for the queen's service and the public good, I do noways doubt but her Majesty will approve it; *for I am very sensible that I take a great deal upon me. But should I act otherwise, the empire would be undone, and consequently the confederacy.*

When I come to Philippsburg, if the French shall have joined any more troops to the elector of Bavaria, *I shall make no difficulty of marching to the Danube.* . . . I shall be, as in all things else, extremely glad to receive your thoughts on all this matter.[1]

This is the first time the word 'Danube' is mentioned in Marlborough's secret correspondence; but it was no surprise to Godolphin.

The full conference the next day met in a tense atmosphere. The Deputies besought the Duke to explain his plan more precisely. On this he took up a position difficult to assail; the plan must be reserved for settlement with the Margrave of Baden. It was not for him alone to prescribe its tactical features before he had even met the eminent soldier at whose side he was to serve. And then in the pause which followed he added with alarming irrelevance, "Care must be taken about the necessary supplies of powder." At this the resistance of the assembly gave way. What else could they do? The only choice open was a campaign on the Moselle in which they would be consulted, or one in which they would be left to themselves. It was the shock they needed. The Captain-General's firm decision "deprived the governing classes of the Netherlands of the will to resist."[2] Having yielded, they gave, like the robust folk they were, the Duke their heartfelt blessing, and promised whatever aid was in their power. They resolved to approve whatever he might decide to be serviceable to the common cause, and ordered instructions to be sent to their envoy in Frankfort, d'Almelo, to help him in every way.

1 Coxe, i, 320.   2 Von Noorden, i, 533.

Nothing, of course, had been proposed to the States-General but the Moselle. The arguments about the impending fall of the Empire and ruin of the confederacy were addressed solely to the proposition that Marlborough should transport an army to Coblenz. If anyone had blurted out the Danube or even the Upper Rhine, the course of history might have been deflected. Marlborough had already set on foot many preparations for supplies, and the necessary agencies of finance centring upon Coblenz and Frankfort, all of which would be necessary to carry a main thrust of the allies up the Moselle. Much of this was bound to leak out. In fact, Marlborough did not seem to care very much if it did. His customary secrecy and reserve seemed to break down upon this aspect. He had already written a letter to the King of Prussia imparting to him the outline of the Moselle operation, going so far as to name dates and places where collisions might occur, and inviting his royal and military opinion thereupon.[1]

While this decision was being extorted from the Dutch, Marlborough had required Wratislaw to secure most explicit pledges from the Emperor that he would proceed against his rebellious vassal with the utmost rigour. He required an Imperial order to the Margrave, "in his own hand or that of the King of the Romans; to put all other schemes aside and to operate with Marlborough against the Elector." He asked also for the presence of Prince Eugene. Wratislaw took this upon his own shoulders. "It is absolutely necessary," he wrote to the Emperor, "that I should have a supporter of his zeal and experience." Moreover, Eugene must be furnished with powers sufficient, in conjunction with Wratislaw, to remove, or even, though this was only implied, to arrest the Margrave, should he falter or abuse his trust. "I once again beg Your Majesty for God's sake not to waste a minute," wrote the faithful and busy Envoy,

for on time depends the carrying out of this plan, and on its carrying out depend the greatness and permanence of your princely house.

1 The Hague, May 5; *Dispatches*, i, 253.

Marlborough, who has come to me as I write these lines, requests me to lay his personal homage at Your Majesty's feet, and assure you that he and his whole army will advance into the Empire with the determination to sacrifice the lives of all or to conquer the Elector. For if that last should not happen, then in England and in Holland he would be lost for ever. But nevertheless he declares that should he see on the part of your Majesty no sincere resolve to suppress the Elector, he would be compelled to withdraw himself and his troops immediately.[1]

And the next day, May 6, Wratislaw wrote to the Margrave in a similar strain to inform him that Marlborough would advance by way of Coblenz and the South. "I assure your Highness," he added, "that Marlborough sets out with the fixed intention of taking a hand in that great enterprise. His own words are: *The issue in this matter is victory or death.*" These were very unusual expressions for the sober-spoken and matter-of-fact Marlborough. Assuredly they did not go beyond the naked truth. While Marlborough was wrestling with the Dutch Deputies the Margrave had already formed independently very similar views. He had in fact written to Wratislaw:

> In the position in which we now find ourselves we can in my judgment do nothing better or more useful than the overthrow of the Elector of Bavaria. So soon as the decision is taken, to unite the armies and crush him by superior force is a matter of two months.[2]

Wratislaw, surprised and overjoyed by this letter, set out post-haste to the Margrave's headquarters at Oettlingen. On May 17 he was closeted for five hours with the Margrave. There was evidently a sting in the Margrave's agreement. He faced the facts; but he placed an uncomplimentary construction on the conditions prescribed. Wratislaw reported to the Emperor:

> In accordance with his obligations to Your Majesty in this grave matter, the Margrave has offered to do everything that can be serviceable to this great undertaking, as he then with the greatest

1 Wratislaw's dispatch, The Hague, May 5, 1704; *Feldzüge des Prinzen Eugen,* vi, 735–737. 2 Röder, ii, 23.

THE EMPEROR LEOPOLD I
From a print in the British Museum

abnegation seeks nothing for himself, but will leave all the honour and gain to Marlborough, if only Your Majesty's service be promoted thereby.[1]

The Emperor for his part had already written on May 15, after praising the zeal and address of his Envoy:

Especially have you done well in giving Lord Marlborough every possible assurance that I cannot now do anything else but seek, in every way and earnestly, to secure that the Elector of Bavaria is brought to recognize his shame and his blunders. Up to now I have not failed to exercise the utmost clemency towards him, only in order that thereby he might amend the presumptuousness and injustice with which he pursues me. But not only has there been no change in his course, but he has indeed abused my clemency. Consequently the time has at last come for him to suffer the operations of justice.

He agreed to the sending of Prince Eugene:

From this decision on my part there should readily be deduced the eagerness with which I take part in this matter, and how greatly I hope for a happy issue, inasmuch as in the present state of affairs I am sending away from myself and my supreme war council a person that I value so highly.[2]

Further, he wrote to the Margrave on May 14:

On the fortunate result of this stroke depends the salvation of us all and the desired object of this war. Because of our paternal anxiety for the Empire, and in accordance with the obligation of the Alliance, *I will not consent to any other operation at the opening of this campaign*.[3]

Marlborough did not belong to the stern and silent type of men of action. On the contrary, he was affable and talkative. People learned from his easy and genial flow of conversation what he wanted them to know. All about him in Holland were spies and go-betweens. Permits to pass the lines of the armies were easily obtained on both sides. Many men must often have been misled by his graceful confidences. Ailesbury is an unconscious witness of

1 Wratislaw's dispatch from Frankfurt, May 22; Klopp, xi, 114.
2 *Feldzüge*, vi, 824.   3 Röder, ii, 27.

his methods at this time. He describes how he visited the Duke at Maestricht and was welcomed in his own apartment, and how later all the generals came in. "There in my presence they were regulating the marches, and my lord asking what general officer would be, of the day, as they term. And then asked if such and such had a good cook, as that they should treat him at supper after marches, whereas a general in chief like him ought to have kept a great table. It was given out for a blind," says Ailesbury (writing long afterwards), "that they were going towards the Moselle to attack France towards the four bishoprics, when indeed they were marching for the Danube."[1] No doubt this incident was 'part of the blind.' Ailesbury was a well-known gossip and had a wide connexion. He was therefore a handy instrument of indiscretion.

The series of unpublished letters which follows describes Marlborough's movements in his own words. They show his feeling that he was going upon a grave and almost desperate adventure; and they breathe a spirit of tranquil and lofty resignation to whatever Fate might impose. We can also see that hitherto Sarah had not been told his real intentions, and how bit by bit the curtain was lifted on the wider scene.

Marlborough to Godolphin[2]

* I expect about the middle of the next week an express from Prince Louis. Till that comes I can't leave this place. Everybody here is very backward in sending what I think absolutely [necessary] for the saving of the Empire, so that hitherto I have only been able to hinder them, from recalling the troops that are already there. You will see by the German letters that the Elector of Bavaria began to encamp at Ulm the 15th of this month and that the Marshal de Tallard was to begin the same day, so that now every post will bring us news. I pray God it be not very bad. I shall use my utmost endeavours to get them all the help I can from hence, being fully persuaded that we shall be undone, *if we can't get the better of them in that country*. I am

1 Ailesbury, ii, 570. 2 Extract.

afraid I shall want the Queen's help in the matter. I have not been free from the headache since I came to this place, and I am afraid I shall not till I get to the army. The English will begin their march next Thursday.[1]

John to Sarah

HAGUE
April 25, 1704

* The wind is so contrary that I must not expect any letters. I shall stay here till about this day senight. I can't yet tell you whether I shall serve in this country or Germany, but if we do not send troops from hence, that country will be undone. However I find great unwillingness here to part with any troops, which gives me a good deal of trouble; for I wish this country so well that I should take pleasure in seeing them do everything that is for their good; but they are, as well as we, so eaten up by faction that I am afraid they will run great risk of being undone.

Whatever becomes of me, I wish you with all my heart, all happiness.

Sarah's conscience had evidently been pricking her about the "paper" she had handed her husband on his departure. Her pride still resisted her heart; but less confidently than before.

John to Sarah

HAGUE
April 29, 1704

* I have this afternoon received two of yours from St Albans, where with all my heart I wish myself. You are so good in one of yours to take notice that I might not like something you had written in the paper you gave me at Harwich. I do own to you that I have had more melancholy thoughts and spleen at what you said in that paper than I am able to express, but was resolved never to have mentioned it more to you after the answer I gave to it, which I hope is come to your hands, for I am impatient of having the copy of my Will. . . .

The people here continue their desires of having me serve this campaign in Flanders, but my own resolution is to go to the Moselle, and if the Service requires, from thence into Germany. The English troops begin to march next Saturday [May 3],[2] and

---

1 On May 1, from their winter quarters at Breda.
2 From their winter quarters. The actual march to the Moselle began on Monday, May 5.

I shall leave this place on Monday. My next will let you know for certain where I shall serve this summer. Where ere it is you have a faithful Servant, *tho' loaded with many faults.*

I desire Ld. Cutts may bring me two Stars, I having none to put upon any clothes I shall make, and if it is not too much trouble to him, a little lickerish, and Rhubarb.

John to Sarah

HAGUE
May 2, 1704

. . . I reckon to leave this place upon Monday [May 5], and in my way I intend to lie one night at my Lord Albemarle's, so that a-Saturday [May 10] I shall dine in the Army on the Meuse and continue there 2 or 3 days, and afterwards join those troops that are designed for the Moselle. But I shall not continue in this country long, *for I intend to go higher up into Germany,* which I am forced as yet to keep here a secret, for fear these people would be apprehensive of letting their troops go so far.

Nothing could have made me *take so much upon myself in this matter,* but that I see the French must overrun the Empire if we do not help them at this time. I am very sensible that if we have not success, I shall be found fault with, by those in this country that will think themselves exposed for want of the troops I shall have in Germany; but I shall have the quiet of mind to know that I have done what I think is the best; and if we have good success, the Empire must own that they are saved by these troops. I have another consideration that gives me uneasiness which is that I shall not be able to hear so regularly from you, and my friends, as when I am in this country; but I am not to be happy in this world. *What ever happens to me* I beg you will believe that my heart is entirely yours, and that I have no thoughts, but what is for the good of my country.

Remember me kindly to my dear Children.

On the eve of his departure from The Hague he received a letter which filled him with joy. Sarah's heart had conquered. She wrote to her husband in love and reconciliation. The Harwich paper was for ever to be blotted out. All her reproaches and suspicions were abandoned. Her one wish was now to join him at the wars.

TREPANNING AN ARMY

John to Sarah

HAGUE
May 5

Your dear letter of the 15th came to me but this minute. My lord treasurer's letter in which it was inclosed, by some mistake was sent to Amsterdam. I would not for anything in my power it had been lost; for it is so very kind that I would in return lose a thousand lives if I had them to make you happy. Before I sat down to write this letter, I took yours that you wrote at Harwich out of my strong box and have burnt it; and if you will give me leave, it will be a great pleasure to me to have it in my power to read this dear letter often, and that it may be found in my strong box when I am dead. I do this minute love you better than ever I did before. This letter of yours has made me so happy that I do from my soul wish we could retire and not be blamed. What you propose as to coming over I should be extremely pleased with; for your letter has so transported me that I think you would be happier in being here than where you are, although I should not be able to see you often. But you will see by my last letter, as well as this, that what you desire is impossible; for I am going up into Germany, where it would be impossible for you to follow me; but love me as you now do, and no hurt can come to me. You have by this kindness preserved my quiet, and I believe my life; for till I had this letter I have been very indifferent of what should become of myself. I have pressed this business of carrying an army into Germany in order to leave a good name behind me, wishing for nothing else but good success. I shall now add, that of having a long life, that I may be happy with you.[1]

Before we set forth on the famous adventure it will be convenient to take leave of English politics for a time. The resolve which Marlborough had taken before leaving England to have done with Nottingham and the letter he had written to Godolphin to that end had now borne fruit. Nottingham did not underrate the quality of his opponents, nor the probable accuracy of Marlborough's information of his designs. He doubtless knew that Marlborough and Godolphin were preparing to drive him from power, and he now resolved to forestall them. Shortly after Marlborough sailed for the

[1] Coxe, i, 322.

Continent Nottingham presented to Godolphin, and afterwards, to the Queen, a very direct ultimatum. It was impossible, he intimated, to continue with a hybrid Ministry. Either it must be Tory or it must be Whig. If it were Tory he and his friends would form a united Administration to serve the Queen and carry on the war as they thought fit. If it were Whig they would oppose the Government by every means in their power. The Queen must choose, and to prove her choice he demanded the immediate dismissal of the Whig Dukes of Somerset and Devonshire from their offices and from the Privy Council. Unless these requests were complied with, he would tender his resignation.

Such language coming from a Minister who commanded a majority in the House of Commons necessarily brought all political affairs to a crisis. But Nottingham did not rightly measure Queen Anne. He counted too much upon the respect and liking which the Queen had for him and, like Rochester the year before, on her personal sympathy with his principles in Church and State. He did not understand that Anne more than anything else wanted her England to win the war, and was prepared to suppress her dearest convictions for that purpose. He did not even now realize that, compared with Mr Freeman and Mr Montgomery, he was only a great noble and a high functionary. Moreover, his challenging procedure and the criticism which his party had permitted themselves to direct against the Queen were bound to rouse her slow but massive combativeness and engage her royal pride, her sense of duty to the nation and of loyalty to her general and the army he was leading so far. We may also suppose that Marlborough, Godolphin, and Mr Speaker Harley had a well-concerted plan of action, and knew where they stood with the Sovereign.

When Nottingham tendered his resignation the Queen desired him to reconsider the matter. But a few days later, instead of parting with the Whig Dukes of Somerset and Devonshire, two Tory Ministers, Sir Edward Seymour and the Earl of Jersey, Nottingham's immediate adherents, were summarily dismissed from their offices. They hastened

ROBERT HARLEY
Sir Godfrey Kneller
Board Room, British Museum.   By permission of the Trustees

indignant to vaunt their wounds to their startled party. There is a curious letter from the Queen to Sarah acquainting her with the royal decision. The grammar is mixed, the style is impersonal, there is a guise of anonymity; but the force and meaning are as lively to-day as when these lines were penned.

> KENSINGTON
> *Thursday morning*
>
> I am just come to this place to get a little air and quiet. I am told by a very good hand that the queen has sent a message to lord Jersey and Sir Edward Seymour which they will not like. Sure this will convince Mrs Freeman that I never had any partiality to any of these persons; for if that had been so, this would certainly never have been done. *Something more of this nature it is believed will soon happen, that will not be disagreeable to Mrs Freeman.*[1]

Something more of this nature that was not disagreeable to Mrs Freeman, in fact, happened immediately. Nottingham was so staggered by the rough dismissal of his friends that he seemed inclined to leave his own resignation in abeyance. The mood of the Tory Party left him no choice. He renewed his request to retire, and was at once shown the door. Officially the Tory Party now went into opposition. But it was soon apparent that there was a considerable body of Tory Members who were indisposed to violent faction in the midst of an adverse war. These Members clustered around the Speaker, and a rift soon opened between them and the main body of their party. It was evident that the immediate sequel to the dismissal of Nottingham must be a system based upon Harley and the moderate Tories, or 'Sneakers,' as they were unkindly called by all true 'gentlemen of England.'

Marlborough must have had a good understanding with Harley before he left England, and he pressed upon Godolphin his prompt appointment to the vacant Secretaryship of State. The new system for the House of Commons pivoted on Harley. The replacement of Nottingham must be made without delay. Any interlude would be not only detrimental, but dangerous. The political foundation must

---

[1] Coxe, i, 312.

be made as solid as possible in view of the stresses to which it would soon be exposed. "By what you say to me," Marlborough wrote to Godolphin from Vorst on May 7, "I take it for granted by the next post to hear Lord Nottingham has given up the Seal, which makes me beg you will take no excuse from 46 [Harley] but that he must immediately come in."

Harley had not gone so far in these serious affairs without facing their logical conclusion. Nevertheless he showed a becoming diffidence, and even affected repugnance to accepting the seals. His scruples were overcome, and on May 18 he added the principal Secretaryship of State to his far-reaching duties as Speaker of the House of Commons. Various minor 'Sneakers' and several Whigs reconstituted the Ministry. Among the former none was more remarkable than Henry St John. His first leap into prominence had been made by his ruthless espousal of the Occasional Conformity Bill. It was he who, with eloquence unmatched then and perhaps thereafter, had expressed the deepest convictions and sharpest appetites of the Tory Highflyers. His second stage had been to ingratiate himself with Harley. His third was to win the regard, almost the affection, of Marlborough. This brilliant being was now flying speedfully upward. He did not worry much more about the Occasional Conformity Bill. On the contrary, he succeeded with alacrity the veteran official Blathwayt—whom we last heard of in the same office in 1688—as Secretary at War. The orthodox Tories were disrespectful about these performances, and found even the term 'Sneaker' unsatisfying; but the youthful St John was dazzled by the glamour of public office, thrilled at being able to lay his hands upon the machinery of war, and fascinated by contact with the great commander whom he set himself to court with all his adulatory magic of pen and tongue.

Thus there was constructed another 'National' Ministry in which Whigs and Tories found their places. But the real Tory Party, dominated by the country clergy, was embattled against the Government, and in direct pursuit of Marlborough

and Godolphin; while the Whigs were not sufficiently represented to bind them as a party. The new Ministry had no
majority in the House of Commons. But the supply for
the year had already been voted, Parliament was about to be
prorogued, and before it met again the war would be lost or
won.

Sarah's reaction to these changes must be marked. Her
view was certainly logical, and perhaps it was true. She
believed that the times were too serious for any compromise
coalition called 'National.' A rigorous Government on a
strict party basis could alone compel discipline and obedience
at home and command success abroad. Her outlook agreed
with that of Nottingham, except that she thought the Queen
should have none but Whigs about her and her two great
Ministers. With the profound instinct of a woman where the
man she loves is concerned, she warned her lord in repeated
letters that Harley and St John were untrustworthy friends
who would in the end betray him. For the sake of these
'Sneakers' he was sacrificing the full, powerful, organized
support of the great Whig Party, the champions of Pro-
testantism and the inveterate foes of France. Thus she
reproached Marlborough for taking half-measures. But
Sarah reckoned without the Queen; and perhaps the Queen
had already begun to reckon without Sarah.

CHAPTER XV

THE MARCH TO THE DANUBE

(1704, May)

THE annals of the British Army contain no more heroic episode than this march from the North Sea to the Danube. The strategy which conceived, the secrecy and skill which performed, and the superb victory which crowned the enterprise have always ranked among the finest examples of the art of war. But a brighter and truer glory shines upon the Man than can be won by military genius alone. Never did lifeboat captain launch forth to the rescue of a ship in distress with more selfless devotion to duty. Not Wolfe before Quebec, not Nelson before Trafalgar, nursed a purer love of his country's cause than Marlborough in this supreme passage in his career. The profound calculations which he made, both political and military, could only present a sum of dangers against which forethought could make no provision. All that gallant army that marched with him risked life and honour: but he alone bore the burden. It was for them to obey the lawful authorities. For him the task was to persuade, deceive, and defy them for their own salvation.

Marlborough was the champion of the entire confederacy, accountable for all time for the common cause and the general deliverance. He could not retire. He could not escape. To withdraw to peace and quiet, ease and affluence; to mingle in the vivid politics of the day; to live the interesting and varied life of an English duke, in days when dukes were dukes: nay, to be happy with Sarah, surrounded in the home he had built and was building at Holywell by children and grandchildren—all were temptations to be put aside. But for what? Ambition? Not certainly in any base sense. He had already all its material rewards. He was only a subject and a servant under a monarchy and

314

patriciate and the House of Commons. He might be the greatest of servants. He could never be more. Monarchies and empires were dissolving or being framed upon the Continent. Perhaps they would be made or marred by his sword. But not for him the prizes of Napoleon, or in later times of cheaper types. His toils could only be for England, for that kind of law the English called freedom, for the Protestant religion, and always in the background for that figure, half mystic symbol and the rest cherished friend, the Queen. But these incentives were respectable. He had to respond to them no matter at what cost in peril or cares. They were also impersonal. A page in history, a niche in Valhalla, and a good conscience to have used well the gifts which God had given: these must be the sole reward of a moral and mental exertion which, for its comprehension and power, has not often been surpassed in history.

But Marlborough felt the greatest compulsion that can come to anyone—the responsibility of proprietorship. It had become his war. He was the hub of the wheel. He was bound to function. He had made the treaties. He had accepted William's bequest. He must discharge it faithfully. He must bring it all to success and safety. The task was his. These foolish-frantic Parliaments, jealous princes, hungry generals, and bitter politicians were all, as he conceived it, in his care. He alone knew the path which would lead them out of their tangles and tribulations, and he was bound to force or trick them to salvation if he could.

Although none of the dangers of his enterprise had been surmounted and its hazards were necessarily imponderable, Marlborough's spirits were high as his coach bore him eastward. He had gathered his army, and wrested it from the Dutch trammels. The British Parliament had been prorogued. With every stage now he would leave England and her jealous politics and Holland with her unreasonable fears farther behind them. The voices of Tory vilipenders and Dutch obstructionists, the endless arguings with councils of war, the wearisome coaxing of the magnates of London

315

and The Hague, the wirepulling and manipulations of their obstinate, faction-ridden assemblies—all fell away. At last he had an army of his own to command. The Government he left behind in England was no doubt weakened and its foes increased by the purge of the High Tories, but at least it was united and coherent. The Lord Treasurer should be able to hold his own till the autumn, and before then the die would be cast in the open field, and the fate of Europe and the war settled one way or the other. Without a victory of the first order and the signal destruction of one of the main armies of France, all was already lost. But he knew himself and he knew his men, and longed earnestly for the ordeal. Moreover, though the sword was in his hand and battle was his quest, there was peace in his heart, for Sarah was kind. One crashing blow to restore the allied cause and then home and quiet, leaving "a good name behind." Thus he mused while the coach rumbled on towards the magnificence of Keppel's country seat, where he would "lie one night" on his way to the army on the Meuse.

Marlborough to Godolphin

RUREMOND
May 9, 1704

* The post going this morning for The Hague I would take all occasions of letting you know where I am. I did also write from Nimwegen, but am in much doubt if those letters will ever come to you. Three deserters are just come to this town. They say the French army was to camp this day at Tongres, but I do not believe it. I shall be with our army at 2 o'clock this day, and shall continue there till the middle of the next week for the English will not be here till Monday, and I design to join them in their fourth day's march from hence. . . .

Marlborough to Godolphin

MAESTRICHT
May 11, 1704

* I came to this place yesterday and have this day reviewed the Army [Overkirk's], which as yet are only 44 battalions and 80 squadrons, but in four or five days time they will be 51 battalions and 92 squadrons, which will be stronger than the French, who have already sent a detachment to the Moselle;

and when they shall be sure that *the English are marching to Coblenz,* which they will know by Friday, which is the day I intend to leave this Army, they will then most certainly send another detachment, which will give these troops here an opportunity of acting offensively. After the 15th of May the surest way of sending your letters to me, will be to Mr Davenant at Frankfort, who will always know how to send them to me. Not having been on horseback for some time, I am so weary that I can say no more.

John to Sarah

MAESTRICHT
May 14, 1704

* As I let slip no occasion of writing when I have an opportunity of sending to The Hague, you will have two or three letters by some posts, and by others none; but I beg you will be so kind and just to me when that happens to believe it my misfortune and not my fault. But when I come higher into Germany I hope to order it so that my letters, and yours too, may come regularly to us.

We have a great many deserters come in [during] the morning, the French army having yesterday marched out of their lines, and, as the deserters say, the general discourse in their army is that when the English are gone, they will attack this Army. But I believe their true design is to alarm these people, and at the same time send a great part of their army into Germany; *for if they should let me get ten days before them, they may come too late.*

I have had so little time to myself that I have not been able to write to my dear children, but pray assure them that I am most tenderly theirs. I shall stay here till Friday, and hope to have letters from you to-morrow, having had none from England since the 21st of the last month. I must make an end, being just going on horseback, to learn more news of the enemy. I shall be sure to write again to-morrow night, till when, my dearest soul, farewell.

Marlborough to Godolphin

MAESTRICHT
May 14, 1704

* I should have given you an account of what had passed with the Pensioner concerning the sparing of five or six thousand men towards the end of this summer before now, had I not been sure that you must know that will depend upon the success we

shall have; for I shall have too many of their troops in Germany for them to spare any till my return, or that I send them some from thence. The Maréchal de Villeroy began yesterday to encamp his army one league on this side Tirlemont. This [Overkirk's] army intends to continue in this camp as long as they make use of dry forage, which will be about ten days longer, and before that time we believe the French will have detached all the troops they intend for the Moselle. I intend on Friday *to join the English on their march*, having already taken all the measures I can with the Generals of this army, *so that my curiosity makes me stay these two days to see what Mons. de Villeroy will do; and longer I can't well stay.* I have had no letters from England since the 21 of the last month, and I am afraid I must not expect to receive them regularly till I come near Frankfort.

A party is this minute come in, which saw the French marking a camp at Montinac, so that they are marched out of their lines. However, we believe their whole body is not yet joined, for yesterday morning the King of France's household was at Louvain.

John to Sarah

MAESTRICHT
May 15, 1704

* I was in hopes to have had letters from you this day, but the Dutch post is come and there are no English letters. I go from hence to-morrow, and hope in ten days to be at Coblenz,[1] where I propose to myself the happiness of finding several of yours. My next will be from Cologne. The French here have not as yet made their detachment for Germany; but I believe they will do it in a few days after they shall know I am gone. I acquaint you with this, flattering myself that you take part in what concerns me so much, as this detachment will do; *for according to the forces they shall send from hence, I shall have the more or less success where I am a-going.* Your kindness has given me so much heart, that if the Germans can hinder the French from joining more troops to the Elector of Bavaria till I get thither, I do not doubt with the blessing of God but we shall have good success, *for the troops I carry with me are very good, and will do whatever I will have them;* I do from my soul wish that we may have a good success for many reasons, but for none so much as that I may end my days in happiness with you, my dearest soul.

1 He was at Coblenz May 25.

THE MARCH TO THE DANUBE

Marlborough to Godolphin

MAESTRICHT
May 15, 1704

* The news here is that the Maréchal de Villeroy has named the regiments that are designed for the Moselle, they will be to the number of 15,000 men.[1] If they send no more, *and there be no misfortune in Germany before I get to the Danube,* I hope we may have success. . . .

Louis XIV had prepared himself to renew the war on all his eight fronts. He and his Marshals in the north and east took it for granted that the initiative rested with them, and from January to March they indulged in the agreeable exercise of choosing where they should throw their weight, what regions to invade, and what fortresses to capture. They surveyed with satisfaction the results of 1703. Trèves and Trarbach, now in their hands, gave them the control of the Moselle. The capture of Landau secured the Upper Rhine. The capture of Kehl and Old Brisach gave them good gateways into Germany. Thus many alternatives were open.

Very long letters were written by the Marshals Villeroy, Tallard, and Marsin to each other and to Chamillart, the Minister of War, and from time to time these letters were answered at equal length by the King. The longest of all were written by Marshal Tallard. In an easy, graceful style, observing the fullest etiquette of old-world gentlemen to one another, and with the profound ceremony due to the first of gentlemen and the first of kings, they discoursed agreeably upon the forthcoming operations. It was a pity the letters took so long to go to and fro; but when one is controlling such great events there should be time for calm procedure. There was no doubt that Max Emmanuel must be reinforced. Marsin's army had received neither recruits nor remounts for nearly a year. He needed strong drafts for all branches, including especially armourers with their flints, etc., to repair the muskets and technical stores. Thus replenished, he and Max Emmanuel believed that they could attack

1 Villeroy actually took 21,000.

Nördlingen and Nuremberg in the early summer and thus make secure the foundation for an advance which would eventually carry them to Vienna. It was settled that Villeroy should stand on the defensive in the Low Countries, and that Germany should be attacked both by Tallard down the Upper Rhine and by Marsin and the Elector down the Danube. The strong combined offensive in the Italian theatre already proposed should at the same time be launched by Vendôme, by his brother, the Grand Prior, and by La Feuillade upon the Duke of Savoy. The first step of all these operations was the reinforcement of Marsin and the Elector. For this Marshal Tallard assumed the responsibility.

Thus the campaign opened in the south. The Elector of Bavaria, with Marshal Marsin, had constructed a strong entrenched camp astride the Danube below Ulm. Here, almost surrounded by ramparts and flowing water, they lay with a Franco-Bavarian army of forty thousand men, representing the depleted units of a much larger force. The first step in the main French design was to raise this army to its proper strength. For this purpose Marshal Tallard had collected drafts of ten thousand men at Strasburg. It was arranged that he should try to pass these troops through the Black Forest towards Ulm under the protection of his own army of eighteen thousand men, and that the Elector should meet them on the way with an adequate force and ample supplies. Accordingly on May 4 the Elector and Marsin, leaving fourteen thousand men around Ulm, marched westward with thirty thousand men and an enormous convoy of wagons, intending to take over the reinforcements from Tallard near Villingen. The army of the Margrave, Prince Louis of Baden, also about thirty thousand strong, was spread along the Upper Rhine mainly in the lines of Stollhofen, while his lieutenant, Count Styrum, with ten thousand men, watched the Elector at Ulm. Styrum thought he had a chance, in spite of his smaller numbers, of striking at the Elector as he wended westward, accompanied by his heavy convoy. But the Margrave, wishing to make sure, set out from Stollhofen with two-thirds of his force to join him, and

320

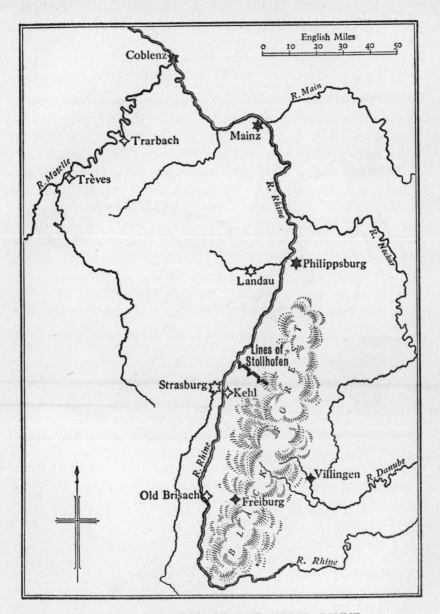

English Miles

0   10   20   30   40   50

Coblenz

R. Main

Trarbach

Mainz

R. Moselle

Trèves

R. Rhine

R. Neckar

Philippsburg

Landau

Lines of
Stollhofen

F O R E S T

Strasburg Kehl

R. Rhine

Villingen

R. Danube

B L A C K

Old Brisach

Freiburg

R. Rhine

FRENCH CONTROL OF THE UPPER RHINE

forbade the attack till he arrived. He united with Styrum on May 19; but it was then too late. The Elector had already reached the neighbourhood of Villingen, and was in touch with Tallard. That Marshal had started from Strasburg on the 13th. He had slipped by the fortress of Freiburg, run-

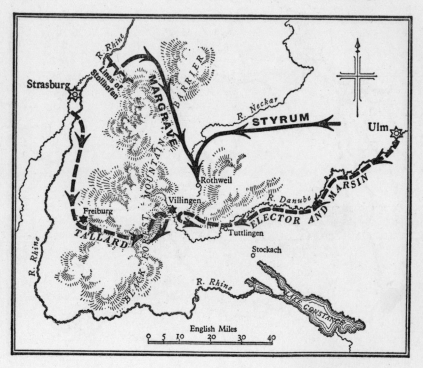

TALLARD PASSES THE DRAFTS TO BAVARIA

ning the gauntlet of its cannon at six hundred yards in the darkness of night without loss of life. He had brought the drafts safely through the Black Forest, and during the 19th and 20th handed them over to the Elector and Marsin.

The united Franco-Bavarian army was now somewhat superior to that of the Margrave, forty thousand against thirty thousand. But the new drafts were not yet incorporated, and the convoy was a burden. The Margrave therefore planned to strike at the Elector while his long columns were passing through the defile of Stockach, in the difficult country north of Lake Constance. This promised great results, for the Bavarians were short of food, and the pass narrow. He was, however, again too late, and after their rearguard had been engaged in a brisk cannonade on May 24, the Elector and Marsin returned successfully

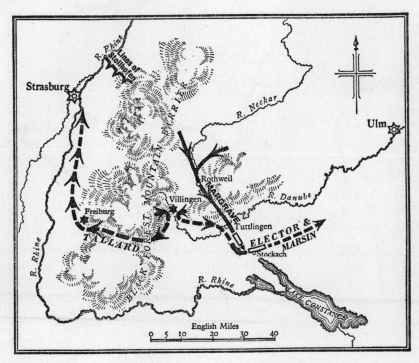

THE MARGRAVE MISSES THE ELECTOR

with their reinforcements to their stronghold north of Ulm. Thus by the end of May Tallard had succeeded in reinforcing the Franco-Bavarian army to a total of fifty thousand men. The Margrave was blamed for his double failure to interfere with this concentration. He continued with his main force opposite Ulm, while Tallard, his mission accomplished, resumed his station on the Upper Rhine. The first move in the French plan was thus completed.

Meanwhile, however, in Flanders, two hundred and fifty miles away to the northward, something had happened which

323

ENGLISH MILES

* Marlborough with the cavalry.
▬ Churchill with the infantry and artillery.

immediately attracted and thenceforward dominated the
attention of all the French commanders. A scarlet caterpillar, upon which all eyes were at once fixed, began to
crawl steadfastly day by day across the map of Europe,
dragging the whole war along with it.[1] During the early
part of May it became apparent to the French that Marlborough was dividing the allied forces in Flanders into two
armies, one of which, under Overkirk, lay around Maestricht,
while the other was assembling at Bedburg and might
amount to twenty thousand men, and certainly included the
bulk of the English. On May 19, the same day when at
the other end of the theatre Tallard was passing his reinforcements to the Elector, this new army began to march
towards the Rhine. On the 21st it was at Kühlseggen. On
the 23rd it was at Sinzig, and evidently moving towards
Coblenz. It was also known that Marlborough was at its
head. The natural conclusion of the French High Command
was that he intended a campaign on the Moselle, with the
fortresses of Trarbach and Trèves as his immediate targets.
The very moment that his movement up the Rhine had become apparent Villeroy, leaving Bedmar with twenty-five
thousand men to face Overkirk, started with twenty-one
thousand men through the Ardennes for the new scene of
operations. He wrote to Versailles explaining that "there

1 This epithet is justified by the variety of tints in red, scarlet, and crimson prevailing in the British uniforms of the period.

was only danger at the point where the Duke in person stood at the head of the allied troops."[1] On May 27 the Marshal was at Arlon, forty miles from Trèves. Tallard was also returning to Strasburg from the south.[2] The French thus conceived themselves not ill-arranged to meet Marlborough along the Moselle; but obviously Tallard could not quit the Rhine until Marlborough was definitely committed to the Moselle. Nor, of course, could the Elector and Marsin begin their march upon Nördlingen and Nuremberg while everything had been thrown into such uncertainty in the north.

The French plan of campaign which had opened propitiously must now be held in suspense. Marsin on the Danube, Tallard on the Rhine, Villeroy on the Moselle, Bedmar on the Meuse—all stood still, waiting with strained attention upon Marlborough's movements. From the very outset, therefore, the initiative had passed from the whole line of French armies to the English commander. The pressure upon Overkirk had been relieved by Villeroy's departure, and Flanders was safe. A respite had been gained for Franconia. But the French hoped that this disconcerting check to their plans would not last long. The Englishman was marching fast, and would surely turn up the Moselle at Coblenz. At this stage we may leave the French Marshals

1 Villeroy to Chamillart, May 18; Pelet.
2 See also general map facing p. 256, vol. IV.

and the Great King waiting and guessing while precious days slip by, and return to Marlborough and his army.

On May 16 Marlborough had set out from Maestricht to overtake his troops. On the 18th, near Bedburg, he passed them in review. It must ever be a source of pride to the British nation that the force which began the famous movement consisted almost entirely of our fellow-countrymen. It comprised at this outset, and for the greater part of the march, 14 battalions, and 19 squadrons, representing England, Ireland, Scotland, and Wales, and the English Artillery, with 20 foreign squadrons, in all about nineteen thousand men. Since these few redcoats changed the history of Europe and indeed of the world, it is right their regiments should be recorded here.

BRITISH TROOPS WHICH TOOK PART IN THE MARCH TO THE DANUBE AND THE BATTLE OF BLENHEIM

Title in 1704	*Later Titles*
Lumley's	1st King's Dragoon Guards.
Wood's	3rd Dragoon Guards.
Cadogan's	5th Dragoon Guards.
Wyndham's	6th Dragoon Guards (Carabineers).
Schomberg's	7th Dragoon Guards.
Lord J. Hay's	2nd Dragoons; the Royal Scots Greys.
Ross's	5th Dragoons; 5th Royal Irish Lancers.
1st Battn. 1st Guards	Grenadier Guards.
Orkney's	1st and 2nd Battns., 1st Foot; the Royal Scots.
Churchill's	3rd Foot, the Buffs; (East Kent Regiment).
Webb's	8th Foot; the King's (Liverpool) Regiment.
North and Grey's	10th Foot; the Lincolnshire Regiment.
Howe's	15th Foot; the East Yorkshire Regiment.
Derby's	16th Foot; the Bedfordshire and Hertfordshire Regiment.
Hamilton's	18th Foot; the Royal Irish Regiment.
Rowe's	21st Foot; the Royal Scots Fusiliers.
Ingoldsby's	23rd Foot; the Royal Welch Fusiliers.
Marlborough's	24th Foot; the South Wales Borderers.
Ferguson's	26th Foot, the Cameronians; (the Scottish Rifles).
Meredith's	37th Foot; the Hampshire Regiment.

Also the Artillery and Engineers.

The actual detachment of the armies and the first few marches from Bedburg were alarming for the Flanders front. Villeroy, with forty-six thousand men still concentrated, was superior to Overkirk, with fifty thousand dispersed on the defensive. He made a demonstration in force toward Huy, and the Veldt-Marshal, believing himself about to be attacked, sent an urgent appeal to Marlborough to return. The Duke, convinced that, since his own movement was now pronounced, Villeroy would have to keep pace with him, sent only a soothing reply and marched on. In forty-eight hours the danger phase had passed. Villeroy was hastening southward, and Overkirk was relieved from all anxiety. On the 22nd Marlborough received a call for succour from the opposite quarter. The Margrave, who believed that Tallard had already returned from the south and was moving to attack the denuded Lines of Stollhofen, sent an alarming message. In response to these opposite tensions Marlborough ordered the Prussian and Hanoverian contingents which were to join him later on his march to strengthen the troops in the Stollhofen lines. As soon as he was certain of Villeroy's southward movement he wrote to the States-General assuring them that Overkirk and Holland were perfectly safe, and urging them to send him the strongest reinforcements they could.[1]

In this he found unexpected support. To his surprise and pleasure he learned that Overkirk and his generals had in fact—on their own motion—already asked the States-General to be allowed to send 8 battalions and 21 squadrons of Danish troops to him. At Bonn, which he reached on the 23rd, he heard that Tallard had succeeded in sending the drafts through to Marsin. This evil news was exaggerated. It was reported that twenty-six thousand reinforcements had joined the Elector. The gravity of

1 Alison writes (i. 147), "Villeroy with the French forces on the Meuse retired before him [Marlborough] to the Moselle, and eluded all attempts to bring him to battle." This reveals the historian's complete misconception of what was happening. Villeroy was not retiring before Marlborough; nor was Marlborough attempting to bring him to battle. The two generals were moving on parallel lines, a hundred miles apart, with the Ardennes between them, and Villeroy was two or three marches behind Marlborough, not before him.

these tidings is revealed in his letters. This was an hour of great personal stress. He did not know yet whether the States-General would allow the Danish troops to join him. If they did not, and if Tallard had really passed twenty-six thousand men to the Elector, he felt that he might reach the Danube only to be "overpowered by numbers." No letter is more grim than the one he writes from Bonn, which fortress he spent the day of the 23rd in inspecting. The only result of these ugly tales and unknown factors was to make him push forward rapidly with the whole of his cavalry in order to emphasize the strategic impression and consequences he knew his march into Germany must produce.

Marlborough to Godolphin

CAMP OF BEDBURG
May 19, 1704

* Having none of yours to answer nor no letters from Germany since my last, I having nothing to write but that I am got hither and in good health, *this little army resting this day*, the Bishop of Raab and several others from Cologne have sent me word they will dine with me. I am very impatient of hearing from you, having none since the 21st of the last month, which were full of the resolution Lord Nottingham had taken [*i.e.,* to go when thrust out]. I confess I must always be of opinion the Queen deserved much better from him.

This minute I have received an express from Mons. Overkirk to acquaint me that the morning I left the Army the Maréchal de Villeroy detached for the Moselle 8 battalions and 16 squadrons [*i.e.,* five to six thousand men]; but they marched no farther than Namur, and as he thinks are come back to the Army. If they are, they must have received orders from Court to attempt something before they let the detachment march. The Dutch army is so well encamped that I do not apprehend the French can do them any hurt, or that they have such a superiority as to undertake any siege. *If they would fool away 7 or 8 days it would be of great advantage to the expedition I am making.*

John to Sarah

CAMP OF KÜLSECKEN [KÜHLSEGGEN]
May 21, 1704

* My express is come back from Cologne without English letters, which makes me very uneasy; for I did not doubt but I

328

should have found some there. I have received this morning an express from Prince Lewis of Baden that the French were using their utmost endeavours to join the Elector of Bavaria, so that I have taken my resolution of taking all the horse with me, and leaving the foot to march with the cannon, so that I hope to be at Mayence the 29th of this month. But you shall hear again of me at Coblenz a-Sunday [May 25], for I hope to have a bridge over the Rhine by that time. Before you receive this I believe you will hear that the French have sent a great number of their troops towards Germany, and I am assured that the Marshal de Villeroy will march with them. *Let them send what they will, I have great hopes God will bless this undertaking*; I am heart and soul yours.

Marlborough to Godolphin

BONN
May 23, 1704

* I left the Army on their march this morning to see this place, and shall join them at their camp this evening. I received by express last night from Frankfort the ill news of the French having joined the Elector of Bavaria at Villingen with 26,000 men; so that if I had not marched with this detachment, the Elector was to have marched to Vienna with an army of 30,000 and have left the rest under the command of the Maréchal Marsin; which they reckon to be 30,000 more; *but I hope they are mistaken, or we shall pass our time ill*; for it is most certain that the Maréchal de Villeroy is marching with the best of the troops from Flanders. So that *if the Dutch do not consent to the strengthening the troops I have, we shall be overpowered by numbers*. For you may see plainly by this march of Mons. Villeroy that they will do all they can to support the Elector of Bavaria.

I think it might be for the service if Mons. de Vriberg were spoke to in the Queen's name; to press the States for the assisting the Empire this campaign with what troops they possibly could. They might strengthen me, and not much weaken their army, if they would draw one-half of their troops out of their garrisons, which they might do, since the French have no army in Flanders, that can give them the least apprehension. I am in such haste that I can only write two words to Lady Marl. and refer her to your letter.

Before this news I had taken the resolution of advancing with

329

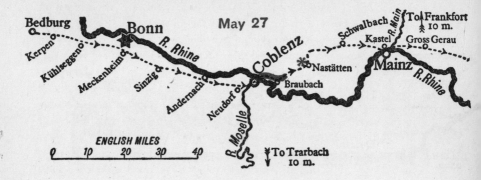

the horse, and now shall do it with all expedition, so that I hope to be at Mayence a-Wednesday night or Thursday morning.

John to Sarah

BRAUBACH
May 27, 1704

* I had yesterday by the Dutch post the ill news of a Packet boat being taken, by which I am afraid I have lost one or more of your dear letters. I had yesterday an express from Prince Lewis, in which he acquaints me that he hopes the next day he may engage the Enemy. I have sent the copy of the letter, so that Lord Treasurer may acquaint you with the contents of it. If flattery could make me happy, Count Wratislaw, that came to me yesterday, has said so much from the Emperor that I am ashamed to repeat it to you; but I hope the Queen will have the good effects of it; for it is certain that if these troops I bring had not come to his [the Emperor's] assistance, he would have run great risk of losing his Crown, which he seems to be very sensible of.

I have also the satisfaction of receiving marks of the friendship of the Dutch Generals in Flanders; for I had an express yesterday from Monsr Auverkerke [Overkirk] to acquaint me that they had written to the States, to desire they might immediately have power to send me 20 squadrons of horse and 8 Regiments of foot: for they were of opinion that no success in Flanders could make amends for any ill accident that might happen to me, for want of having more troops. I know you are so concerned in anything that makes me easy or uneasy, that I would not omit

330

Duke's army was following the right bank of the Rhine. He had crossed the Main. The Hessian artillery which the Landgrave had prepared for a campaign on the Moselle had already arrived at Mannheim. But, most significant of all, bridges were being constructed across the Rhine by the governor of Philippsburg. Here, then, it seemed, was the Englishman's object at last exposed. His campaign was to be in Alsace, and the strong fortress of Landau, taken and re-taken already in the war, fifteen miles from the river opposite Philippsburg, on the Queich stream, was no doubt the first objective. Hence the Hessian artillery at Mannheim, and the pontoon bridge by Philippsburg. Hence the recent reinforcements by the Prussian and Hanoverian detachments of the thinly held Lines of Stollhofen.

This prospect was not unwelcome to the French. On the contrary, it offered them simpler and less menacing proposi-tions than a campaign on the Moselle. Tallard was already near Landau. Villeroy had been marching towards him ever since he heard that Marlborough had turned across the Rhine at Coblenz. The two Marshals, who now each had at least twenty-two thousand men, were in a position to form a strong army to dispute the siege of Landau or resist an invasion of Alsace. Moreover, once this fascinating enemy had engaged

333

himself before Landau or otherwise in that region, the Elector and Marsin could begin their offensive in Germany, with the capital of the Empire as its final goal. "We shall know for certain," thought these experienced soldiers, "once Marlborough has crossed the Neckar." And to the Neckar he was evidently making his way. So once again they paused and watched and waited. Tallard alone spoke of a possible design which might reach to the Danube.

Marlborough had been received with the highest ceremony and a triple salute of cannon by the Elector of Trèves, most of whose country was in the hands of the enemy, and he dined with him in the castle of Ehrenbreitstein on the 26th, while his cavalry and dragoons were defiling beneath them across the floating bridges. At his camp at Neudorf he had been joined by Wratislaw on behalf of the Empire, by M. d'Almelo, the envoy of the States-General, and, perhaps most important of all at this moment, by Mr Davenant, the English agent at Frankfort. Frankfort now played an important part in his schemes. It was his advanced financial base. Here were those ample English credits, so faithfully fed by Godolphin, which enabled the English commander to pay cash for everything and to supply all ranks with their pay and allowances. On this depended the discipline and smooth movement of his army. The German countryside and townsfolk had seen and heard much of war, but an army that paid its way, pillaged nothing, and seemed so orderly and good-tempered, was a novel experience. And since they recognized this army for their deliverers they hastened with not unnatural enthusiasm to aid its march and supply.

Once across the Rhine the scarlet caterpillar progressed amid flowers and blessings. The British troops felt the same thrills as rewarded their descendants when at the end of 1918 they drove the enemy before them through Belgium and the liberated provinces of France. But now it was no devastated region but the beautiful, smiling Rhine valley in the glory of summer which welcomed the marching columns of horse and foot with every sign of gratitude and admiration.

334

Then, as in later times, the costly excellence of the British equipment attracted attention. Until late in the nineteenth century a 'Marlbrouck' meant in these districts a wagon of exceptional strength and quality. Bouquets and waving of ribbons, friendly helpful hands, and bands of smiling women and girls—"some of them much handsomer," says Captain Pope characteristically, "than we expected to find in this country"—cheered the long marches.[1] High and low, from prince to peasant, the Germans greeted their rescuers. And around all an embracing forethought, at once sure and easy, provided for all their needs.

In this surprising journey nothing seemed to have been forgotten. Parker says:

> We frequently marched three sometimes four days successively and halted one day. We generally began our march about three in the morning, proceeded about four leagues or four and a half by day, and reached our ground about nine. As we marched through the countries of our allies, commissars were appointed to furnish us with all manner of necessaries for man and horse; these were brought to the ground before we arrived, and the soldiers had nothing to do but to pitch their tents, boil their kettles and lie down to rest. Surely never was such a march carried on with more order and regularity and with less fatigue both to man and horse.[2]

But Marlborough's agent, Mr Davenant, with the English gold and credits at Frankfort, had much to do with this. The Duke had been able to make very considerable arrangements in Frankfort which nevertheless wore the appearance of being directed to the Moselle. He was able to tell General Churchill to order from Frankfort all the replacements and spare equipment which were necessary. A complete outfit of new shoes for the whole army had been secretly prepared at Frankfort for issue to the troops. The saddlery of the cavalry was similarly kept in the highest condition, and in every particular the British and all other forces in the Queen's pay were maintained as they deserved. These continual evidences of design unfolding day after day bred in all

1 Cowper Papers, *H.M.C.*, iii, 36.   2 Parker, pp. 80–81.

ranks that faith in their commander which, once rooted, is hard to destroy, while at the same time the eyes of a grateful population convinced the soldiers of the righteousness of their cause. Their professional spirit was strengthened by a new morale, and while Marlborough's stinginess kept strict account of all expenses, the housekeeping of the army was good and ample. Well might he write to Sarah, "The troops I carry with me are very good, and will do whatever I will have them."

"I send to-morrow to Frankfort," Marlborough wrote to Godolphin,

> to see if I can take up a month's pay for the English, and shall draw the bills on Mr Sweet; for notwithstanding the continual marching, the men are extremely pleased with this expedition, so that I am sure you will take all the care possible that they may not want.[1]

Thus this march is remarkable among military operations both for the detail in which it had been prepared and the secrecy and mystery in which it was shrouded from the enemy. Alike for its audacity and forethought, alike for its strategic swiftness and day-to-day comfort, it was a model which in those days had no copies. We wonder how it was done when organization by our standards was so primitive, and the staff employed so small. None of those large departments of A (Adjutant-General), G (General Staff), and Q (Quartermaster-General) existed. In fact, the full classification was not to be made for two hundred years of military history. Four or five men, each with no more than as many clerks and officers around them, handled the whole affair. Cadogan, Cardonnel, Davenant, stand out almost alone at this stage as Marlborough's managers. He had picked them all carefully and tried them long. He must have kept the whole central grip in his own mind largely without any written record. All were men of high quality in their different functions, and each accepted without question the orders they received from their chief. No doubt they consulted together

1 Mainz, May 29; Coxe, i, 331.

COLONEL WILLIAM CADOGAN
Louis Laguerre (?)
National Portrait Gallery

where necessary, but not one of them at this time, except Cardonnel, knew where he was going or what he meant to do. Each functioned perfectly and with confidence within the limits of the task assigned from week to week, nor questioned arrangements, the purpose of which could not be seen.

Not less remarkable was Marlborough's Intelligence. In these days between Coblenz and Mainz in the camp at Neustadt Mr Cardonnel received an important letter from a friend at Celle. The letter and its enclosures have vanished, but their purport can be judged by Cardonnel's answer. "This serves," he wrote, "chiefly to thank you for your two letters which accompanied Mons de Chamillart's Memorial and du Breuil's examination. With regard to the former, you know already that the most considerable point they concerted—viz., the junction—has had its effect, without a blow being struck, before the Prince of Baden had joined the troops, and while he had given positive orders that they should not act before his arrival: *we find, however, the utmost designs of the enemy, in this memorial, and I hope we shall be able to traverse them.*"[1]

This fragment opens a loophole on Marlborough's elaborate secret service. The agent in Celle, a man named Robethon, had raised himself from a humble origin to become the confidential secretary of the Elector of Brunswick. Here he was well placed with the approval of his master to gather information, and Marlborough kept him supplied with large sums of money for several years with excellent results. He had now forwarded the entire French plan of campaign to Cardonnel. Napoleon's historian makes the following sub-acid comment: "We must conclude from this significant paper that the feeble Chamillart, occupying the post of Louvois without having either his vigour or his talent, had let himself be robbed of the secret of the campaign plan. Nothing is beyond the reach of the power of gold, and it looks as if Marlborough, although blamed for avarice, knew how to spend money to some point. As clever at piercing the hidden designs of his enemy as in beating him on the field of battle, he united the cunning of the fox to the force of the lion."[2]

1 Lediard, i, 300.   2 Dutems and Madgett, *Histoire de Jean Churchill*, i, 293.

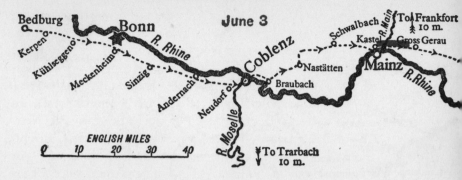

Here was the French plan, part executed and the rest to come, filched or bribed from the cabinet of the War Minister in Paris, deciphered in Celle,[1] sent to Cardonnel by long circuitous routes through France and Germany, and laid upon Marlborough's camp table in his tent at Neustadt. Oddly enough, this priceless information added nothing to his knowledge. He had learned it already by his finger-tips. It only confirmed what his occult common sense had divined. But it must have been none the less very reassuring.

Thus the columns rippled along the roads as the scarlet caterpillar beat the ground rhythmically with its feet. Up the hills and down the hills, through the forests and gorges, across the Main and across the Neckar, always wending on, while the Great King and his Marshals readjusted their views from week to week, and Europe from one end to the other became conscious of an impending event.

Marlborough had insisted that Wratislaw should be at his side as his *liaison* with the Emperor, the Margrave, Eugene, and the German princes. "For as I have revealed my heart to you," he wrote to the envoy on May 20, ". . . I depend for good success largely on your zeal. . . ."[2] Wratislaw rejoined him at Neudorf, and here the Duke made it clear that he expected him to make the campaign with him. Wratislaw feared that if a disagreement occurred between the generals the blame would be thrown on him. But Marlborough would have none of this. Wratislaw was in the business,

1 *Dispatches*, i, 285.   2 *Ibid.*, i, 269.

and must take the rough with the smooth. He stirred the Elector of Mainz, a sincere devotee of the Empire, in whose palace they were entertained a few days later, to back his demands. He had already made formal application to Vienna through Mr Stepney.[1] "I must acquaint you that as I am now going to Prince Louis and have no manner of acquaintance either with him or his generals, . . . I have prevailed with Count Wratislaw, though he be very impatient to return home, to go along with me for some time." The Emperor decided that Wratislaw must abide with Marlborough. "He ought to be there," said the Emperor, "to ensure that Marlborough undertakes and completes the operations decided upon."

On June 3 Marlborough's cavalry, now reinforced by various allied contingents from the German states to eighty squadrons, crossed the Neckar at Ladenburg by the floating bridge and encamped on the other side. Here he halted for three days.

John to Sarah

WEINHEIM
June 2

I take it extreme kindly that you persist in desiring to come to me; but I am sure when you consider that three days hence will be a month that the troops have been in a continual march to get hither, and we shall be a fortnight longer before we shall

1 *Dispatches*, i, 288.

339

be able to get to the Danube, so that you could hardly get to me and back again to Holland, before it would be time to return into England. Besides, my dear soul, how could I be at any ease? for if we should not have good success, I could not put you into any place where you would be safe.

I am now in a house of the elector palatine, that has a prospect over the finest country that is possible to be seen. I see out of my chamber window the Rhine and the Neckar, and his two principal towns of Mannheim and Heidelberg; *but would be much better pleased with the prospect of St Albans, which is not very famous for seeing far.*[1]

From his next camp at Ladenburg he wrote the letters which revealed for the first time his true destination both to the States-General and to his brother. The Queen of England, he told their high Mightinesses, had commanded him to go to the aid of the Empire, and accordingly he was marching to the Danube. He appealed to them to allow their troops in his army—the Danish contingent and certain Dutch detachments he had collected on his march—to share the honour of this memorable expedition. To Churchill he sent orders to march direct upon Heidelberg, as the Ladenburg road was difficult for the cannon.

On June 6 Marlborough advanced to Wiesloch, only a day's march from Philippsburg and the Rhine. He was now within thirty miles of the enemy at Landau, and he knew that both Villeroy and Tallard might be very near that fortress. Moreover, the moment was come when the final veil must be lifted to the French. Hitherto Marlborough had always possessed the power to return at superior speed to Flanders. He had gathered a mass of boats on the Rhine, and by embarking his infantry therein could transport them back downstream at a rate of at least eighty miles a day. It was this curious feature of the military problem which, while it comforted the Dutch, was so baffling to Villeroy. Till Marlborough had passed at least Coblenz he could not be sure that the whole march was not a feint to lure him from Flanders, whither he could only return at one-eighth Marlborough's

1 Coxe, i, 333.

potential speed on the current of the Rhine. This possibility had renewed itself at Mannheim. Now, however, the next march would remove all protecting doubts. Marlborough therefore halted for three days to allow Churchill with the infantry and cannon to overtake him. It was not till the 7th, when his brother was only two marches away, that he moved again, this time in the direction which finally revealed his purpose. He turned sharply east to Sinzheim, which no doubt he remembered from the days of Turenne, and headed openly for the Danube. Once again the messengers sped to the French headquarters.

The news that Marlborough had crossed not only the Rhine but the Main created a profound sensation at Versailles. The King insistently directed the two Marshals together to frame and submit to him a plan of succour for the Elector in the event of the armies of Marlborough and the Margrave actually uniting. As soon as Villeroy was sure that Marlborough was not coming up the Moselle he had crossed that river, and marched through Alsace towards the Upper Rhine. On June 7 the Marshals met in conference at Zweibrücken. Together they commanded between fifty and sixty thousand men. They had before them the King's demand for a plan in case Marlborough should really go to the Danube: and now the news reached them that this was certainly where he was going.

While the Marshals had waited and wondered, while they interchanged anxious messages with Paris, while they canvassed every possibility, the strategic situation had been gradually but remorselessly transformed. All Marlborough's calculations had been justified. Villeroy had not attacked the weakened Dutch, but had been drawn south, first to the Moselle and then to the Upper Rhine. The Dutch had been obliged by the force of facts to accept and condone Marlborough's movement and to reinforce him against their wishes up to the limits he required. He was now in Swabia with the power to concentrate nearly fifty thousand men, and in sure and easy contact with the Margrave, whose forces at Stollhofen and opposite Ulm, together with

341

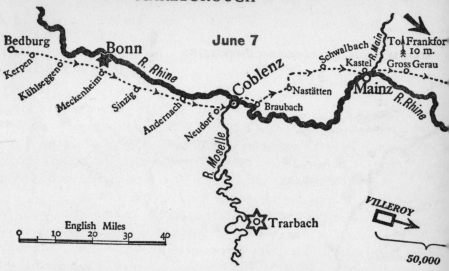

various detachments, were of about the same strength. Allied armies of about a hundred thousand men stood in harmonious relation in a central position between the Rhine and the Danube, while the two enemy armies, though not much inferior in numbers, lay at opposite sides of the circle, separated from each other by distance and stronger forces, and able to reinforce or join each other only by long and painful détours; and each was liable meanwhile to be attacked by overwhelming strength. Finally, Marlborough could soon, if need be, discard the whole of his communications by the Rhine and establish a new direct line of communication north-east behind him into Germany.

It was with consternation that the French chiefs felt the weight of these facts upon their well-trained military minds. Villeroy and Tallard understood plainly the peril in which the army of the Elector and Marsin lay. That army, gathered for the march to Vienna, was now exposed to attack within a fortnight by very much stronger forces, many of whom had marched across Europe for that express purpose. Bavaria, the deserter state, lay open to invasion by the confederates her ruler had so grievously wronged. The two Marshals saw how easy it would be for Marlborough to leave one-third of the combined forces to hold them off

on the Rhine, while he threw his main weight against their comrades on the Danube. But what to do?

The story of the next fortnight is one of futility and paralysis in the French High Command. The Marshals thrust their burden back upon the King. They sent him not one plan, but four, each with its own memorandum setting forth the grave or destructive objections to it. In mid-May they had been choosing between prizes: now there was only a choice of evils. Tallard began his covering letter with a disconcerting sentence. "In view of the superiority of the enemy forces between the Rhine and the Danube, assistance to Bavaria is so difficult as to appear almost an impossibility." In short, the Marshals avowed themselves completely baffled. Only the King could decide.

Louis XIV favoured the boldest of their alternatives—namely, to try to force the Rhine below Stollhofen and march down the Neckar valley towards Stuttgart. He expatiated on this in his letter of the 12th, but, puzzled himself, he gave no positive orders. He invited further comments, to which the Marshals replied in two separate papers on the 18th. They made it clear to him that they would take no responsibility. "Your Majesty," wrote Villeroy, ". . . understands war better than those who have the honour to serve you."

343

One has to search the annals of war to find so utter an obfuscation of a competent command. Yet the process by which it had been produced was, like many great things, simple and inevitable. How could they know that Marlborough would disdain the Moselle before he had crossed the Rhine at Coblenz; how could they be sure he would not double back to Flanders before them while he was still in touch with his flotillas on the Rhine; how could they

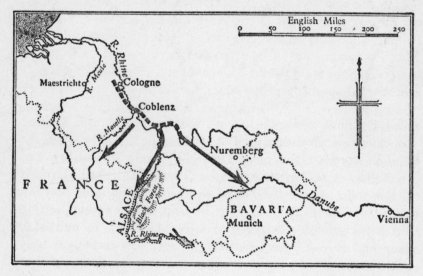

MARLBOROUGH'S SUCCESSIVE THREATS

know that he was not interested in Landau till he turned east at Wiesloch? And by that time it was too late. We have no doubt that he had foreseen these successive stages, inherent in the operation, a long time before. These enduring uncertainties were, in fact, the mechanism by which alone he could reach the Danube. Thus the tables were completely turned, and nearly all the strategic advantages the French had enjoyed in the middle of May had been transferred to their opponents by the end of June. And this by manœuvres of almost equal forces without a shot fired in either siege or battle.

As early as June 5 the Elector had heard that Eugene was

in the field. He immediately divined that he had been sent from Vienna to attack him. He even foresaw the exact plan of campaign which would be used against him. That same day he wrote his supplication for help from Louis XIV. Marshal Marsin supported him by a more explicit letter two days later. It was no longer a question, said the Marshal, of strengthening the Franco-Bavarian army for offensive action, but of saving the Elector from being forced out of the war and the French troops with him from being cut off and destroyed. If the King did not send a new army to help him, but, on the contrary, his enemies received one, Max Emmanuel would in despair embark his wife, children, and treasure on the Danube to seek safety with the Hungarian rebels. "Monsieur," wrote Marsin, "judge of the condition of a prince who can fall back on no other resource to save his family!"

A third appeal was made by General Legalle, who reached Versailles from the Franco-Bavarian army on June 22 to plead their cause in person. He was received in audience by the King. Louis, deeply moved by his advocacy, demanded a written statement. The document exists in the French military archives. Legalle declared that Marlborough was not advancing to strengthen the army on the Upper Rhine, but against Bavaria. As Bavaria was a completely open country the enemy could enter with two armies—one down by the Danube, the other high up the Iller—"and in a very short time devastate the defenceless land." Moreover, the Elector's health was precarious. "Were he to die, *his troops would desert to the enemy the very next day.*" The disappearance or submission of the Elector would transfer 35 Bavarian battalions and 45 squadrons to the hostile armies, and the fate of all the French troops already in Bavaria would be sealed.

Legalle proceeded to urge a definite action. At any cost and without delay another army must be sent to the aid of the Elector through the Black Forest and preferably by the Kinzig valley. On this the King made up his mind. He consulted the Marshals, who were shirking their re-

345

sponsibilities no further. On June 23 he sent his orders to Villeroy.

It is then my intention that you, Marshal Tallard, and General Coigny should divide all my troops which you and they command in Alsace into three corps. That of Marshal Tallard, which is to advance over the mountains, should consist of 40 battalions and 50 squadrons which I have chosen . . . in the appended list. . . .

The second army which you command should advance to Offenburg, observe the enemy, retain them in the lines of Stollhofen, follow them into Alsace, or join Marshal Tallard with the whole or a part if they move all their troops towards the Danube. This army should be composed of at least 40 battalions and 68 or 70 squadrons.

The corps which Coigny is to command should consist of 10 or 12 battalions and the same number of squadrons; and will safeguard Alsace. The Swiss regiments, even my Swiss Guards, will form part of this corps, as I have no intention of forcing them to cross the Rhine against their will. . . .

You are to keep this plan as secret as possible . . . in concert with Marshal Tallard.[1]

The Marshals had asked for orders, and now they had got them. But when on June 27 they sat over these orders at Langenkendal, they were filled with deep misgivings. Villeroy was deprecatory, but Tallard was outspoken. His complaint was bitter. The superior armies of the enemy between the Rhine and the Danube, he protested, would at any time be able to join together, while the French and Bavarian forces would be "always separated, in the air, and dependent on what the enemy decides to do." The infantry assigned to him was perhaps sufficient, but with only 50 squadrons of cavalry he declared his task impossible. Fifty more squadrons were required, and also the presence of an army in the Rhine Valley strong enough to prevent Eugene from leaving it. Unhappily, these forces did not exist. Thus Tallard.

I venture to say that in the circumstances Your Majesty can come to no decision which would not encounter extraordinary diffi-

1 Pelet, iv, 496–7.

culties in view of the numerous hostile fighting forces between the Rhine and the Danube, which owing to their means of communication are always able to join up together, whereas the troops of Your Majesty and the Elector, always separated and without means of communication, are in the air. I shall therefore be entirely dependent on what the enemy decides to do, the more so as, being without contact with Bavaria, I cannot expect any help from that quarter.

If the army which Your Majesty has assigned to me could maintain itself independently—that is to say, if I had fifty additional squadrons of cavalry—and if at the same time an army were stationed in the Rhine valley, sufficiently large to hold Prince Eugene from entering Alsace or to follow him [if he went eastward], the Empire would fall: but as Your Majesty cannot do this, it is waste of time to discuss it. I venture only to say that with fifty squadrons of cavalry, which I am to have, a campaign cannot be undertaken. My infantry is sufficient, and in regard to that I have no misgiving.[1]

Nevertheless both the Marshals obeyed. Tallard crossed the Rhine at Kehl, and began his southward march around the long curve to Villingen on July 1. Villeroy followed him and took up his station at Offenburg. Thus at last a decision had been wrung from the French. But Marlborough had also moved.

1 Pelet, iv, 507.

CHAPTER XVI

MARLBOROUGH AND EUGENE

(1704, June)

MARLBOROUGH at Wiesloch credited the enemy with more clarity of view and decision than they possessed. He thought it probable that their answer to his march would be either a violent attack upon the Lines of Stollhofen or that very bridging of the Rhine and thrust into the valley of the Neckar towards Stuttgart that Louis XIV had favoured but had not resolved. He must set up a shield upon the Upper Rhine strong enough to give him time to come to conclusions with Bavaria. Moreover, his own position was complicated because the Danish reinforcements which the States-General had sent after him, without which he had not enough strength, were still nearly a fortnight behind him.

Towards the end of May Prince Eugene had left Vienna for the Margrave's headquarters at some distance before Ulm. Marlborough now sent Wratislaw to the Imperial camp to explain the situation and procure compliance with its needs. It is plain that he wished to have Eugene with him on the Danube, and that the Margrave should undertake the defence of the Rhine. But one or the other must go to the Rhine at once.

"Having received intelligence yesterday," he wrote to Godolphin on June 8,

> that in three or four days the Duke of Villeroy, with his army, would join that of the Marshal de Tallard about Landau, in order to force the passage of the Rhine, I prevailed with count Wratislaw to make all haste he could to prince Louis of Baden's army, where he will be this night, that he might make him sensible of the great consequence it is to hinder the French from passing that river, while we are acting against the Elector of Bavaria. I have also desired him to press, *and not to be refused*, that either prince Louis or prince Eugene go immediately to the Rhine. I am in hopes to know to-morrow what resolution they have taken.

348

If I could decide it by my wishes, prince Eugene should stay on the Danube, although *prince Louis has assured me, by the count de Frise, that he will not make the least motion with his army, but as we shall concert.*[1]

To Wratislaw he said:

The army on the Upper Rhine must be strengthened, and either the Margrave or Prince Eugene must take the command there. *A General of great experience and vigilance* is necessary, because undoubtedly, whilst we shall be weaker there, the enemy will be stronger, against which we have the advantage of the Rhine. I should be very glad if the Margrave, being the most experienced, took command there.[2]

We may note the diplomatic touch about the need of having the most experienced general on the Rhine.

On June 8, while the Marshals at Zweibrücken were inditing their four alternative staff papers to Louis XIV, Wratislaw reached the Margrave's headquarters at Aermingen. Prince Eugene had already arrived, but the conversation was begun between Wratislaw and the Margrave alone. The Margrave agreed at once that the army on the Upper Rhine must be strengthened. On the question of who should go there he remarked casually but decisively, "You will have great difficulty in persuading the Prince of Savoy to take the command." At this moment Eugene entered the room: Wratislaw began his story over again. Marlborough, he said, considered that the army on the Upper Rhine must forthwith be reinforced. Either the Margrave or Prince Eugene must take command of it. Here the Margrave broke in, "Try to persuade the Prince to do so. For in the army he is the only man who could be entrusted with a command so responsible *and subject to so many risks.*" The reference to the "many risks" was shrewdly calculated. Eugene's temperament and sense of military honour were evidently well known to the Margrave. He knew he was leaving no choice open. Eugene answered as a soldier: "The Emperor has sent me into the Empire to serve under the command of his Lieutenant-General, and

---

[1] Coxe, i, 336.　　[2] Wratislaw's dispatch, June 13.

as I have never made difficulties about going wherever duty called me, I am quite ready to carry out the order of the Lieutenant-General. But I must remind you that, as our weakness and the enemy's strength there are quite well known, I must have left with me sufficient troops to put me in a position *to attack* the enemy."

The Emperor had had heart-searchings about Prince Eugene. He had determined to leave the decision to that Prince, who, indeed, had been accorded latent powers superior to the Margrave. But as the Emperor pondered over Eugene's character, which he knew so well, he feared that if a choice rested with Eugene, he would certainly choose for himself the most dangerous station. The Emperor could not bear the thought of this. In a rescript to Wratislaw he wrote:

> Subsequently I have come to the conclusion that the matter might be very harmful to my service. For the loyalty, zeal, and great valour of the Prince would at all times cause him to go wherever the danger was greatest. But that I cannot possibly allow. I will not permit the risking of the life of such a man, who is so competent and for so many reasons merits so well the respect and regard of myself and all my hereditary house.[1]

Therefore Eugene was not to decide for himself where he would fight, but only the generals together. However, the question had been settled by the Margrave's pointed remarks. And there are no grounds for thinking, as most English writers, following Coxe, suggest, that it was ever reopened. Marlborough, who learned of it the next day, announced it accordingly to the Duke of Würtemberg, the Prince of Hesse, and General Scholten by letters written from his camp at Mundelsheim on the morning of the 10th before he met Prince Eugene. There can be no argument about this.

Marlborough to the Prince of Hesse

MUNDELSHEIM
June 10

An adjutant has just come from Prince Eugene, whom I expect every minute; it is now five P.M. and he has notified me that he

---

[1] June 20. *Feldzüge*, vi, 739.

350

PRINCE EUGENE OF SAVOY
Jacob van Schuppen
Rijksmuseum, Amsterdam

will come to dinner here. *He is going to command on the Rhine,* where his presence is indeed necessary. . . .[1]

The Margrave, having secured his main point, made no difficulty about distributing the forces. He transferred to Prince Eugene all the Würtemberg troops in Dutch pay and offered the whole of the Prussian corps of eleven battalions and twenty squadrons, if they were found willing to go. What followed shows the curious conditions of these times. The Margrave sent for the Prussian commander, Prince Leopold of Anhalt-Dessau, and tendered him the choice of serving with the main army or with Eugene. If he opted for the main army, he was warned that he might be sent into districts where it would be impossible for the Margrave to guarantee his troops a daily bread-ration. Anhalt-Dessau put this issue bluntly—"Starve or obey"— to his generals. They decided to go to the Rhine. The fortresses and garrisons in the Black Forest, Freiburg, Villingen, Rothweil, and some smaller places also passed to Eugene.

The command and the partition of the forces being thus determined, the Margrave opened a third topic. He mentioned that he had received approaches from the Elector. This roused the suspicions of Wratislaw and Eugene. So he had been in personal touch with Max Emmanuel during all the abortive operations which had enabled the French and Bavarians to combine their armies. The Margrave explained the nature of the Elector's proposals: how he "wanted to play Ulm into the hands of the Empire," to join the allies with sixteen thousand men and "treat the French if they would not agree in such a way that they would never forget it," always provided that the conditions offered to him were "sufficiently good."[2]

The Margrave said that the negotiations would first of all be concerned with a personal meeting between him and the Elector; and the Elector had said he would welcome at this meeting

1 *Dispatches,* p. 303.
2 Wratislaw's dispatch to the Emperor, June 14, 1704; *Feldzüge,* vi, 825.

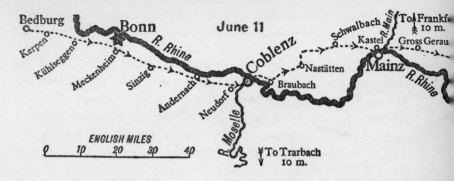

the presence of Prince Eugene. What did his two colleagues
think of this? Both of them were stiffly reserved and adverse.
If the Elector wanted a settlement let him first of all
make a definite offer. Whatever he said, he could not
be trusted. Obviously it was to his interest to gain time
by any means. The Margrave did not challenge this view.
He allowed the matter to drop. But when Eugene and
Wratislaw pressed him to come with them at once to
Marlborough's headquarters he demurred on the pretext
of posting the army better, "which may well mean in fact,"
wrote Wratislaw to the Emperor, "in order to communi-
cate further with the Elector. . . . Although we cannot
advance anything definite, we are of opinion that the Margrave is unwilling to attack the Elector vigorously or to do
him injury."[1]

In the evening of Tuesday, June 10, Eugene with
Wratislaw reached Marlborough's camp. The Duke received
his illustrious comrade with the highest military honours,
and after a banquet described as "magnificent" the two
generals spent several hours in each other's company. Then
at once began that glorious brotherhood in arms which
neither victory nor misfortune could disturb, before which
jealousy and misunderstanding were powerless, and of which
the history of war furnishes no equal example. The two
men took to one another from the outset. They both thought
and spoke about war in the same way, measured the vast

<hr />

1 Wratislaw's dispatch; *ibid.*, 826.

forces at work by the same standards, and above all alike
looked to a great battle with its awful risks as the means by
which their problems would be solved.

Both, moreover, possessed the highest outlook on the
war; for Eugene, though in the field, was still head of the
Imperial War Council, and Marlborough was not only
Commander-in-Chief of the English and Dutch armies, but
very largely a Prime Minister as well. They could therefore
feel towards the whole problem a responsibility different
from that of the leaders of individual armies, however large.
It must have been very refreshing to Eugene after his toilsome discussions at Vienna and with the Margrave, and to
Marlborough after the long, paralysing obstructiveness of the
Dutch, to find themselves in such perfect harmony upon the
essentials of their task. Each felt the relief which comes from
the shadow of a great rock in a thirsty land. In the midst of
the intrigues, cross-purposes, and half-measures of a vast, un-
wieldy coalition trying to make war, here was the spirit of
concord, design, and action.

Strangely different were they in appearance and manner;
the Englishman with his noble, symmetrical features and
pink-and-white complexion, with his languid courtier air and
quizzical smile, and with that sense of calm and power which
was his aura: the French-Austrian-Italian death's head,
vibrant with energy, olive-dark, fiery like a banked furnace;
Marlborough bland, grave, affable, cool: Eugene ardent, stac-
cato, theatrical, heroic. Nor was the contrast of their lives

353

less marked. Marlborough, the model husband and father, concerned with building up a home, founding a family, and gathering a fortune to sustain it: Eugene, a bachelor—nay, almost a misogynist—disdainful of money, content with his bright sword and his lifelong animosities against Louis XIV. Certainly quite different kinds of men; yet when their eyes met each recognized a kindred spirit in all that governs war. They were in action, as has been well said, "two bodies with one soul."

Next day, the 11th, Marlborough's march was to Heppach, and Eugene rode with him. In the meadows between the road and the river the whole of the English cavalry, nineteen squadrons, were found drawn up for Eugene to ride along their ranks. They were indeed a spectacle to greet a military eye. Everything was in excellent order—men, horses, equipment, and uniforms in perfect condition, a little travel-stained, rather fine-drawn, but all that soldiers should be. "My Lord," said Eugene, "I never saw better horses, better clothes, finer belts and accoutrements; but money, which you don't want in England, will buy clothes and fine horses, but it can't buy that lively air I see in every one of these troopers' faces." "Sir," said Marlborough, "that must be attributed to their heartiness for the public cause and the particular pleasure and satisfaction they have in seeing your Highness."[1]

These compliments, which were intended for the public, are all that has come down to us of Marlborough's prolonged conversations with Eugene on this their first meeting. But it is clear that they came to much closer grips behind the scenes. The two men were together from Tuesday till Friday, and the more they talked over what they had to do the better they understood and liked one another. "Prince Eugene," wrote Marlborough to Sarah, ". . . has in his conversation a great deal of my lord Shrewsbury, with the advantage of seeming franker. He has been very free with me, in giving me the character of the Prince of Baden, by which I find I must be much more on my guard than if I was

[1] Hare's Journal.

to act with Prince Eugene. . . ."[1] We know how much Marlborough was attracted by Shrewsbury, and the charm exerted by "the King of Hearts," as he was always called. Nothing could be more expressive to Sarah of Marlborough's esteem for Prince Eugene than his use of this comparison. The fullest confidences were interchanged between the two chiefs. Here and now they resolved one way or another to bring matters to a supreme trial with the French before the campaign ended, and, although they must at first be separated for a time, to combine for that purpose. This desultory but costly and possibly fatal warfare of sieges and manœuvres of nicely balanced forces, advancing and retiring according to the rules of war, exercising strategic influences upon each other with many bows and scrapes at the public expense, could only lead to destruction. It must be made to give place to a bloody punch and death-grip; and on this they would stake their lives and honour, and the lives of all the soldiers they could command. Surveying the general war, we can see that matters had now come to such a pitch that, without a great victory in two or three months, the Grand Alliance was doomed. Something had to be produced outstanding, and beyond the ordinary course of events, which would transform the scene. Safety and self-preservation demanded the stake of all for all. On that day they must be together.

Nothing could exceed the candour with which the character and qualities of the Margrave were canvassed. Marlborough expressed complete distrust of him and of his military abilities. Eugene revealed that if the Margrave did not do his duty "the Emperor was determined to stamp out the mischief with the utmost vigour." They did not by any means, however, exclude the possibility of negotiating with the Elector. Marlborough dwelt on the dangers of conducting a negotiation through the King of Prussia. They all agreed that Wratislaw should obtain authority from the Emperor to treat with him, if needful, on the spot. Marlborough wrote forthwith for such powers from London;

1 Coxe, i, 341.

but he was already in all but form a plenipotentiary for England.

Marlborough to Godolphin

GREAT HEPPACH
June 11, 1704

* Yesterday the Prince Eugene came to me. *He is to command on the Rhine,* where he will have all the Prussians, the Palatines, and other troops that are to make a body of 30,000 men. But I am very much afraid the French will force their passage before the Prussians can arrive, for they begin their march but this day from the Danube. They must have ten days for their march, and those troops of the circle of Swabia which are on the Rhine must have a long time to go to the Danube. I could not forbear telling P. Eugene that if we should have made such counter-marches in Flanders when the enemy are ready to put their projects in execution, we should have been very much censured. He agreed that it would have been a much better time if this had been done immediately after the reinforcement had joined the Elector of Bavaria; but the truth is that *P. Louis had no thoughts but that of having a strong army,* I hope with the design of having it in his power to beat the Elector. . . . P. Eugene marched with me this day, Prince Louis having sent me word that he will be with me to-morrow [actually the day after], so that when we have agreed upon the method, we shall open the campaign. *P. Eugene will take post for the Rhine.* . . . I find by P. Eugene that everything here is in a worse condition than I could have imagined, although I thought them very bad.

It may so fall out that the service may suffer, by my not having the powers of treating.

On this day also he wrote to Harley congratulating him on becoming Secretary of State.

Meanwhile the Margrave was approaching. He was, as arranged, reinforcing the Rhine front at Stollhofen from his army opposite the Elector, with 9 squadrons and 15 battalions, perhaps twelve thousand men. On the morning of the 13th he was a day's journey from Heppach. No pains were spared to gain his good-will. Cadogan with a gallant escort went to meet him on the road, and Marlborough, Eugene at his side, received him with the utmost ceremonial. Again compliments were exchanged for the benefit of the armies. Prince Louis spoke with soldierly frankness. "Your Grace is come to save the Empire and give me an opportunity to vindicate my honour, which I am sensible is in some manner at the last stake in the opinion of some people." This reference to the muddled operations in the Black Forest and at the Pass of Stockach might well have disarmed the fierce professional criticism by which the Margrave was assailed. Marlborough said in reply, "I come to learn from your Highness how to do the Empire service; for men must want judgment who do not know that the Prince of Baden has not only, when his health would permit him, preserved the Empire, but extended its conquests as well as secured its own [territory]."[1]

The three generals met before the Lamb Inn at Gross Heppach under a great tree still distinguishable in the nineteenth century. Marlborough was the eldest: he was fifty-four. Prince Louis was fifty, and Eugene not yet forty-one. In military rank the Margrave stood first, next Marlborough, and then Eugene. Marlborough was the only one who was not a royalty. He was the only one who had never gained a battle. He could not compare in military renown with Prince Louis, still less with the famous Eugene. Still, there he was, the Englishman, with his commanding personality, his redcoats, and the army he had led so far to aid the Empire. Thus he counted for something. Indeed, he became naturally and at once the presiding authority: and this was virtually implied in the conditions he had exacted before he committed himself to the adventure.

Later they came to business. The Margrave had long had his plan prepared against Bavaria. It was the one which Legalle had already explained to King Louis. It required two armies, together overwhelming, each strong enough to defend itself. With one army he would cross the Danube above Ulm, then pass the Iller by its numerous fords, and engage the Elector from the south, while the other army broke into Bavaria across the Danube somewhere from the north. Marlborough agreed with this now conventional pincer operation. He agreed also that the Margrave should be the southern and he

1 Lediard, i, 308.

the northern claw. But the Duke of Würtemberg had not made the Danish cavalry march as fast as was expected. They were still nearly a fortnight behind, and until they arrived there were not enough troops to form two adequate armies. They must act at first as one, for, considering the pressure they must expect upon the Rhine, there was not a day to be lost. The merging of the armies raised directly the question of the command.

This problem was serious and delicate. By custom the Margrave, the Lieutenant-General of the Emperor and first general of the Empire, would, especially on the soil of Germany, have had precedence. But Marlborough had not come all the way from the North Sea with what was probably the best disciplined and equipped army in the world in order to renew under Louis of Baden the vexations he had suffered from the Dutch Deputies. He had therefore before he started obtained conditions which, although by no means ideal, were not so unsatisfactory or absurd as has been represented by so many writers. On April 4 the Supreme Council of War at Vienna had considered the proposals of the Margrave, who was

> content to divide the command with the Duke of Marlborough and arrange matters on the same footing as they were with the Elector of Bavaria and the Duke of Lorraine in Hungary and the Reich . . ., and in the event of his being attacked by the enemy the Duke of Marlborough could join the Lieutenant-General's army and share the command with him. And so that that should be no stumbling-block on the question of the parola [the watchword of the day] . . . your Imperial Majesty could send the parola to the two commanding generals and it could then either be given by each to his army or to his wing if the armies were together or alternatively could be given out by each of them on alternate days.[1]

We see therefore that there was never any question either of Marlborough or his army coming under the Margrave's orders or of the two commanders taking it in daily turn to command the combined forces. The two generals had

[1] The Archduke Joseph's report to the Emperor, April 12, 1704; *Feldzüge*, vi, 728.

THE MARGRAVE OF BADEN
From an engraving after the painting by John Closterman
British Museum

to work together as commanders of independent forces of equal status; and they agreed at Gross Heppach that the orders of the day which had been settled beforehand and the parola should be issued in turn from the tent of each of them. Furthermore, while the titular honours and appearance of the command were thus equally shared, there was a definite understanding and assurance that the prevailing direction of the campaign lay with Marlborough, who had the largest army and had come at great personal risk to rescue the Empire.

On the 15th, when the conferences had ended, he wrote:

> But at the same time they [Eugene and Wratislaw] have assured me that their master would not suffer him to do hurt, either by his temper, or by want of good inclinations. After I have said this, I must do him the justice, that I think he will do well; *for* [and this is a striking phrase] *he must be a devil, after what he has said, if he does otherwise*.[1]

It was agreed at Gross Heppach that the Margrave, with his army north of Ulm, should hold the Elector; that Eugene, with less than thirty thousand men, should at Philippsburg or Stollhofen confront the Marshals, who were found to have sixty thousand on the Upper Rhine, and that Marlborough should traverse the mountains with his whole force, and join the Margrave as quickly as possible. Eugene was deeply conscious of the weight he had to bear. "I realize very clearly," he wrote on June 14 to Starhemberg,

> that I am placing myself in a serious *impegno* . . . yet I have not in the present circumstances been able to decline this dangerous command.[2]

And so, in Marlborough's words to Godolphin, "After we had taken the necessary resolutions for putting in execution what had been projected against the Elector of Bavaria, yesterday in the afternoon Prince Eugene went for the Rhine, Prince Louis to his army, and your humble servant to his place."[3]

Meanwhile Marlborough's march had produced its reactions both in Holland and England. The States-General

1 Coxe, i, 343.   2 *Feldzüge*, vi, Suppt., p. 55.   3 Coxe, i, 343.

had, it is true, promptly acceded to his request to allow their troops and reinforcements to go to the Danube. But they naturally felt entitled to throw the whole responsibility for what might happen upon the commander. By concealment and stratagem he had forced their hand. He had created a position in which they had no choice but to wreck the campaign or support him against their wishes and judgment in an obviously most disputable adventure. Heinsius had been glad to see the decision ultimately carried in Marlborough's favour, but under-currents of resentment and alarm ran through the whole Dutch oligarchy and its military advisers. "On his head be it," was the general view.

In England these feelings were even more intense. The Tories were outraged in their party principles by this carrying of the war and of the Queen's troops into the heart of the Continent. Such measures were contrary to their whole theory of British policy. No authority had been given by Parliament for any such surprising transference of the army to a new and remote theatre. The influential ex-Ministers threatened fury and retribution upon the Captain-General, who had broken loose not only from prudent methods of warfare, but from proper Parliamentary control. These reproaches were not confined to violent partisans. A letter in the French archives says:

> The moderate party has decided to frame articles accusing Marlborough of having arbitrarily [*de sa propre tête*] changed the seat and measures of the war: of having withdrawn [*avoir éloingné*] forces capable of defending the country at a perilous moment: of having thrown doubts upon the fidelity of Prince Louis of Baden [*entré dans une méfiance de la fidélité du P*^{e}*. Louis de Bade*].[1]

No doubt there was some exaggeration in this, but Seymour pithily expressed the views of the hunting squires. "If he fails we will break him up as hounds upon a hare."

And fail he surely would in this mad escapade. It was lucky indeed that Parliament, with its Tory majority in the Commons and hostile Whigs, was not in session. The

[1] *Correspondance politique, Angleterre, t.* 214, f. 113, *et seq.*

chiefs of the Opposition consoled themselves meanwhile with the belief, or even secret, subconscious hope, that a disaster was impending. It was worth while to wait for the supreme opportunity which would probably come their way. They could not bring Marlborough back now before some awful trial of strength occurred. An overwhelming case would come into their hands when the famous, invincible armies of France baffled, defeated, or destroyed the presumptuous general and lukewarm Tory. This arch-dissembler had brought the Occasional Conformity Bill to nothing. He had struck a covert blow at the Church of England in her stress and tribulation. He had used his favour, and his wife's favour—that poisonous Whig—to pervert their own Tory Queen. All the true leaders of Toryism had been driven from her councils at his instigation. A wretched set of moderates and trimmers of both parties clustered around Godolphin and Harley. They might be strong enough to maintain themselves in office until this hideous gamble with the Queen's armies in a far-off European quarrel had met its fate. But thereafter vengeance would be wreaked upon the whole gang of hardy intriguers. A day would come, and soon, when this reckoning could be made.

Neither were the Whigs, as we have seen, content or loyal. True, they did not disapprove of Continental warfare, and they had some representation in the Government: but what folly it was, at a time when all Toryism was rabid, not to rely upon the great party which had sustained King William and saved the cause of civil and religious liberty! Moreover, it was their own cause that was at stake. They it was who would suffer as a party by a disaster in the field. If Marlborough failed a Tory triumph was inevitable, and meanwhile the Whigs had scarcely any share of the offices. A colourless central combination built around the placemen of the Crown and favourites of the Court was a precarious foundation for policies the audacity of which might well break the strongest Government. And why, inquired the Whigs, was this course adopted? Why were they not fully trusted? Clearly

361

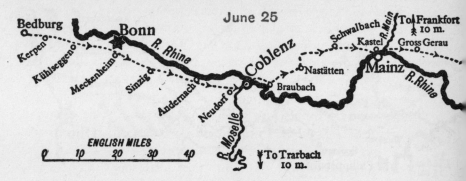

because Marlborough and Godolphin were at their old tricks again with the Jacobite exiles.

Lediard prints some instructive letters from Cardonnel's widely gathered correspondence.[1] Lord Stamford, for instance, wrote on June 2:

> . . . I can assure you, it has been a very great mortification to the Party to be so crossed and exposed, when nothing could stand against them in the House of Commons. . . .
>
> . . . I must own your reasonings upon the changes at court [i.e., the dismissal of the High Tories], to be the same with our most judicious, honest men here, that is, to be very chimerical, and will not, in all human probability, attain the ends aimed at, but may have a contrary effect; Whatever My Lord Marlborough does abroad (which for the sake of Europe, I heartily wish may be well) Yet his foundation being rotten here, and his not increasing his friends, may exasperate his enemies to that height, that it may push them on beyond the rules and measures, which have been kept amongst them hitherto.

This refers to the general understanding of both parties, apart from their views, to support the war and vote supplies. Stamford continued:

> You know when two sets of people agree in a third design, tho' they personally hate one another, and have still concurred in the main, to prevent a third [i.e., the enemy] reaping any benefit; yet such things may be done, that may occasion an entire breach, that so those rules may be no more thought of. This I look upon to be our case.

1 Lediard, i, 318–320.

362

A letter written by an English gentleman at the Court of Hanover to a compatriot in another German Court also came into Cardonnel's hands.

> I am sure, that there is a greater party forming against My Lord Treasurer and My Lord Marlborough, than ever there was against King William's Ministers, and what the consequence may be, I cannot tell. Affairs will yet go worse, if their Enemies prevail; but much will depend upon My Lord's success in Germany, and no King could wish for a more noble opportunity to relieve not only Germany, but Europe, than this that he is employed upon, or that could be more glorious for himself. If the Elector of Bavaria is reduced, it will stop the mouths of his enemies, and they will not be able to hurt him in England; But if he fails, he will be railed at in Holland, and accused in England, for the loss he must suffer in such an expedition, and I much apprehend the consequence everywhere.

And, again (June 25):

> My Lord Marlborough has joined the troops under Prince Lewis of Baden, not far from Ulm, and the success of this affair will either gain him a great reputation, and very much shelter him from his enemies (which are not few) or be his ruin.

These tidings and doubtless many others came daily to Marlborough's headquarters as they rolled forward, march by march, and formed a background to his thoughts while he pondered upon the impugned loyalty of the Margrave, strove to conciliate and work him, and measured from hour to hour the anxious, obscure strategic scene.

363

The first step was to join the two armies. Marlborough had still to traverse the hilly country of the Swabian Jura before he could enter the Danube basin. This required enormous exertions from Churchill's foot and artillery. The defile of Geislingen, through which he must pass, was narrow, and even in good weather extremely difficult for wagons. Of course it poured with rain for ten days. Men and horses floundered and struggled forward. Meanwhile the Margrave's army was well placed to cover the exits from the mountainous regions on to the Danube plain. But the Margrave was greatly weakened by the departure of the troops he had sent to Eugene for the Rhine. There was always the danger that the Elector and Marsin would attack him before Marlborough could get clear of the hills and join him in the plains. While this task was at its worst the States-Generals were led to believe that Villeroy was returning to the Netherlands, and demanded a part at least of their force for the defence of Holland. They did not get them.

Because we have turned aside to discuss strategy and politics, the reader must not lose the sensation of a continuous march. Marlborough could ride on ahead and have two or three days to transact his affairs. But the scarlet caterpillar crawled onward ceaselessly. It averaged about ten miles a day for six weeks. Napoleon's march a century later from Boulogne to Ulm over much better roads was considerably faster. But Marlborough's aim was not entirely speed. The Danes anyhow were lagging behind him. Everything depended upon the timing of passing successive critical points in relation to the knowledge and movements of the enemy, and on the fitness and spirit of his troops at the end of their march. All his strategic requirements were satisfied by the pace they made. To Versailles and to the French Marshals, as from time to time they received their news, it seemed that Marlborough was marching with "great strides" to the Danube, and that nothing could intercept or overtake him.